Beyond *Papillon*

Beyond Papillon

The French Overseas Penal Colonies, 1854–1952

Stephen A. Toth

UNIVERSITY OF NEBRASKA PRESS
LINCOLN AND LONDON

Source acknowledgments
for previously published material
appear on p. x.

© 2006
by the Board of Regents
of the University of Nebraska
All rights reserved
Manufactured in the
United States of America

Library of Congress
Cataloging-in-Publication Data
Toth, Stephen A.
Beyond *Papillon* : the French overseas penal colonies, 1854–1952 / Stephen A. Toth.
p. cm.—(France overseas)
Includes bibliographical references and index.
ISBN-13: 978-0-8032-4449-8 (cloth : alk. paper)
ISBN-10: 0-8032-4449-5 (cloth : alk. paper)
1. Penal colonies—France—History. 2. Penal colonies—French Guiana—History.
3. Penal colonies—New Caledonia—History. I. Title. II. Series.
HV8955.F8T68 2006
365'.34—dc22
2005028930

Set in Minion by Kim Essman.
Designed by Ray Boeche.

Contents

Illustrations

Maps

Photographs

Following page   58

Tables

Acknowledgments

This book would not have been completed without the generosity of many people whom it gives me great pleasure to acknowledge. The late William B. Cohen was a kind and generous man who eagerly shared his invaluable insight into the French colonial world. His personal example of hard work helped me understand how a scholar practices his craft. I also owe a special debt of gratitude to Rachel G. Fuchs, whose encouragement and advice helped me choose my profession many years ago. Her love of France and all things French is infectious, as countless others can attest.

I benefited from fellowships while a graduate student at Indiana University, including the Leo Solt Dissertation Fellowship and the Hill Fellowship. I am also happy to acknowledge the support I received in researching parts of this book subsequent to my doctoral dissertation, in particular a Scholarship, Research and Creative Activities Grant from Arizona State University in the summer of 2002. With such support I made numerous forays into the Archives d'Outre-Mer in Aix-en-Provence, where the administrative records of the French overseas penal colonies are held. I am most grateful to the staff of this institution for their efforts in assisting in my research. Ismet Kurtovitch at the Service des archives de la Nouvelle-Calédonie in Nouméa was a great help as well in locating many of the photographs that appear in this book.

My thanks also go to the organizers and participants of a number of academic conferences and seminars who provided the opportunity to rethink this work on many occasions. I thank those who have contributed over the years, in sometimes unintentional ways, at the University of Melbourne (Rudé Conference, 2004); Yale University (Howard Lamar Center for the

Study of Frontiers and Borders); Marquette University (French Historical Studies Conference, 2003); the University of California, Los Angeles (Western Society for French History, 2000); the University of Liverpool (Association for the Study of French History, 1997); and the University of Delaware (Hagley Fellows Program on Modernism and Technology).

Some portions of the book have appeared previously in journal articles. I therefore acknowledge with appreciation the permission to adapt and reprint the following: "The Desire to Deport: The Recidivist of Fin-de-Siècle France," *Nineteenth-Century Contexts* 25, no. 2 (2003): 147-60; and "Colonization or Incarceration? The French Penal Colony in New Caledonia," *Journal of Pacific History* 34, no. 1 (1999): 59-74. (The journals can be accessed at www.tandf.co.uk/journals.)

This work has also benefited greatly from the attention and inspection given to it by the anonymous readers at the University of Nebraska Press. Whatever shortcomings the reader may find reflect my own failure to address the many cogent comments and points these individuals first raised. I would also like to thank Jim Le Sueur, who took an initial interest in the manuscript, and the staff of the press, who shepherded it through the publication process.

Finally, I must express my thanks to those closest to me who have been pillars of support for so long. Sean Quinlan has been not only a dear friend but an insightful reader and commentator on this work. My parents, Andrew and Betty Toth, have helped support me, both financially and emotionally, through the years, and I cannot thank them enough. This book is a testament to their love and patience. Meredith, you have made life that much sweeter over the past three years. Thank you, ma belle femme.

Introduction

For most people, the French overseas penal colonies typically call to mind the motion picture *Papillon*, based on the best-selling eponymous novel of former convict Henri Charrière and so named for the butterfly tattooed on his chest. Even today, long after its theatrical premiere in 1973, images of a defiant and determined Steve McQueen running through the jungle and evading his cruel captors linger in the collective subconscious. Indeed, with the advent of VHS, cable television, and worldwide film distribution, it is likely that Charrière's story has never really stopped playing since its original release more than three decades ago. As a result, two generations of viewers have learned of the penal colonies only through the distorted lens of a self-aggrandizing autobiography and Hollywood movie magic.[1] Therefore the *bagnes* (the word originally referred to the dockyard prisons of the early modern period in France and would later be extended to the overseas penal colonies of French Guiana and New Caledonia) are distant and exotic, ensnared in myth and legend.[2]

Until recently, scholarly treatments did little to address this lacuna. Most works on the subject fell into one of three camps: those that touched upon the *bagnes* only within the more general framework of the history of crime and punishment in France; those that examined the penal colonies within broader colonial or national histories; and those that focused primarily on the features which made the institution an affront to humane penal policy and a place of unparalleled misery for those unfortunate enough to be held within its confines.[3] The picture that emerged from this historiography was unchanging, undifferentiated, and ahistorical. We knew the penal colonies only in relation to other modes of incarceration or in terms of their inherent cruelty and barbarism.

There is evidence, however, that the penal colonies are being examined in new and exciting ways. Anthropologist Peter Redfield has juxtaposed the *bagne* with the Ariane space program in an effort to explain French Guiana's uniqueness, both in terms of its nature and culture and in terms of its complex place in French memory and contemporary consciousness.[4] French Guiana was a "laboratory of modernity," an epistemological and geographic site that allowed for the experimentation and dissemination of French knowledge and power.[5] In this vein, the penal colony is a small but important part of a much larger story surrounding the intersection of technology and colonial development in the nineteenth and twentieth centuries.

For historian Alice Bullard, the primary purpose of the penal colony in New Caledonia was to inculcate a French national identity among the exiled Communards and the Kanaks (the indigenous people of the island).[6] Through their control of the *bagne*, and by extension their control of daily life in the colony, officials "civilized" by using the "body"—both metaphorically and corporeally—as a site of discursive and violent intervention. Such efforts were self-legitimating, as they were aimed at two populations who were seen by those in the metropole as manifestations of a fundamental physical, mental, and moral deficiency. With the Communards and the Kanaks as the primary focus, however, little attention is paid to the common-law convicts who composed the vast majority of the population of New Caledonia in the late nineteenth and early twentieth centuries.

Of course, the specter of Michel Foucault hovers above these and most other works that touch upon issues of deviance and social control. Although Foucault had little to say in regard to the *bagne*—noting simply that it was "a rigorous and distant form of punishment" that was "of no real economic or colonial importance"—his work on the prison was paradigmatic.[7] Through his analysis of the normalizing techniques that emerged in conjunction with the factory, army, and school, Foucault uncovered the various strains of a nineteenth-century discourse that cohered into a mechanism of imprisonment (i.e., the penitentiary) that was conceived not simply to punish but to reform criminals. Thus the body was the focus for a new kind of power relation, and corporal punishment gave way to the meticulous observation, investigation, and control of the human subject.

Although Foucault's analysis enlightens, it also elides, as he conflates rhetoric with administrative practice. By privileging the voices of juridical and social-scientific authorities, Foucault indulges in his own fantasy about the power of intellectual discourse itself. What results is a caricature of the modern prison, a vast, gray, monolithic institution, mechanically ordered and rigidly stratified through the ever-invasive panoptic gaze of professionals and staff. In this sense, all historical contingency and nuance is absent from his account.

This leaves to historians the task of tracing how the various strategies of normative reason embedded within such institutions were actually implemented and diffused. As David Garland has cogently pointed out, however, one must keep in mind that "there are elements of the penal system which malfunction and so are not effective as forms of control or else are simply not designed to function as control measures in the first place."[8] This was nowhere more apparent than in the colonial prisons of French Indochina. As historian Peter Zinoman has recently discovered, these were not sites of methodical bureaucratic control but rather premodern jails that had the unintended effect of imbuing in its prisoners—through their shared sense of suffering at the hands of an "antiquated and ill-disciplined" penal regime— a distinct national identity that actually helped to facilitate and strengthen anti-French sentiments.[9] Given that they had always been seen as the "Other"—colonial subjects whose identity and culture were problematized and marginalized—those who happened to be both Indochinese and "criminal" were beyond the pale.[10] Therefore a disciplined and well-ordered penal system that was focused on the rehabilitation of its prisoners was simply irrelevant to French authorities.

This was not the case with the *bagne*, however, as it was seen as having a rehabilitative purpose separate from its social function as a mode of punishment and permanent exile. Simply stated, the penal colonies were founded on the fantasy of regenerative work and labor in faraway, unoccupied (devoid of French citizens, if not indigenous peoples) lands. In this sense the French penal colonies had much in common with Britain's Australia. Both systems were inextricably tied to colonial ambitions, as they shared the same basic idea of making convict labor productive in the colonies and, after a period of probation, allowing convicts to establish themselves on the land. But from this notion came an inevitable and ultimately insoluble dilemma: should the penal colony serve positive colonial development—through such mechanisms as concessions of land to prisoners as would-be pioneers—or should it be punitive and harshly disciplinary? No system could equally serve both imperatives, and therefore penal colonization was always an uneasy, forever-shifting, and in some ways unworkable compromise between reform impulses and social-defense advocates of severe treatment of prisoners.

Indeed, transportation ran counter to the contemporaneous notion of reformative punishment, which attempted to recover criminals for the state by making them productive members of society. For instance, individuals such as penal reformer John Howard complained that by shipping the malfeasant to Australia the state lost any possibility of benefiting from his recovery and that his punishment would no longer serve as a criminal deterrent.[11] The founder of the panoptic prison, Jeremy Bentham, was similarly critical of the Australian penal colonies, also charging that they offered little in the way of criminal deterrence and that they were far too costly for the state.[12]

While British policymakers eventually came to this same basic conclusion and officially halted shipments of prisoners to New South Wales, Port Philip (Victoria), and Van Diemen's Land (Tasmania) in 1840, 1850, and 1853, respectively, the French landed their first shipment of common-law convicts in Guiana in 1852. Historian Colin Forster has attributed the belated effort at penal colonization to colonial or territorial envy, as France had lost most of its overseas empire in 1814 and was in desperate search for another. In addition, the establishment of penal colonies was a way for the navy to extend its interests abroad. Certainly after the defeat of Napoleon I and throughout the 1820s and 1830s, the navy was "pitifully weak" in comparison to the army in terms of both strategic importance and prestige. As Forster has cogently argued, a newfound colonial empire based on penal colonization was attractive because it would require a concomitant expansion of the navy for transport, provisioning posts, defense, and management.[13]

While the navy got its wish in 1852, the same basic dissonance as to the raison d'être of penal colonization in Australia fatally undermined the French system as well. Indeed, there was a profound tension between theory and praxis as the carceral ideal embedded within the written directive of the Ministry of the Marine (later the Ministry of the Colonies)—which oversaw the entire operation from France—was openly questioned, often challenged, and sometimes superseded because of perceived "local" imperatives. With its intricate and multiple layers of bureaucracy, the penal colony complex operated, not in a vacuum, but in an environment involving many areas of contestation. By examining the various collusions, alliances, and conflicts among multiple parties, one sees not a monolith of surveillance and success but rather a deeply contingent and often fractured domain. Whereas Foucault depicts an ever-encroaching normative discipline as the historical dialectic of the penitentiary, the history of the French penal colonies was driven by a continual and often contentious fratricidal struggle that belied a pervasive will to power among those within the administrative apparatus itself.

Given their remote location and great distance from France, local authorities had immediate and total control over life in the penal colonies. Unlike the Benthamite panopticon, in which adherence to the regimented and monastic existence of the cell was intended to be conducive to reflection, remorse, and repentance, prisoners in the penal colonies were housed in communal barracks and shackled together by chains. While corporal punishment was not a part of the penitential regime, officials routinely engaged in beating and torturing the *bagnards*, even mandating public executions for those guilty of legal and disciplinary infractions while in their charge. It was not therefore architecture but rather administrators and guards who were the linchpins and ultimate moralizing agents of the penal colonies.

To determine how these individuals, faced with the exigencies of everyday life in these far-flung colonial outposts, construed and constructed their own *bagne*, I explore daily reports, internal memoranda, and administrative correspondence. From the multiple vantage points of administrators, guards, and physicians, I uncover alternate and oppositional understandings that reflect particular institutional practices and circumstances. Yet such a focus only tells half the story.

To fully understand the penal colonies, one must move, as David Rothman has argued, "Back and forth, and in and out" of the asylum to free society—or, in the case of the *bagne*, between metropole and colony.[14] In this regard I situate the penal colony at those historical moments in which its image is highly contested. As such, I am interested in uncovering the means by which the institution was understood and the rhetorical frameworks that conveyed this understanding. Toward this end, I bring together intellectual conceptualizations and cultural representations in what historian Pieter Spierenberg has termed a "mentalities" approach in which one reconstructs "the wider context of historical processes which may be relatively independent of the motives of prison founders."[15]

Given its approach, this book takes a different path than those that have gone before it. Although I do not dismiss Foucauldian insights regarding modern forms of punishment—as we shall see, there are some points of commonality between the penal colonies and the penitentiary—this study aims to be part of something different: a multilayered social and cultural analysis that focuses on the will of civil society and the will of those who actually lived and worked in the *bagne*. Interwoven within the history of the *bagne* lie the integral moments that gave it meaning.

In this context, chapters 1 and 2 examine the intellectual and cultural milieu of mid- to late-nineteenth-century France in order to understand why penal colonization appeared as a solution to a perceived rise in crime and petty recidivism. In chapter 3 I explore the establishment of an idealized prison regimen intended to rehabilitate and reform the *bagnard* as well as the various means by which prisoners subverted the regime. Through prisoner letters, diaries, biographies, autobiographies, and novels, one sees the outlines of a distinct prisoner subculture that was a site of resistance and struggle. In the following chapter I move on to discuss how, through a variety of internal bureaucratic struggles and ill-conceived policy initiatives, penal colony officials unintentionally undermined the very institution they were charged with administering. Thus the focus of chapter 4 is the highly pitched battle between authorities and local physicians, with the latter seeking to disentangle convicts from the prevailing penal colony structure and reintegrate them within a physically hygienic environment in which they would play a more significant role as normalizing agents. Chapter 5 connects the brutality and violence of penal colony guards to their liminal status and traces the process by which they were subsumed by an occupational model in which they possessed, willingly or not, many of the functional characteristics of the military. Turning back to the metropole in chapter 6, I explore fin de siècle criminological representations of the *bagne* and how their prosaic notions led not only to a reconceptualization of the penal colony but also to a fundamental shift in administrative power on the local level as well. In chapter 7 I delineate how the birth of modern journalism—with its focus on the lurid and the sensational—created a transnational awareness and dialogue condemning penal colonization, forcing officials into a period of critical reexamination and ultimately leading to the closure of the *bagne* in the years immediately following the end of World War II.

As an institution that existed for over a century and in which more than one hundred thousand individuals were imprisoned, the *bagne* played a crucial role in the history of modern France. In utilizing its institutional life as a prism through which to examine broader historical themes such as urbanization, industrialization, militarization, bureaucratization, crime, colonialism, modern medicine, the social sciences, modern journalism, and popular culture, we can view its central importance. What may not be as clear, however, is that in exploring the conjuncture/disjuncture between the "lived" and the "imagined" we not only move beyond mythic and monolithic characterizations of the *bagne* but also shed light on how power, discipline, and punishment were construed and enforced in these prison outposts.

Beyond *Papillon*

1. Back to the Future

France and Penal Colonization

By the mid-nineteenth century the banishment of political prisoners overseas had long been the policy, if not the actual practice, of penal administration in France. During the Revolution, dissidents were deported to the territorial holding of Louisiana, where they were not incarcerated in any way upon their arrival but simply required to live in a designated area for a specified length of time. Indeed, most of those exiled were later pardoned and repatriated. Although deportation for political offenses was an official part of the Napoleonic Code of 1810, it was something of a dead letter, as a suitable overseas replacement for the former American territory could never be found.[1]

The event that impelled the French state to reevaluate its position on penal colonization was the Revolution of 1848. To forestall continued political unrest and to lessen the burden on a penal system charged with housing the twelve thousand June Days insurgents sentenced to prison terms by Louis Napoleon's hastily convened tribunals, the president issued an emergency decree to transport these individuals to a "fortified enclosure" outside continental France. Although a number of possible locales were discussed, including Senegal, Madagascar, and even the arctic Kerguelen Islands, it was eventually decided that the insurgents be relocated to Algeria.[2]

Not until 1854 was legislation passed that formally established the South American territory of French Guiana as a destination for common-law criminals convicted of felonies. Heretofore they had typically served as *galériens* (oarsmen) on the galleys, which, given the brutal conditions aboard these vessels, was akin to a death sentence. Advances in design that allowed for more efficient sailing, however, made the ships and the convicts necessary for their propulsion obsolete, and the management and maintenance of the convicts who endured years of arduous rowing was turned over to the Ministry of the Marine.

In 1748 the government's Mediterranean galley fleet was decommissioned, and prisoners were sentenced to *travaux forcés* (hard labor) in such port cities as Toulon, Brest, and Rochefort.[3] The vast majority of prisoners were sent to Toulon, where they were paired together in chains on board the old galleys moored as hulks in the harbor until they had rotted away, at which time the prisoners were placed on pontoons. At the other locales, men were housed in shore prisons. The latter were not jails with cells but barracks-like structures where inmates were chained to their *tolards* (long wooden planks) at night. These crowded, dirty, and disease-ridden quarters were the site of "violence, trafficking, and sexual deprivation," as there was "no efficient supervision" of the men.[4]

In the ports, the prisoners helped build, repair (attending to masts and ropes), and provision ships. Convicts typically worked twelve to thirteen hours a day for a wage of ten to fifteen centimes, which they spent on extra food and wine.[5] Those possessing some mechanical skill had the opportunity to engage in more delicate tasks, such as joinery, drilling, and the caulking of ships, but most were "needed to carry heavy loads, turn wheels, drive pumps, and pull cables."[6] The prison population in the dockyards was about fifty-four hundred in 1789,[7] not including the *forçats libérés,* those freed at the end of their prison term. Whatever their original offense, it was generally agreed that those who completed their sentences were a significant source of crime and disorder in the port towns. Indeed, local officials complained of escapes and the frequent theft of tools and materials that were resold by prisoners to free workers.

Moreover, statistics compiled in the *Compte générale de l'administration de la justice criminelle*—the first government-sanctioned retrospective study of crime—seemed to indicate that France experienced an unprecedented wave of crime during the first half of the nineteenth century. Indeed, the twelve years between 1825 and 1837 saw a 39 percent growth in the number of criminal offenses and reported investigated crimes. As official crime statistics also pointed to a dramatic increase in the percentage of those accused of both repeat felonies (15.5 percent from 1826-30 to 26.2 percent in 1846-50) and misdemeanors (3 percent from 1826-30 to 17 percent by 1846-50),[8] concern arose over the apparent emergence of a permanent criminal class.[9] Individuals such as the famed prison inspector Louis Mathurin Moreau-Christophe characterized the figures as "a symptom of an active perversity; the indication of an imminent social peril."[10]

This discourse was rooted in a profound demographic shift that swept poor and uneducated workers out of the rural countryside and into the streets of Paris and other urban areas in search of employment and a better life. Indeed, during the nineteenth century the number of people living in urban areas in France almost tripled. According to historical sociologist A. R. Gillis, "urban France (considered as a settlement of at least 2,000 people) contained just over six million people in 1821, which was about twenty percent of the total population. By 1900, almost sixteen million people lived in urban areas, or forty-one percent of the population."[11] Moreover, inadequate measures taken by municipal and state authorities regarding sanitary living conditions exacerbated an already unhealthy lifestyle.[12] This not only made poverty and social dislocation more visible but led social theorists to attribute the "moral decay" of the new social class to the urban environment. The expanding problem of crime signified the deleterious effect of the city on individual morality.

Thus a widespread perception arose that it was in the burgeoning urban centers of nineteenth-century France where "irreligion, ignorance, selfishness, the contagion of example . . . all the vices of man are rampant. . . . [I]n the confused mixing of social classes, and the overturning of all ideas of subordination and duty, one sees immorality, prostitution, and poverty in our cities."[13] Viscount Louis Hermann Brétignières de Courteilles, a prominent philanthropist and penal reformer, agreed: "There are signs of malaise and ferment in the heart of the city where . . . pauperism has increased because of heavy industry. . . . [A]ttacks on property also continue to multiply, and there is a continual and sustained increase in misdemeanors and felonies."[14]

Social theorists did not believe crime to be absent from provincial France, but they regarded the crimes committed by the denizens of urban and rural areas as qualitatively different. In general, they viewed the criminal activity of the countryside as less dangerous and premeditated than that of the city. Journalist and penal reformer Léon Faucher explained this difference as one of environment: "Two different types of condemned criminals can be distinguished: the people of the city and those of the countryside; the precocious crime that grows in the cities as in a hothouse, and the occasional, almost childlike crime that occurs in the open air, and in the freedom of the fields."[15] Faucher's opinions on crime and punishment are crucial for the history of the penal colonies, as the Chamber of Deputies appointed him in 1848 to examine the problem of recidivism, and he would serve as minister of the interior in 1849 and again in the spring and summer of 1851.[16]

Recidivism was also perceived as a quintessentially urban phenomenon. In this regard the prominent penal theorist Benjamin Appert remarked: "Why are recidivists more numerous among *condamnés* from the large cities than the countryside? . . . [T]here is a shameful culture of vice and the practice of all types of dissolution and debauchery in the large cities. It is in this impure cesspool of society that exist almost all the criminals who are terrifying society with their misdeeds."[17]

Given such perceptions, many penal reformers advocated "colonizing the interior of the country with ex-convicts."[18] Utilizing a very broad definition of industrial worker and a much narrower one for agricultural laborer, Charles Lucas, the inspector general of French prisons, hypothesized that although there were two agricultural workers for every one individual employed in the city in 1700, this ratio had been completely reversed by 1830.[19] While Lucas's conclusion was erroneous, given that the height of rural under-population did not occur until the 1840s, commentators nevertheless suggested that former prisoners be sent to undeveloped rural areas of southern and southwestern France, where they would be given land and equipment to begin new lives as subsistence farmers.[20]

Commissioned by the French government to examine the penal system of the United States, Gustave de Beaumont and Alexis de Tocqueville issued a report that examined the relative merits of the Auburn and Pennsylvania modes of imprisonment. While opposed to the principle of penal colonization, the authors were nonetheless enamored with the idea of replacing the police surveillance to which newly released prisoners were subjected with terms of service in agricultural colonies. "If such colonies were established," argued the famed penal theorists, "no idler could complain of not finding labor; the beggars, vagrants, paupers, and all the released convicts whose number continues to increase, and continues to threaten the safety of individuals and the tranquility of society could find a place where they would contribute to the wealth of this country by their labor."[21] According to physician and penal reformer Michel Louis François Huerne de Pommeuse, such labor would "regenerate both physically and morally; the criminal would thus reenter society as a useful member, instead of being debased and a burden. . . . [C]olonization transforms generations of criminals into veritable citizens. . . . [I]t attacks crime at its roots."[22]

This notion of "internal penal colonization" was also based on the apparent success of an auxiliary penal institution that emerged during the 1840s: the Mettray agricultural colony for delinquent boys.[23] Established on a thousand-acre estate in the Indre-et-Loire by Frédéric Demetz, a young Parisian magistrate, the colony was structured around small "families" of forty or so inmates, each family living in a separate house with a "guard-father" who was responsible for their own agricultural production and upbringing. The goal of the institution was the rehabilitation of criminal youths through agricultural work and military discipline in a "family" setting. As its rehabilitative success became public—at government inquests, Demetz claimed that Mettray had a recidivism rate of 14 percent, in comparison to 75 percent for state penitentiaries for children—it spawned the establishment of fifty other agricultural colonies during the 1840s and eventually led to the passage of legislation in 1850 that made the private agricultural colony the most common form of incarceration for juvenile criminals in France.[24] By 1853, half of the minors under correctional care lived in agricultural colonies, giving these institutions a quasi-monopoly during the Second Empire.

Despite the apparent success of Mettray—the institution was closed in 1939 following charges of inhumane treatment—and the various calls to "arm the detainees with pick and trowel without fear, as work in the outdoors will provide a powerful palliative," plans for establishing such institutions for adult offenders did not come to fruition.[25] Nonetheless, the allure of agricultural life, idealized as the "natural occupation of man, that which satisfies him more than all others and which always calls to mind feelings of gratitude and love for providence," remained strong for French penal theorists.[26] As historian Jacques Petit has cogently argued, one sees the government of the Second Empire begin to reorganize prison work in the outdoors for the first time, with the idea "of the virtue and redemptive value of the land" never far from view.[27] Perhaps more to the point, C. R. Ageron characterized the penal strategy of agricultural colonization as "happiness for the poor and tranquility for the rich," as social exclusion connoted security in the minds of economists and publicists.[28]

To many observers in mid-nineteenth-century France, crime appeared as a moral pathology to which the "lower orders" of the city were particularly susceptible. Since the "urban poor give in to their passions and do not work," it seemed only "natural" to contemporaries such as social scientist Honoré-Antoine Frégier that "they always have been and always will be the most productive seedbed for all sorts of malfeasance: it is they whom we refer to as the dangerous classes . . . they are a fit object of fear and danger for society."[29] Indeed, as Louis Chevalier has pointed out: "This was unquestionably a class struggle, but it was carried on by means of a struggle which its contemporaries themselves described as a struggle of race, a conflict between two population groups differing wholly from each other, but above all in body, a difference not merely social but biological."[30]

A general concern with environment undergirded explanations of criminal causality that variously touched upon themes of class, morality, and physiology. Thus reformers began to argue that for a penal regime to be effective (i.e., to rehabilitate) it must offer a fundamentally new way of life for those incarcerated. The seeming increase in recidivism appeared to demand a reconfiguration of the offender's prison experience. In the old and crowded jails held over from the ancien régime, conditions were bleak, filthy, and disease-ridden. Many reformers railed against what they considered to be the "corrupt air" circulating within the confines of the prison. Physicians such as Guillaume Ferrus saw this befouled air as the result of not only the overcrowded and dirty conditions within the jails but also the insalubrious emanations of the urban-industrial milieu in which they were located. Indeed, Ferrus advocated that all prisons be relocated to isolated rural areas where such "pollution" was not so prevalent.[31]

Prisoners were also forced to depend on charity or their families for food, bedding, and clothing. Most of their time remained unoccupied, and officials made no attempt to separate the different classes of convicts; thus children and those accused of minor offenses were often confined in the same quarters as hardened criminals.[32] In such institutions, according to Faucher, "the criminal finds jail to be like home . . . the traditions and the vices of the jail are those of the street, and there is a corruption mutually taught."[33]

In this context, one sees the birth of an organized prison-reform movement in France. Steeped in Christian notions of charity and inspired by the ideals surrounding the Revolution and the Declaration of the Rights of Man, upper-class members of Restoration society promoted the idea that punishment should be nothing more than the deprivation of liberty and that decent living conditions for all prisoners was a fundamental responsibility of the state. Proponents of penal reform believed that improvements in the prison system were necessary not only to demonstrate to prisoners that the state whose laws they had violated was just and compassionate but also to forestall the damage occasioned by their return to society. Consequently, the weight of sentences shifted from corporal punishment to imprisonment, and an emphasis on vengeance and deterrence was broadened to include reform.[34]

By embarking on an active campaign of prison visitations and publicity, groups such as the Société de la morale chrétienne and the Société royale pour l'amélioration des prisons set the stage for the prison-reform bill of 1832, which stipulated that the penal administration provide inmates with the basic necessities.[35] The piles of straw that had been used as bedding were replaced by cots, and convicts were regularly provided clean clothing and bed linen. Prisoners were also given access to "elementary instruction, religious services, and rudimentary libraries."[36]

Prisons were designed according to type of prisoner and length of sentence. Nine *maisons centrales* (housing those sentenced for more than two years) were established, and the various departmental prisons (*maisons d'arrêt, maisons de justice,* and *maisons départmentales*) were charged with confining those awaiting trial or serving sentences of less than one year. Thus long-term and short-term offenders would no longer be held in communal quarters.[37]

Aside from more humane prison conditions, the primary agent of spiritual redemption for the prisoner was to be work. Raised with the notion of work as the fulfillment of Christian duty, penal reformers were convinced that productive labor was the true path toward moralization. For instance, Moreau-Christophe characterized work as "embodying all the punishment of imprisonment, in the sense that work is the necessary condition of man on earth; that is, nothing is owed him unless he earns it."[38] Prisoners were employed in a variety of tasks, such as the production of uniforms, bedding, clothing, and shoes, in order to meet the needs of not only the institution itself but also of private entrepreneurs who often organized and supplied such efforts as part of a profit-making enterprise.[39]

Because improvements in the penal system implied that the prisoner could be reformed, rehabilitation was to serve as the guiding principle for all prisons and houses of detention. In this regard, however, the dockyard *bagnes* were seen as lacking. Jacques François Bosourdy, a naval physician, commented that "although the legislator today seeks to establish laws of repression for crimes that punish the guilty, but also make them better through a penitence and a restoration of honest sentiments and good virtue in the soul, . . . the [shipyard] *bagnes* serve only to leave the prisoner with a sentiment that is completely depraved and a heart that is full of an invincible passion for crime."[40] Indeed, authorities viewed penal servitude in the ports as functional only because it mobilized large numbers of laborers as cheaply as possible, not for any reformative influence that such work might have upon the convict. With the notion of rehabilitation introduced into the penal equation, however, the Ministry of the Marine came under increasing criticism from those penal reformers and theorists who complained that prisoners were not employed in tasks that inculcated a sense of contrition. Given that Ministry officials had been complaining for years that "there was not enough work in the ports to keep the men busy" and that it was "a frightful burden" for the navy to meet such demands, this should not have been altogether surprising to critics.[41]

Nevertheless, individuals such as Baron Jean-Marguerite Tupinier, a counselor of state and director of ports, charged that "one sees in all the recesses of the arsenals, prisoners engaged in the most easy tasks; most of the time they are half-asleep or chatting; one sees ten to twelve men nonchalantly loading or unloading small carts, while others simply stand by and watch."[42] Penal administrator Édouard Proust remarked that with "the introduction of machine labor in the arsenals . . . forced labor has nothing forced or painful about it except in name.... [T]he easy labor of the prisoner is now accomplished outdoors amid the workers of the port; the *bagnes* have lost their power to intimidate."[43]

In addition, given the crowded conditions in the ports, the *bagnes* were subject to the same criticism as the prisons of the old regime, namely, that they were breeding grounds for deviant and criminal activity. Benjamin Appert spoke of "a contagious corruption that reigns in the *bagne*.... [T]he young prisoners are thrown pell-mell among the old, without regard to age; the *bagne* is a school of crime with tutors who teach their students brutality, violence, and vice."[44] Similarly, physician and penal reformer Almire Lepelletier de la Sarthe described the *bagne* as "a workshop that prepares them for greater crimes; it propagates perversity. Once they leave, they are monsters, wretches who are dumped upon society."[45]

Although the *bagnards* were tethered to one another by manacle, poorly clothed, ill-fed, and prone to disease (particularly typhus), it was not a sense of indignation over conditions in the dockyards but rather concern over their supposed attractiveness to prisoners held in traditional jails that helped to galvanize support for the eventual liquidation of these *bagnes*.[46] According to prison administrator Maurice Alhoy:

> Of all jails, those which merit the name the least, are the *bagnes*. ... In return for a bout with the chain, the *forçat* can communicate freely with his counterparts ... in spite of the fact that he is to be at hard labor, he is rarely tired. He can work for a savings; [he] finds upon entering the *bagne* a frugal nourishment that is preferable to the coarse dishes which satisfy most of his countrymen ... one sees assassins happy to find themselves in the *bagne*; they have what they want: life, shelter, and little work; they live in relative tranquility. ... Those who have visited the *bagnes* have seen in these establishments the picture of a happy criminality and an establishment of charity in favor of thieves and assassins.[47]

Moreau-Christophe maintained that "life in the *bagnes* is preferable to life in the prison. If one wants proof, look at all those who would prefer a punishment to hard labor rather than the isolation of imprisonment. In my visits to Bicêtre [a prison near Paris] I have listened to many *condamnés* plead to be transferred to Brest or Toulon."[48] Lucas similarly spoke of the "*condamnés* who beg to be transferred from the *maisons centrales* to the *bagne*. . . . [T]hey do not fear the infamy attached to the *bagne* and always ask for a transfer just as one would solicit an amelioration or even a pardon."[49] "The *bagnards* are more happy than the majority of our countrymen," argued Lepelletier de la Sarthe. "There are many who are less well-fed, and who do not have a bed that is preferable to the common plank of the *bagne*."[50]

The navy saw in such pronouncements an opportunity to be rid of the shipyard *bagnes,* whose regimen had been criticized for not being harsh enough and whose oversight it had always disdained. In this regard, Baron Portal, minister of the marine, once complained: "The *forçats* today number around 12,000. This is a frightening charge for the navy. Not only is it very costly, it corrupts the population of our shipyards."[51]

In this context, a commission of naval officers headed by Admiral Armand de Mackau concurred with the newly crowned emperor—following Louis Napoleon's coup of 1851—that the *bagnes* be permanently closed and that common-law convicts be transported overseas. Because of its proximity to France, however, Algeria had always been seen as an unhappy compromise among adherents of penal colonization, particularly among those supporters in the navy who were also well aware that the North African colony was under the control of the army. So for a time the issue of where these common-law criminals were to be transported remained unresolved. It was only after considerable research and debate—over such possible sites as Haiti, Cuba, the Dominican Republic, and even Texas—that French Guiana emerged as the locale of choice.[52]

This is somewhat surprising given that the French had failed to establish themselves in Guiana despite the fact that their presence reached all the way back to 1604 with Daniel de la Ravadière's search for Eldorado, the mythical city of the Incas. Over the course of the next fifty years, numerous mercantile companies failed in their efforts to settle colonists at the site of present-day Cayenne. Under the patronage of the Duc de Choiseul, the French prime minister, a settler colony was finally established at Kourou in 1763, where all but nine hundred of twelve thousand French colonists died of yellow fever in the first years after their arrival.[53] Those few who survived slowly developed a rudimentary plantation system, growing rice and sugarcane. Despite utilizing slave labor imported from West Africa, however, the colony was barely self-sufficient. With the abolition of slavery in 1794 the economic situation was dire, as the colony had lost its chief source of labor. As plantation production dwindled, and faced with the burgeoning slave economy of the American South, the only French colony on the South American continent appeared to be on the brink of extinction.

Yet voices emanating from the colony indicated that such unhappy results were a thing of the past. For instance, in an unsigned editorial that appeared in the colonial newspaper *Les Antilles,* the author remarked:

> With all exaggerations of fear, many speak of French Guiana as peopled only by serpents, tigers, and wild animals . . . that the inhabitants must live everyday in fear of venomous and ferocious beasts in an excessive heat and destructive climate. They charge that we have sent these people not to a place of exile but to their death. To these fears one must insist that the climate of Cayenne is one of the best in the world; the heat is not brutal . . . without doubt while there are abundant rains that are the cause of intermittent fevers, they are not dangerous, particularly if one is treated with quinine early on. . . . As for the venomous or ferocious animals, there are many, that is true. But they inhabit the forests in every sense, and I have rarely encountered such reptiles here. Others can attest to what has been written here and the truth of those words. We have written this for the poor mothers, for the faithful wives, and for those deported themselves, that they should not despair. . . . Yes, it is hard for everyone, but the actual circumstances of the country that is destined to receive the penitentiary are far from cruel.[54]

It would appear that such concerns were misplaced, as once the emperor called for volunteers to be transferred from the shipyard *bagnes* to French Guiana in 1852, some three thousand prisoners applied. (Two-thirds of these men set sail that same year, while the remainder would settle during the next two years.)[55]

These men were divided into two basic categories: the largest group was the *transportés*, or common-law prisoners sentenced to hard labor under the law known as *doublage* (which required that the prisoner serve a sentence equal in length to that which he had served in France); the *déportés*, or those individuals convicted of espionage or conspiracy, made up the second group. As we shall see in the next chapter, a third category was added in 1885 with the *rélégués*, or those individuals who had already served their sentences for numerous misdemeanor offenses in France and were forced to reside in the penal colony indefinitely.

All of these prisoners were first shipped to the island of St. Martin de Ré, off the coast of Normandy, where they were typically held for weeks or sometimes months before embarking on their journey overseas. Once the first penal settlements were established in French Guiana, one by one the old shipyard *bagnes* closed: Rochefort in 1852, Brest in 1858, and Toulon in 1873.[56] A new era in French penology was born.

In these early years the colonial *bagnards* were a relatively small portion of the total French prison population. For instance, in 1860 there were 21,493 prisoners housed in national prisons, 20,744 prisoners housed in departmental prisons, and 8,538 prisoners housed in juvenile institutions, or a total of 50,775 prisoners housed in France. In contrast, there were 5,597 convicts in French Guiana in that same year, or slightly over 11 percent of the total prison population. While the total number of *bagnards* remained nearly steady during the last half of the nineteenth century, with an average of approximately 5,400 inmates, the total number of individuals incarcerated steadily declined, as there were only 9,603 prisoners housed in national prisons, 17,235 prisoners housed in departmental prisons, and 4,599 prisoners housed in juvenile institutions, or a total of 31,437 prisoners in 1900. (This reduction in prisoners was largely the result of the decriminalization of certain felonies and the increasing use of fines for certain fiscal and forestry offenses.) Thus the overseas *bagnes* held slightly over 17 percent of the total prison population by the turn of the century.[57]

The first penal colony settlements were established on the Îles du Salut, off the Guianese coast, in 1852.[58] These are the three offshore islands of Diable, Saint-Joseph, and Royale. Île du Diable, or Devil's Island, the smallest of the island chain, was utilized exclusively for political prisoners such as Alfred Dreyfus, while the larger two islands were reserved for those guilty of disciplinary infractions such as escape or repeated refusal to work on the mainland. Île Saint-Joseph housed fifty-two cells, two *cachots* (dungeons),

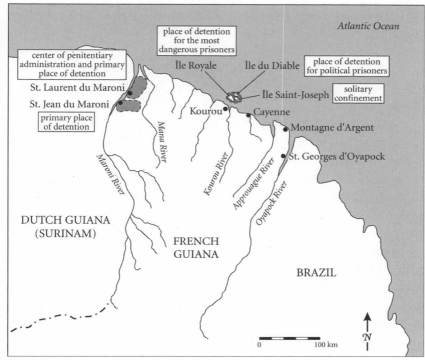

Penal establishments in French Guiana

and an infirmary, while Île Royale had fifty-eight cells and eight *cachots*.
Built in 1853, the first jungle camp—called Montagne d'Argent, as it stood
on a small hill near the Brazilian border—was a jumping-off point for deforestation and rudimentary road building.[59]

Conditions in these early days of penal colonization were made more
difficult by the presence of yellow fever. Indeed, hundreds of prisoners succumbed to the disease in French Guiana during the early years of transportation. Reports of yellow fever traced the continued extension of camps into
the interior near the hamlets of St. Marie and St. Augustine, where prisoners
were housed in lean-tos and exposed to mosquitoes while clearing trees and
building roads. A *médecin* (physician) first class by the name of J. Orgeas,
who would later write a lengthy tome on public health in the tropics after
completing his stint as a penal colony physician in French Guiana, estimated
that in 1855 the life expectancy of a convict housed on the relatively salubri-

ous Îles du Salut was one year, seven months, and six days, whereas in the interior camp of Montagne d'Argent it was a mere eight months and fifteen days.[60] At the latter camp, at which a coffee plantation had been established, mortality reached a high of 63 percent in 1864, forcing its abandonment the following year.[61]

Among the 6,288 prisoners transported to French Guiana between 1852 and 1856, 3,574 cases of yellow fever resulted in 1,721 deaths: more than 27 percent of the total prison population.[62] This pattern continued for the next five years as annual rates of prisoner mortality from yellow fever in French Guiana ranged from 8.40 percent in 1858 to 9.90 percent in 1859, 8.30 percent in 1860, 8.00 percent in 1861, and 7.60 percent in 1862.[63] This compared unfavorably with mortality in metropolitan French prisons. Indeed, mortality in some of the most infamous *maisons centrales* in France were much lower, with annual rates during this same period of time averaging 4.85 percent in Riom, 4.64 percent in Gaillon, 4.4 percent in Melun, 4.13 percent in Clairvaux, 3.98 percent in Chiavari (Corsica), and 3.75 percent in Fontevrault.[64]

Of course, it was unknown at the time that the bite of the *Aedes aegypti* mosquito endemic to tropical regions such as French Guiana was the principal vector of the disease. During the early years of settlement yellow fever ravaged those penal colony establishments located near standing bodies of water where mosquitoes bred. Initial symptoms of the disease typically include headaches, fever, vomiting, and the presence of albumin in the urine. After a brief period in which the fever subsides, the victim begins to hemorrhage from mucous membranes, to vomit blood (the characteristic black bile of yellow fever), and eventually to suffer jaundice, due to the destruction of liver cells. Recovery, when it occurs, provides immunity from future attack, but the swift-moving infection often kills its host.[65]

The disease afflicted penal colony personnel and settlers no less than prisoners. From 1852 to 1856 there were 886 deaths from yellow fever among the 4,254 civilians in French Guiana—more than a fifth of the total free population. This figure does not take into account, however, those functionaries stricken with the illness who returned to France for convalescence. Thus, of the 358 personnel shipped back to France during this period, 306 ultimately died from yellow fever. When these individuals are taken into consideration, the total proportion of those who succumbed to the illness rises to 28 percent, nearly identical to the rate of prisoner deaths.[66]

Given the startling number of deaths, officials determined that a change in the location of the point of arrival was necessary. In 1857 the tiny mainland village of St. Laurent du Maroni, some twenty-five miles from the coast on the Maroni River, was chosen as the site for a "penal city" through which all the prisoners were processed (i.e., medical examination, prisoner classification, and labor assignments). Indeed, St. Laurent would serve as the ostensible capital of the *bagne* for the next eighty years, "as two-thirds of the convict population would serve their time there."[67] Upon arrival, these penal colony pioneers found little on the ground and were immediately charged with building the jails and barracks in which they would live and work.

Soon, however, there were reports that another disease had taken hold in the interior: malaria. Of course, malaria had long been a scourge for Europeans as it spread from Egypt and Asia Minor to southern Europe and the Mediterranean owing to the increased commerce in that part of the world and the fact that habitats for the mosquitoes that carried malaria were found there. As with yellow fever, it was transmitted by the mosquito—in this case the *Anopheles* genus—and characterized by "intermittent high fevers and a general weakening of the body," which most often resulted in death for those who had not developed a resistance through a lifelong exposure to the disease.[68] The disease would eventually make its way to the New World with the settlement of Europeans and slaves in the sixteenth century.

The first report of malaria came from St. Georges, which was about twenty-five miles from the mouth of the Oyapock River.[69] Of the 248 prisoners who made their way to this site, on which a sugar and coffee plantation was to be put into operation in April 1863, only 147 were still alive by March of the following year. More striking was the fact that, unlike the metropolitan prisoners, none of the thirty-three conscripted black workers from the French Antilles who accompanied the convoy fell ill. This startling divergence in the morbidity (i.e., the rate of disease or portion of diseased people in a population) of blacks and whites attracted the attention of physicians and administrators. In the annual reports produced by the Ministry of the Marine there always appeared comparisons in mortality between the two

races. In the case of St. Georges it was noted that while the rate of morbidity
from malaria among Europeans in the year following the first outbreak was
21.6 percent, for black prisoners and personnel it was only 5.2 percent, and
in 1865 it fell to 3.2 percent.[70]

As it was still not known that resistance to malaria stemmed from long-
term exposure to the disease and that the mosquito was its principal vector,
the high mortality of Europeans seemed to confirm the long-standing shib-
boleth that race, climate, and salubriousness were inextricably intertwined.
This notion that the physical constitutions of certain races were inherently
incompatible with particular environmental conditions was firmly embedded in mid-nineteenth-century medical thought. It was widely believed that
while those emanating from the more torrid regions of the globe could not
adapt to the rigors of colder climes, the heat and humidity of the tropics
was similarly inimical to the European physique.[71] It was in this vein that
the chief physician in French Guiana remarked: "Because of the numerous
attempts to colonize French Guiana, it is possible to appreciate the influence
of the climate on metropolitans. The maladies that are prevalent in the country have an intimate connection with the climatological and geographical
constitution." In this context, he believed, "What has passed in St. Georges
during the course of the last few years demonstrates that the different races
are endowed with an aptitude that allows them to survive in their own climate. One thousand Negroes cultivating the earth around Moseau would
live no longer than 1,000 Europeans cultivating the earth in French Guiana.
. . . Different races are not apt to contract the same maladies. . . . Malaria
principally strikes the white race. Blacks are very nearly free of the affliction.
. . . In this regard blacks enjoy an immunity that is nearly complete."[72] It was
in this context, as Redfield has pointed out, that the black prisoners were
shifted to camps in "unhealthy" areas to clear and drain land.[73]

This crude biological determinism—what French biologist Jean Boudin
termed "non-acclimatization"[74]—was also invoked as an explanation for
what seemed to be a low birthrate among the few convicts who served their
prison terms and married indigenous women or whose spouses joined them
in French Guiana upon their release. Although data from this early period of
penal colonization are not substantial, Orgeas found in his study of public
health in French Guiana an "enormous" number of infertile or "sterile"
households in and around St. Laurent between 1859 and 1884. The "primor-

dial and general cause of this phenomenon," according to the doctor, was "the non-acclimatization of the white race. In the middle of this unfavorable milieu there are a high number of miscarriages . . . which are at least as numerous as those pregnancies that come to full term."[75]

For those children born in French Guiana, local physicians held out little hope for survival. In a report from 1866, a chief physician characterized young children as being "infiltrated by a general lethargy between the ages of two and three. It is at this time that they become prone to intermittent fevers and are taken to the hospital where most die. We do not speak here of all children in Maroni, fortunately there have been exceptions, but in sum, this young generation seems to have little hope of a future."[76] Orgeas also saw no future for the French in French Guiana, proclaiming that "a child born in France has a much better chance of reaching the age of five years than a child in Maroni. One must conclude that the white race of *transportés* living in French Guiana and cultivating the soil will be the only generation to do so."[77]

Thus the Ministry of the Marine made the decision to halt the transportation of metropolitan prisoners to French Guiana in 1867 and to rely exclusively upon the more temperate Pacific island holding of New Caledonia. A total of 17,229 prisoners were transported to French Guiana between 1852 and December 1866. Of these, 16,523 were of European descent, with 394 emanating from the colonies. In addition, 212 convict women were shipped from the *maisons centrales* in France, although they were not held in the *bagnes* but instead placed in a nunnery that was managed by the Saint-Joseph of Cluny sect of the Catholic Church.[78] Without question, the first attempt at penal colonization in French Guiana had ended in failure, as "nearly half" of all prisoners transported to the *bagnes* between 1852 and 1866 died of disease.[79] The outbreak of malaria at the camp of St. Georges merely proved to be the catalyzing event that led officials to a different shore.

New Caledonia had long been viewed as a potential settler colony. This is evident in the report of a ship's surgeon on a voyage of exploration aboard the *Alcmène*: "On the day when New Caledonia, now thoroughly untamed, becomes the fief of a civilized people, it will in my opinion, rapidly progress to prosperity. The excellence of its climate, its fertility, its wholesomeness, and its many riches are all guarantees of success for colonizing ventures on this great island."[80] At this time New Caledonia had only 430 settlers, most of whom were mining prospectors not intent on remaining permanently in the South Pacific, and some 800 military personnel.[81] But the lure of New Caledonia, no matter how illusory, proved far too great for French officials to ignore. The first shipment of 250 *forçats* arrived on the Isle of Nou in May 1864. By 1870 there were 2,451 prisoners in New Caledonia,[82] and by 1885, when the first shipments of *rélégues* arrived, the prison population reached a relatively staggering 9,997.[83]

Four main penitentiary sites were established: Île Nou (1867-1913); Presqu'île de Ducos (1870-80); Île des Pins (1870-80), for the 4,500 Communard deportees exclusively; and Îlôt Brun (1870-1913), a disciplinary establishment where the *cachots* and punishment cells were located. The penitentiary administration was located in Bourail on Île Nou, and all the prisoners were processed through this depot before being transferred to the Grande Terre (main island).[84]

Aside from the penitentiaries, work camps for logging and road building existed in and around the island. Penitentiary farms were also estabished west of Nouméa, where vegetables and fruits were cultivated in order to meet the needs of the institution. Sugarcane was harvested on Île Nou, which had some 425 hectares of fallow land at its disposal. With some twenty-five hundred prisoners by 1885, this island also housed a variety of workshops in which those prisoners who had some practical labor skills—as in carpentry or metalworking—worked in sawmills or forges or as wheelwrights.[85]

Once these institutions were established in New Caledonia's relatively temperate climate, it was decided that "French Guiana should receive only Arab and African prisoners whose constitutions are resistant to the climate of the colony, since their health does not seem to change greatly under the sudden change in temperature they must undergo."[86] Indeed, in the years immediately following the cessation of European prisoner transportation to French Guiana, overall rates of hospital admissions and mortality dropped (see tables 1.1 and 1.2).

While these figures do not differentiate between white and black prisoners, officials attributed the decline in mortality to the immediate abandonment of the interior jungle camps and the slow transfer of European convicts to New Caledonia. Physicians and Ministry officials were very pleased with the apparent salubrity of the new penal colony in the South Pacific. In the annual report on transportation produced in 1867, it was noted that of an

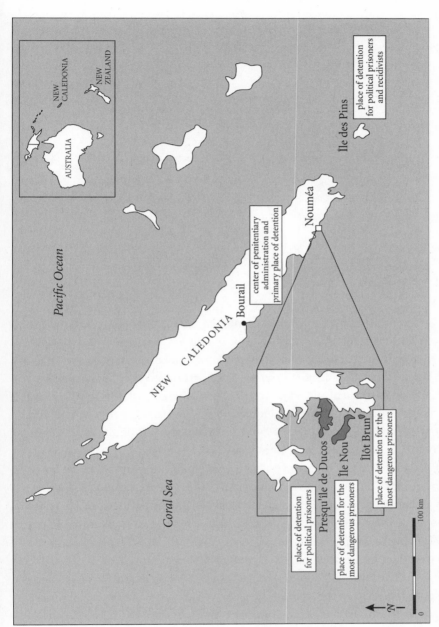

Penal establishments in New Caledonia

Table 1.1. Hospital Admissions in French Guiana, 1868–1870.

Year	Average number sick by day	Average prison population	Number of trips	Percentage
1868	504	6,906	183,914	7.3
1869	482	6,500	175,722	7.4
1870	386	5,805	141,064	6.6

Source: *Notice sur la transportation en Guyane et en Nouvelle-Calédonie* (1868–1870), 17.

Table 1.2. General State of Mortality in French Guiana, 1868–1870.

Year	Average prison population	Deaths by illness	Percentage	Accidental deaths
1868	6,906	384	5.5	48
1869	6,500	324	4.9	26
1870	5,805	275	4.7	25

Source: *Notice sur la transportation en Guyane et en Nouvelle-Calédonie* (1868–1870), 17.

average number of 247 *transportés* on the island, only three had died in 1864 and 1865. In this context, New Caledonia was seen as "exceeding all expectations. . . . We have found here a situation far superior to that of the [shipyard] *bagne* of Toulon, reputed until this time to be the most healthy penal establishment in the metropole."[87] In the long history of the penal colonies, this notion that individuals could flourish only in a climate like that of their ancestral origin would be one of the last points upon which doctors and administrators would agree.

Whether based upon rehabilitative sentiment or political expediency, the initial effort to remove malfeasants from France did not reduce the incidence of crime. As historian Gordon Wright has pointed out, there did appear to be a decline in the overall crime rate in the decade immediately following the implementation of penal colonization in French Guiana. As we shall see in the next chapter, however, this apparent success was illusory, and the leitmotif of disorder in both the prison system and society at large would reemerge in the writings of social critics and theorists as the misdemeanor recidivist became a dominant figure in the cultural landscape of fin de siècle France.

2. The Desire to Deport

The Recidivist of Fin de Siècle France

Like their predecessors in the first half of the century, fin de siècle com‑
mentators would also locate a source of disorder in the prison system and
in French society. However, it was no longer the felonious criminal but
rather the petty recidivist who served as the dominant figure in the cultural
imaginary. Despite the fact that the attempt to rid France of its most dan‑
gerous malfeasants resulted in only a temporary reduction in the incidence
of crime, the beggar and vagrant were thrust into the same penal colony
web inhabited by the murderer and rapist. With the Relegation Law of 1885,
those individuals convicted of four misdemeanors, such as theft, swindle,
abuse of confidence, offenses against public morals, morals crimes against
children, and vagrancy and begging with aggravating circumstances (i.e.,
while carrying a weapon), were relegated to the *bagnes*. The commission
of two misdemeanors plus five convictions for simple vagrancy also led to
relegation. It was therefore not the gravity of the crime but the repetition of
the same or similar acts that constituted legal grounds for transportation.[1]

The elaborate effort to transport common-law criminals overseas marks
an important break in the development of juridical and penal ideas in France.
In the period of the Revolution and Empire there had been a general—albeit
halting—move away from arbitrary penalties over whose application the
magistrate had little discretionary power and toward a more individualized
form of punishment. For instance, the penal code of 1791 for the first time
allowed judges to vary the length of criminal sentences according to the
circumstances surrounding the commission of a crime. This was followed
by legislation passed in 1832 that permitted juries to consider extenuating

circumstances and to recommend reduced penalties for criminal infractions.[2] Thus it was individual criminals, not individual crimes, that were
punished.

Penal philosophy and practice also underwent significant change during
the first half of the nineteenth century. The Napoleonic Code of 1810 drew
up a scale of offenses and prescribed for them prison sentences of different
lengths, establishing a hierarchy of punishment. This system of justice was
to accompany a program of rehabilitation. It marked a shift away from the
older, and more brutal, non-utilitarian punitive structures to penal institutions designed to make its subjects more efficient, productive, and docile.
Punishment was to be proportionate to the crime committed; anything
more would be not only cruel but also useless in reforming the prisoner.
The objective was no longer the vengeance of the sovereign but rather the
"normalization" of the subject.[3]

In this context, how does one account for the appearance of the Relegation Law, which—by mandating that all those meeting the aforementioned
conditions, regardless of circumstance, be banished for life after already
serving out their prison sentences in France—not only compromised the
discretionary power of judge and jury but also negated the principles of
individualized and proportionate punishment? I seek to answer this question by situating petty recidivism within larger processes of criminological
and social-scientific definition. Serving as a focal point around which a
variety of intellectual and cultural anxieties swirled and accreted, recidivism
appeared to require an institutional solution not found within the prison
system, namely, what to do with the habitual criminal who had become
an object of terror and contempt in fin de siècle France. By examining this
configuration of knowledge, we not only uncover the premises that shaped
and legitimated the decision to transport the recidivist overseas but also
disclose how the practice spoke powerfully to a profound sense of crisis in
society at large.

There was a growing belief in late-nineteenth-century France that the
repression and punishment of criminals was a failure. Commentators found
that recidivism was on the rise, despite efforts during the first half of the
century to rehabilitate the malfeasant through the implementation of a separate, cellular regime. This was especially true of the government-sponsored

Haussonville Commission. Appointed by Parlement in 1871 and headed by the prominent social Catholic Viscount Othenin d'Haussonville, the commission investigated the state of crime and punishment in France following the horrific events surrounding the Paris Commune. It determined that in less than two decades the number of individuals who committed crimes within the first year of their release from prison had nearly doubled, from 34,901 in 1851 to 65,211 in 1868.[4] Studies subsequent to Haussonville's also noted this phenomenon. As reflected in the *Compte générale de l'administration de la justice criminelle* of 1880, statisticians found that whereas 16 percent of those charged and sentenced to prison terms between 1826 and 1830 were repeat offenders, the figure had risen to 51 percent by 1881.[5]

As troubling, and perhaps more perplexing for observers, was the number of those convicted of minor offenses such as vagabondage and petty theft. French law recognized three categories of criminal offenses: *contraventions* (misdemeanors), which were judged by the *tribunaux de police*; *délits* (moderately serious offenses), which were judged by the *tribunaux correctionels*; and *crimes* (felonies), which were judged by the *cours d'assises* in which a jury sits.[6] What seemed to be remarkable to observers was that between 1850 and 1880 the rates of recidivism for theft and begging were 60 and 70 percent, respectively, or nearly double that for felonies during the same period.[7] Thus, while misdemeanors accounted for only 17 percent of all crimes charged in 1850, this number had risen to 46 percent by 1900.[8]

Given the development and growing authority of statistics in the nineteenth century, it is hardly surprising that contemporaries viewed such numbers so uncritically.[9] However, much of this increase, both relative and absolute, was due to improvements in policing. Indeed, during the Second Empire one sees the birth of a modern police force, particularly in the cities. Borrowing from the structure established by the London police, Louis Napoleon tripled the size of the Parisian police force, quadrupled its budget, started a training program for its agents, and introduced a modern organizational structure in 1854.[10] Of course, the direct effect of this was a precipitous rise in minor offenses. This category of offenses ballooned from a yearly average of 248,690 in 1846–50 to an average of 538,441 in 1866–70.[11]

The recidivism rate was also the result of a major innovation implemented during this period. With the creation of *casiers judiciaries* (individual dossiers) for each criminal passing through the court system in 1850, the criminal record of every offender was available to all magistrates. Kept in both the home department of the offender and at the Prefecture of Police in Paris, these files contained biographical data.[12] This not only eased the task of identifying recidivists but provided invaluable information to those government officials charged with estimating the rate of recidivism. It is not coincidental that the recidivism rate jumped sharply with the introduction of the *casier*. Nevertheless, the belief that the rate of crime and recidivism was swelling caused great social concern.

Rather than crediting an expanded police force and greater judicial oversight for an increased awareness of the problem, the Haussonville Commission attributed recidivism to "the insufficiency of our penitentiary regime from a moral point of view." Upon delivering the final report of the commission to Parlement in 1875, Haussonville declared: "We are not men who are moved by the condition of the malfeasant, and propose to improve his condition. No, gentlemen, to the contrary, we are inclined to believe that the penitentiary system is neither moral nor repressive enough."[13] In his critique of the prison system, Haussonville pointed to a "floating population that moves between prison and freedom, and which likes to receive prison sentences at the beginning of winter in order to be free in the spring. Vagabonds, beggars, and violators of parole hide from the police until the first snow and then allow themselves to be arrested because they know that in prison they will find themselves food, a blanket, and a society which agrees with them."[14]

The reformed and rehabilitative prison would come to generate much criticism among other criminal theorists searching for explanations of recidivism. Indeed, there was something of an ideological backlash against the utilitarian punitive structure of the early nineteenth century. In this regard, Camille Aymard, a Parisian attorney, argued: "When one visits a departmental prison . . . one understands that for the miserable placed there, life is often less painful and more secure when behind prison bars. How many are there among them, who were deliberately arrested at the beginning of winter and implored the court to inflict a sentence that would last until the following spring? For those already hardened by crime . . . what is a few weeks of detention? A happy accident which assures them lodging, food, and clothing, and a time of rest in their life of adventure."[15] In this sense, the rather arcane academic debate over penal reform took on a new and practical urgency: what was to be done with "this compact army, an association against society; a league against the law, a refractory body whose profession threatens public security"?[16] As article 271 of the Penal Code stipulated that it was a crime to not have a permanent or certain domicile, these men had to be punished, or, in the words of penal administrator M. James-Nattan, "bowed and broken."[17]

Lurking beneath such prosaic generalizations lie the reality and the perception of the vagabond. As historians Matt Matsuda and Jean-François Wagniart have argued independently, the vagabond was a cultural creation, an archetype that reflected the anxieties of the age.[18] This was certainly the case in the criminological and social-scientific discourse of the day. The physician Armand Pagnier considered the vagabond's itinerancy to be "atavistic," "harkening back to the needs of the primitive hordes in constant search of game, with the difference being that today his game is society."[19] Indeed, A. Rivière, an attorney, described vagabonds as "worn-out beings... their inertia always stronger than any of the measures employed to combat it. Their only faculty is obstinacy, and their inveterate aversion to work is a veritable infirmity that seems to be impervious to all medication."[20]

Anxiety over the vagabond was only heightened by a pervasive model of decline which assumed that a first minor criminal transgression would inexorably lead to a chain of more serious crimes. In this sense, Gustave Macé, a former prefect of police, argued that "every vagabond contains the stuff of a criminal, and will sooner or later become one."[21] Similarly, pastor and penal reformer Elie Robin maintained that "after a first condemnation the vagabond inevitably commits a second, then a third offense, and he then becomes a recidivist. . . . He will then engage in more serious crimes such as theft. . . . Vagabond, beggar, recidivist, thief, he goes around in a fatal circle."[22] Thus reduced to the level of abstraction, the vagabond was troubling not only for his state of being but also for his potential future criminality.

Criminal theorists argued, however, that the French system of justice could no longer fulfill its punitive function, as prison sentences for petty offenders were too short for true expiation to take place. The "brevity of prison sentences," wrote penal administrator M. Choppin, "not only weakens efforts to morally amend the *condamné*, but at the same time is an inconvenience for society, which must face these individuals who commit new crimes nearly immediately after they are out of the hands of justice."[23]

Haussonville also made note of this phenomenon: "In 1869 there were 40,000 prison sentences of less than one month pronounced: applied in this fashion, the punishment of prison has lost all of its intimidating character, with the result that the guilty have become all too familiar with this punishment."[24] Emile Yvernès, chief of the statistics bureau for the Ministry of Justice, expressed a similar thought: "Imprisonment to a short term is completely lacking in moral effect and serves as neither a mode of repression, nor example, nor amendment. It seems that these figures demonstrate the necessity of a more severe repression."[25]

In this context, the famed French jurist Gabriel Tarde maintained that "the growing feebleness among judges and juries who offer clemencies every day" is the result of "individuals who are impregnated by a pseudo-liberalism and an emotional sensibility that benefits criminals."[26] Critics such as Aymard also attributed this reticence to enforce an "afflictive" term of punishment to a society in which "everyone is filled with the detestable philanthropic sentimentalism that has characterized the nineteenth century; one fears being called a barbarian if not adhering to this so-called ideal . . . with the result being that the application of punishment is made with too much softness, too much humanity, and that the effect of intimidation which was once produced has now disappeared completely."[27] Paul Cuche, a professor of law at Grenoble and the author of a book on penitentiary science, inveighed similarly:

> Punishment has been weakened by a progressive softening of morals, especially among the well-off class from which magistrates are recruited. Thanks to the prodigious development of science and industry, our material life has surrounded us in comforts that our fathers never knew. Thus, physical suffering increasingly frightens us as we ourselves suffer less. . . . Our civilization is invaded little by little by this sickly sensitivity which has dulled our emotions . . . and now strongly exceeds the measure of what one could call humanity. . . . Today, as the surgeon

anesthetizes the sick in order to operate, we would like to bring about moral recoveries without pain. . . . If we continue in this way, penal intimidation will soon be no more than a memory, with the result being that the vast majority of delinquents will be subject to a kind of moral hygiene that will demand only the temporary sacrifice of their liberty. . . . At this time the criminal profession will offer such an appeal that the most powerful levers society has to offer will not stop its development.[28]

Such opinions were based on the widely held notion of "less eligibility,"[29] the belief that beggars and vagabonds should experience more discomfort in the institution designed to punish than those who supported themselves through their own thrift and industry. The very presence of a reformed prison diminished the value that the state placed on the moral efforts of the poor. In this understanding, penal reform was recast as mawkish in inspiration and dangerous in effect. In their reformative zeal, the "humanitarians" of the early nineteenth century had overlooked the deterrent effect of punishment, which, by the force of example, was to hold sway over the rest of the community.

Jules Leveillé, a Parisian professor of criminal law and member of the Chamber of Deputies, believed that French society had already reached this crucial juncture. Perhaps the most politically active criminal theorist of the day, he fostered a reputation as a "tough law-and-order man," largely based on his advocacy of a more severe disciplinary regime in the penal colonies.[30] According to Leveillé, "The prison, such as we have made it, in its sickly sentimentality, clumsy and inefficient with public funds, does not intimidate, and is very expensive for our budget. In my opinion, the prison, if left alone, will no more stand up to the needs of modern society than a stone would to a rifle and the needs of our modern wars."[31] Deterrence had been minimized at a great risk to society at large through the insertion of reformation into the concept of punishment.

Although critical of a prison system they believed did not sufficiently deter recidivism, many theorists were also convinced that such incorrigibility was a harbinger of social collapse. In this regard Haussonville and others perceived something quite sinister in the rising incidence of petty recidivism. It was not merely a failed prison system but also an unsettled and agitated individualism at the heart of French society that was to blame for this social pathology.

In support of this general contention, the educator, social theorist, and solidarist politician Alfred Fouillée argued that crime in late-nineteenth-century France was the product of a moral crisis brought about by the spectacle of wealth. This spectacle reinforced acquisitive instincts, the disintegration of the family, and the destruction of traditional morality. It was not economic deprivation but rather the "ease with which we can satisfy our desires that has led to the vices of our children." According to Fouillée, "Crime is by far, especially in France, less frequent in the poorer regions. The wealthiest regions of our nation are the most avaricious and present us with a youth that honor that fact. . . . Rural Brittany has less crime because wealth was attained slowly and laboriously."[32] Henri Joly, a member of the law faculty at Paris, argued similarly: "The departments where there are the most poor people are to all viewpoints the most honest. Poor thieves never steal for the satisfaction of fantasy or flirtatiousness, but instead for pressing needs. At present the rising movement of crime follows the increase in the general well-being and elevation of salaries."[33]

Here we see the same rural-urban dichotomy posited by earlier social theorists, but with a slight variation. As in the first half of the century, there was a sense that French society was violently changing under the stresses of industrialization and the growth of cities. Aided by a railway system that had grown from 26,327 kilometers in 1882 to 64,898 by 1910 under the Freycinet Plan of 1879, and spurred by such factors as the phylloxera epidemic of the 1860s and a general downturn in the agricultural economy, France experienced massive rural-to-urban migration.[34] This phenomenon was not seen as the simple result of a changing socioeconomic pattern but rather was attributed to the "irresistible pull of displays of luxury which dictate one's behavior."[35] "Attracted to the great cities by the prospect of luxuries and pleasures . . . these migrants," according to Paris attorney Augustin Delvincourt, "find only misery . . . and are quickly reduced to a life of crime."[36]

In this context, the contrast between the "disordered" city and the morally upright countryside was manifest in contemporary social-scientific discourse. For instance, we see the social theorist G. L. Duprat decry that "unlike agriculture, which asks for the continuous effort and patience of robust people who live day by day, bit by bit, this life has been abandoned little by little by most of those in the countryside for the great cities which inspire the continual desire for a better existence."[37] The penologist Adolphe Prins told a similar story: "The emigration from the country to the city increases our army of criminals and multiplies the chances of crime. When the sons of peasants leave the plow for the workshop and come to seek fortune in the furnace of the great cities, they follow the spirit of adventure; they must have, at any price, a means of subsistence, and as competition is great and temptations arise at every step, the prisons profit by this oversupply that the country gives to the city."[38]

Such critiques were a way of negating the urban environment, an almost visceral reaction to the "modern" world in which the city's differences from the countryside were perceived as pathological. Unlike the bucolic vision of the rural village where individual lives depended on the "natural" cycles of agriculture, the character of the city was determined by the necessities and attendant moral unpleasantness that accompanied commerce and trade. As such, contemporary social theorists demonized the city, imagining it as an orgy of unrelenting moral depravity and decadence, while they portrayed the countryside as less a place than an idea of place.

By examining the effects of economic and industrial progress on the entire social order, theorists were calling into question the value system of fin de siècle France. A new leitmotif of mass consumption as social disruption was now deployed to describe the complications arising as the result of socioeconomic change. It was therefore "not capitalism that is demoralizing," according to Tarde, but "the moral crisis that accompanies the pressure of change from artisan production, or from some particular mode of the latter to some other mode. . . . In short, criminality and morality are less dependent upon the economic state of a country than upon its economic transformations."[39]

As the urban milieu was the locus for this economic transformation, it was seen as the preeminent breeding ground for this new, pathological *mentalité*. In part this can be tied to the contemporaneous discovery of the unconscious, of what theorists considered the innate human compulsion to imitate. Indeed, this notion of human nature was quite prevalent in fin de siècle social-scientific circles. For instance, Gustave Le Bon, perhaps the greatest bowdlerizer of "crowd psychology,"[40] maintained: "Man, like animals, has a natural tendency to imitation. Imitation is a necessity for him, provided always that the imitation is quite easy. It is this necessity that makes the influence of what is called fashion so powerful. Whether in the matter of opinions, ideas, literary manifestations, or merely of dress, how many persons are bold enough to run counter to fashion? At every period there exist a small number of individuals that act upon the rest and are imitated by the unconscious mass."[41]

In a manner similar to Le Bon's, Tarde argued that imitation passed not only from one person to another but from one class to another. This was fostered by an "envy" symptomatic of social changes that had brought the classes closer physically and economically, allowing not only the communication of ideas and values but also the pursuit of luxury and happiness.[42] In particular, it was in "cities where contact is close and life is active and exciting" that "imitation is most frequent and changes often." Tarde defined this phenomenon as "fashion," which he contrasted with "stable groups, family and country," where contact is less frequent and imitation less pronounced.[43]

Duprat also believed that the city was a space in which "the heterogeneity of elements contribute to a ruined and unscrupulous collective consciousness . . . the city has modified the ancient spirits, transformed old mores and habits, and made the collectivity more unstable and less harmonious. . . . In their dream-like state . . . demoralization occurs because of the ominous influences of an aggregate of elements too recently integrated. . . . [T]hus it takes little time for the peasant to become the most scurrilous of citizens . . . astute, daring, and deceitful.[44] Similarly, magistrate Louis Albanel argued:

> While there certainly still exist peasant personalities of high
> repute, simple and strong of spirit . . . who know how to conform
> themselves to the situations they are in . . . the experience of our
> day obliges us to believe that they form a minority and that there
> are many more who are lured to the city by false mirages. . . . The
> country man leaves his village—where he earned a low salary,

it is true, but sufficient in general to live—in search for superior
wealth in Paris; but he soon understands that it is much more
expensive to live there than in the country, and while he earns
more he is obliged to spend more. . . . After arriving in the city
with its rich hotels, and its department stores with their sump-
tuous displays . . . the peasant soon feels ashamed and awkward
and succumbs rapidly to the temptation of luxury.[45]

It is not surprising that these notions of "imitative" human behavior
were articulated in the wake of the events surrounding the Commune. All
social order—individual and collective—seemed to have been obliterated,
leaving nothing but the fear of being completely unmoored: the terror of
an erupting chaos. Haunted by this fear of impending cataclysm and social
anarchy, many social theorists foresaw the imminent collapse of French society as they knew it. Indeed, with images of violent and unruly mobs easily
manipulated by unscrupulous leaders still fresh in the collective memory,
antisocial behaviors of all kinds were characterized as having an almost
epidemic quality about them.[46] Thus, at the same moment that there is a
heated debate about who would enjoy the privileges of legal and economic
enfranchisement in France, we see theorists such as Tarde argue that

the social revolution has increased the number of persons without a class, of those who are restless, a hotbed for crime, and of
vagabonds whose number has quadrupled since 1826. And as
charitable instincts have not made much headway in our bus-
tling society, the condemned who are still honest after having
committed their first crime—discharged prisoners wavering
between the example offered by the majority of society, honest
but inhospitable, and that of the little criminal fatherland which
is quite ready to naturalize them—end by necessarily taking this
direction as unwed mothers naturally turn to prostitution.[47]

In this understanding, recidivism and revolution were related phenom-
ena. Indeed, Haussonville believed that the vast majority of the Communards were criminal recidivists.[48] The city was a space that favored the trans-

mission of both criminal and revolutionary impulses among the laboring poor. In the eyes of contemporary social theorists, today's recidivist in all likelihood becomes tomorrow's social revolutionary.

Amid these generalized fears of social disorder in fin de siècle France, a belief emerged that moral character and psychological features were to some degree tied to biology. Indeed, it is noteworthy that the growing fixation upon the petty recidivist becomes particularly evident when not only economic but also military forces threatened national stability and unity. After the shocking defeat at the hands of Bismarck, the discussion about recidivism was often linked to anxieties about national and racial decline. While a united Germany was growing at a rate of four hundred thousand per year, France's population remained static. As such, many contemporaries felt that this "de-natality" foreshadowed the moral and physical degeneration of the population.[49]

As such, crime was a preeminent signifier of national degeneration. Operating within the paradigm established by Jean-Baptiste Lamarck in the eighteenth century and refined by Benedict Augustus Morel between 1857 and 1860, many theorists saw crime as the result of a fatal interaction between heredity and milieu.[50] Simply put, because of the adaptive qualities of the human race, individuals—if exposed to a pathological environment—would be inclined to dysfunction and would also pass on a predisposition for antisocial behavior to their progeny. Thus a retrogressive process is depicted whereby the degenerative influences of "diet, toxins, climates, disease, and moral depravities" are manifest in the criminal acts of successive generations.[51]

Building his theories in this intellectual context, Le Bon maintained that there were two distinct groups of criminals. The first were those with a hereditary disposition to crime: those "whose vicious natures are regularly transmitted from father to son, and who generally end up in prison, the *bagne*, or on the scaffold. It is among them that the largest number of criminals are recruited." The second group of criminals in Le Bon's schematic, however, had no "hereditary aptitudes for crime" but rather displayed "acquired traits" that were transmitted from the unhealthy sociocultural milieu and displaced onto the nervous system of the individual. Such malign influences could transform "the most virtuous man into a villain capable of any crime." Le Bon blamed the spread of these "lesions" of the nervous system on the insalubrious effects of civilization's recent progress.[52]

Once again the specter of "modernity" rears its head, and it is in the newly reified urban morass—with its attendant social pathologies—that a biological catalyst for crime is located. In effect, the constitutional defects of the recidivist resulted from the deleterious physical and social environment of fin de siècle France. Thus, the physiological and psychosocial interpretations of crime—while very different—were synchronous and often inextricably intertwined. Indeed, many French criminologists and social theorists relied upon the same curious admixture, as did Le Bon in formulating their explanations of crime. Although not adhering to the strict anatomical determinism of Cesare Lombroso and the Italian school of criminology, they nevertheless eschewed a strict mind-body dualism, arguing instead that the moral and intellectual qualities of the mind were subject to the primacy of the body itself.

Although some theorists explicitly rejected the idea that crime was the consequence of genetic and biological deficiencies—primarily because the logical corollary was that rehabilitation was impossible—one also sees in contemporary criminological theory the growth of a recidivist archetype. Physically weaker than "normal" men and thus forced to make do with a severe handicap throughout their lives, these "degenerates," according to psychiatrist Charles Féré, "compensate by taking the fruits of more productive laborers; that is, through crime."[53] Criminologist Henri Joly characterized the petty offender as "preternaturally attracted by a life of adventure, by the taste for forbidden fruit, and by gross charms and pleasures they cannot afford or merit. . . . [T]hey have no fear of the law, and are a very real danger."[54]

If a sentence to a metropolitan prison could not dissuade the petty criminal—degenerate or otherwise—from repeating his crimes, it appeared to many that the only alternative was exile to one of the overseas *bagnes* previously reserved for France's most serious criminals. Haussonville was one of the earliest proponents of the idea: "Transportation should be applied to criminals such as the beggars and vagabonds who comprise the veritable river of recidivists flooding our streets; those useless to the world and themselves . . . whose numerous convictions are proof of their incorrigible perversity, and justify this measure. Finally, the fear of transportation would provide a salutary effect upon those too familiar with the prisons in the metropole."[55] The director of the *maison centrale* in Fontevrault believed that the mere prospect of "being sent six thousand leagues from the metropole without hope of return should be enough to diminish the number of recidivists. The latter are still French, and, despite their miserable existence here, would never want to leave their native soil."[56] Lying beneath the argument for deterrence, however, were two additional—and quite contradictory—impulses to expel the recidivist that were tied to the aforementioned models of criminal causality.

The basis of the first motive was the continued belief among fin de siècle theorists and legislators that penal colonization was the path to national expansion and their nostalgic faith in the power of the land to rejuvenate the denizens of a corrupt urban society. Like their predecessors more than thirty years earlier, these individuals retained a misty image of an idealized preindustrial French village in which agrarian pursuits offered a sense of moral purpose and a well-ordered way of life. Anxiety about the destabilizing moral effects of "modern" society only heightened their intense romantic longing for the supposedly more "natural" social relations of the farm. No longer viewed as exuding civilized values, the city—with its various spectacles of wealth and conspicuous consumption—was seen as a locus of moral turpitude. Speaking in this vein, the director of the colonies, M. Michaux, remarked that "it is through agricultural work and the spectacle of nature that the spirit is calmed. Ownership, marriage, paternity: these are the means by which one is influenced; transportation brings about the regeneration of men because it takes them away from our degraded and infamous metropolitan society, to make them pioneers of a new colonial society."[57]

Just like his felonious cohorts, the recidivist would be an agent in the service of France's larger colonial project. Through his labor he would pay his debt to the mother country while simultaneously increasing the domain of her rule. Exile could therefore be justified on the grounds that it was a process of resocialization that would eventually allow for the reinsertion of the recidivist into the civil society of the colonies.

Such reasoning ran counter, however, to the second motive behind the transportation of the recidivist, which was based on a clear desire to permanently rid *la mère patrie* of an incurable "social evil." In this almost eugenic framework, Armand Pagnier argued that a steadily evolving society must dispose of "its refuse and dead weight," by which he meant anyone too slow—mentally, physically, or morally—to keep up with "incessant progress."[58] Nor was he alone in such thinking. Social critic H. LeChartier declared it "imperative" to isolate the country's better nature from the vicious elements in the streets and to "purify Paris by removing those perverted beings teeming its gutters . . . who pose a permanent danger for public security." LeChartier compared vice to contagion, to gangrene: "a living plague that has attached itself to the flanks of society."[59] Such biological metaphors were not mere rhetorical devices, notes Robert Nye, but suffused all discussions of crime, including the debate surrounding the transport of recidivists in fin de siècle France. It therefore seemed imperative to contemporaries such as Delvincourt—fearful of the physical degeneration of the populace—that the social body of the French nation "be rid of this sickness."[60]

At the basis of both the sociological and biological interpretations of crime were the fundamental assumptions that society was primary to those who compose it and that the social organism has needs which supersede those of the individual. In essence, crime came to be seen as an attack upon the social body. Thus the mantra of "social defense" became transcendent in the fin de siècle discourse on recidivism. For instance, criminal theorist F. Desportes maintained that all forms of criminal punishment should be viewed as "a means of defense whereby society . . . must protect itself from attacks by malfeasants; its goal should be to make it impossible for them to do harm."[61] Similarly, Alexandre Lacassagne, a professor of legal medicine from Lyon, argued that "the idea of punishment must be changed to the idea of protection."[62] Le Bon agreed that it was time to abandon punishment with the hope of rehabilitation; instead, the country must resort to protecting itself from the internal threat of criminality by expelling offenders to "our faraway colonies in Africa, Asia, and Oceania where civilization does not yet exist."[63]

By virtue of their shared emphasis on the importance of milieu in their explanations of crime and recidivism, social theorists provided a language that proponents of transportation could draw upon in political debate. It was therefore as a means of public hygiene and national self-preservation that French legislators looked across the seas and expanded the penal colonies. In this context, the parliamentary sponsor of the legislation to transport recidivists, René Waldeck-Rousseau, argued:

> As for those who have done nothing to surmount the difficulties of existence, who have abandoned themselves to their instincts and appetites; those individuals are in a state of revolt not only against the particular laws of society, but against the most elementary principal of natural law. . . . Everyone recognizes that the first duty of the state is to assure the security of those who comprise it . . . and it has the right to inflict the punishment of transportation upon incorrigible recidivists to safeguard public security and prevent these fatal infractions from reoccurring in the future. . . . [I]f all citizens have the right to legitimate self-defense, does not society itself?[64]

As a means of public hygiene, then, under the guise of national self-preservation, French legislators once again looked across the seas and expanded the penal role of the colonies. With strong public support for the measure, and after three years of haggling between Opportunists and Radicals who favored transportation and various elements of the socialist left and monarchist right initially aligned against such a plan, the Relegation Law was passed in 1885.[65]

In the year following its passage, 1,610 petty recidivists were exiled to the penal colonies. Although this number would reach an all-time high of 1,934 in 1887, it steadily declined to 632, or less than 1 percent of the total criminal population, in 1900. It is likely that this decline was due to the hesitancy of judges to apply the perpetual punishment. A total of 8,931 individuals were sentenced and transported overseas during the nineteenth century, or nearly 35 percent of the 25,600 total sentences to relegation handed down between 1885 and 1938 (the year all shipments of prisoners was halted).[66]

Although they retained their civil rights, most *rélégues* could not fend for themselves and therefore had to live in detention camps.[67] If they did so, they were legally compelled to work and were "subject to all the discipline and vigor of the penitentiary establishment." Those who refused were expelled from the penitentiary and were not provided a means of existence. If they could not locate employment or a means of subsistence, they were "considered to be in a state of vagabondage," a crime that was, ironically enough, punishable by imprisonment in the *bagne*.[68]

There were certainly points of disjuncture between the 1854 legislation, which formally established the penal colonies, and that of 1885, which extended such penalties to petty recidivists. The former contains a clear tone of idealism—however self-serving or self-legitimating—that is clearly absent in the latter. Penal colonization appeared to mid-nineteenth-century legislators as a means to remove criminals from the corruption and degenerative forces found within cities and to rehabilitate them in the hard work of forging the colonial empire. This labor, along with indoctrination in a moral ideology based on Rousseau's concept of the countryside's redemptive value, would stamp out the dissipation inherent in urban life. Convicts would be restored to an upright moral life by being close to nature and participating in an idealized vision of a rural France that no longer existed.

This scheme made the prisoner an agent in the service of France's larger colonial project. Through his labor he would pay his debt to the mother country by helping to increase her empire's domain. Thus penal colonization was seen not simply as the banishment of dangerous and undesirable individuals to a faraway locale but as a process of resocialization that would eventually allow for their reinsertion in the civil society of the colonies.

With the 1885 law, however, we see a specification and refinement of more generalized fears of social disorder. As economic advances kept extending the scale and complexity of modern life, petty crime was seen as part and parcel of a pathological ethos in which impulses and desires went unchecked. By the late nineteenth century, the long-standing conflation of economic standing and morality gave way to a deterministic perception of an interrelationship between crime and changing material and status desires.

In this new determinism, petty recidivism was the most tangible manifestation of the individualist ethos at the heart of modern society. Protecting society against the threat necessitated permanent exile. Given the pervasive and prolonged sense of crisis in the French prison system, penal colonization offered a way for social theorists and politicians to negate their immediate environment by turning their attention toward an institutional site seemingly untouched by moral decline. Removed from the deleterious milieu of the city and isolated in the pastoral realm (so it was imagined) of the overseas penal colonies, the criminal might still be invested with a sense of moral purpose and values of good conduct. If not, however, the health and integrity of the metropolitan body would be preserved.

3. Life in the Penal Colony

The View from Above and Below

In the initial days of penal colony settlement, each encampment had only a skeletal staff, and the camp commandant had broad, sweeping powers over day-to-day activities. He was to oversee the procurement of all material provisions, the construction of all buildings, the matriculation of all *condamnés*, and the management of "all the employees and agents who are in charge of assuring the strict application of work rules, discipline, and good behavior" in the camp. Finally, he was to keep the Ministry of the Marine abreast of events through memoranda and correspondence forwarded by his office.[1]

Ministerial and colonial officials, however, voiced immediate complaints regarding the actions of camp commandants. Drawn from officers active in the navy, many of these commandants were characterized by officials as "incapable," and "incompetent." For instance, the governor of New Caledonia complained: "The importance of the position necessitates that establishments be placed in the hands of intelligent and energetic men who will exercise these qualities in a distinguished manner, which I regret to say has not been the case. So far they seem to lack the calm and necessary patience to deal with the complaints addressed to them, many of which, unfortunately, are well founded."[2] Although prior military training would seem to be the ideal training ground for a camp commandant, whose raison d'être was vigilance, obedience, and a strict adherence to routine, it was his inability or unwillingness to complete the administrative functions of his position that incurred the wrath of his superiors.

This aspect of the relationship between the metropole and the colony was fraught with miscommunication and mistrust from the start. Lacking

an administrative arm with which to oversee and coordinate local activities, ministerial officials found themselves at odds with local commandants
intent on conducting affairs in their own manner. This is evident in the
following dispatch to the governor of French Guiana, in which an administrator cited the behavior of a particular commandant as typical: "In his correspondence he nearly always responds in an irreverent, ironic, or aggressive
form. . . . On September 30 he submitted a note that was without address,
without salutation, without signature, and in which he remarked that he
found such reports an inconvenience. He has not communicated with the
Ministry for forty days."[3] There were even complaints among ministerial
officials of commandants who exhibited "a puerile orthography in their
reports . . . many instructions read 'pentenciere' [*sic*]."[4]

Various governors of French Guiana—there were five in the first ten years
of settlement—complained about having to mediate disputes between ministerial officials and local commandants over their various and sometimes
conflicting views as to how the *bagnes* were managed. As civilian chief of the
colony, a position that entailed the oversight of his own administration—a
military officer in charge of colonial defense, a budget director, a director of
the interior, and a justice official—he saw such efforts as above and beyond
the call of duty. In this vein, Governor Baudin once complained that he
had repeatedly been "called to regularize relations and details between the
Ministry and various commandants. . . . In the middle of these antagonisms,
I have worked ardently for two years in the difficulties of directing a service
which itself constitutes a colony."[5]

In response to such complaints, the Ministry of the Marine created a new
administrative apparatus in 1867, with offices headquartered in St. Laurent,
French Guiana, and Nouméa, New Caledonia. At the top of the new penitentiary administration was a director, who, while "personally responsible
for the acts of his subordinates," was also to ensure that "good order and
discipline" was maintained in all penitentiary establishments. Although the
director was still under the supervision of the governor, his responsibilities
included making "certain" that ministerial initiatives were adhered to with
regard to the distribution of all *condamnés* among the various penitentiaries;
organizing prison labor; granting land concessions to released prisoners; and
nominating all agents whose salaries did not exceed two thousand francs
per year. He was also charged with formulating the annual transportation

budget and maintaining "correspondence with the Ministry and all other exterior establishments."[6]

With this reorganization, camp commandants saw their powers more circumscribed and scrutinized. Although all officers, noncommissioned officers, military employees, and agents in the penitentiary were still subordinate to the commandant, he was specifically instructed not to "modify, approve, or reject the propositions of the Director or the Governor." In addition, a procurer general was charged with making annual penitentiary inspections in which he was to hear grievances and complaints from *condamnés* and personnel; he would then address a report to the Ministry that also contained the observations of the director of the penitentiary administration as well as the governor.[7]

The bureaucratic hierarchy within each penitentiary was also refined at this time. The commandant now had under his direct authority an assistant chief, who, "in the case of absence or impeachment, assumed the authority of the Commandant." In particular, he was charged with the day-to-day affairs of the office staff. As an intermediary he was to ensure that the commandant "be met with only those demands that are asked of him." In addition, an agricultural agent was appointed to each penitentiary in order to "direct all agricultural work, and assure that it conforms to the written and verbal instructions given by the Ministry and approved by the Governor. . . . He supplies every day to the Commandant, information on the state of agriculture, and any demands of material he deems necessary. He also designates to the Commandant any need for men he may have for various tasks."[8]

This attempt at "bureaucratization" was an effort on the part of authorities to improve coordination and communication between local and metropolitan officials, whose relationship up to this point had been ill defined. The new institutional structure now bore some of the characteristics that Max Weber would later ascribe to a "modern" bureaucracy in which "a relation is established between legally instated authorities and their subordinate officials which is characterized by defined rights and duties, prescribed in written regulations . . . [and] authority relations between positions are ordered systematically."[9] The emphasis was on improved administrative efficiency through the dispersal of tasks and responsibilities among numerous individuals. In the Ministry's view, the commandant now had the proper administrative distance to act in the efficient and judicious manner of a manager. What he lost in terms of his own independence and flexibility he gained in administrative and clerical support from the newly created office of director.

This nascent bureaucracy—a quintessential feature of the vast disciplinary apparatus that Foucault has so aptly outlined with the birth of the modern penitentiary—was necessary to deal with the concomitant efflorescence of documentation pertaining to the *bagnard* (files, records, physical and psychological findings, etc.). Upon their arrival in the prison depots of St. Laurent, French Guiana, or Bourail, New Caledonia, all the prisoners were counted and given a number. This number was determined sequentially and served as the key component for future identification and surveillance purposes by authorities. Once the various documents were summarized by a commission of ministerial and naval officers, a newly reconfigured dossier was collated with the prisoner's matriculation number and then transcribed by local clerks; a copy was then sent back to the Ministry of Justice in Paris.

The new dossier included a form that detailed such basic information as name, height, weight, eye and hair color, age, and notable scars or tattoos, as well as a set of fingerprints (beginning in the early twentieth century). There was also a section in which the prisoner's forehead, skull, and ears were measured. Although this was initially an effort on the part of penal colony authorities to determine potential future criminality—based upon the dubious science of phrenology—it was primarily utilized as a means of identification. Aside from this standardized form, the prisoner's dossier was divided into three categories: judicial, penitential, and health. The judicial portion outlined the prisoner's life preceding his sentence to the penal colonies: prior crimes and sentences; prior profession or trade; general aptitude or skills for work; and, in the judgment of authorities, the possibility of his reformation and rehabilitation. The second section contained the recommendation of the committee as to what type of work in the penal colony the prisoner might be best suited, given the elements contained in the preceding segment. In the third section, a physician delineated the prisoner's general state of health following a medical examination.

After studying the dossiers, the local commission placed the convicts into three general classes: those who were deemed the least amenable to reha- bilitation were placed in the third class; those more inclined to rehabilita- tion (i.e., those with some mechanical skills or aptitude) were placed in the second class; and the remainder were advanced to the first class. Those in the third class were typically classified as *bon pour stère*, which meant they were fit for cutting timber in the outlying work camps that eventually spread throughout both French Guiana and New Caledonia. There, prisoners were charged with cutting one *stère*—a cubic meter of wood, or about thirty-five cubic feet—each day.[10] They were also forced to work in silence, and between 1852 and 1881 they were encumbered by a ball and chain. Those of the second class were not constrained to the ball and chain but rather were employed in camp workshops where they made prison garments, cooked in prison kitchens, or dispersed to local public works projects. Those in first class were allowed not only to speak but to work in the homes of local officials as *garçons de famille* or gardeners. Rules stipulated, however, that to advance to this class a prisoner had to serve at least two years in second class and to obtain the approval of the governor, who determined if the prisoner's be- havior warranted such a post. In practice, almost all prisoners were placed in the third class upon arrival.[11]

To work in silence had long been a feature of prisons in France (the idea was based on the early modern "collective" model of imprisonment outlined in chapter 1). As inmates lived and worked together there was the ever-pres- ent possibility of "moral" contagion passing from one convict to another by word of mouth. By enforcing strict rules of silence, only the orders and com- mands of prison guards were heard. Again, the intention was to inculcate habits of labor and obedience in the prisoner and to limit any opportunity for collective defiance or disobedience.

Those in the first class earned fifty centimes per day, although half of this sum was withheld by the penal colony administration and placed into a nest egg, which the prisoner was entitled to upon the completion of his sentence. Those in the second class earned twenty centimes per day, with the same provision for savings. Prisoners of the third class were awarded five centimes per day. A prisoner deemed "incorrigible" by authorities for various disciplinary infractions and therefore imprisoned in the *cachots* was not paid. The infamous *cachots* were cells of little ventilation and no outside light where prisoners suffered from bouts of anemia and hookworm, usually from a lack of medical attention and a proper diet.

Those sentenced to the penal colonies under the Relegation Law of 1885 were also not paid by the state, as—at least in theory—they were free to seek employment with civilian employers. They were burdened, however, with a paper trail that was very similar to the one that followed their felonious cohorts. In addition, the *rélégue* was required by law to carry a *livret du rélégue*, which was, in part, a passport. Although he was free to reside and work in or near the penitentiary centers of Cayenne or St. Laurent or in and around Bourail or Nouméa, it was a criminal offense for a *rélégue* to not have this book in his possession at all times, as he could not legally travel from one locale to another without having it stamped by authorities.[12]

Aside from basic information such as date of birth, height, weight, color of hair and eyes, and notable scars and tattoos for identification purposes, this book contained sections that delineated the *rélégue*'s trade or profession prior to his conviction in the metropole, marital status, all of his past crimes (including those committed while in the penal colony), the location of the tribunal that formalized his sentence to relegation, and the date of his liberation. It also contained pages that served a purpose similar to that of a résumé. After completing a brief survey that described their enterprise, where the business was located, and how long it had been in operation, past employers were asked to describe the nature and duration of work performed by the *rélégue* and to evaluate his skills and labor. Given that civilian employers preferred to rely upon conscripted convict labor that was cheaper and seemingly limitless, the few books contained in extant prison dossiers often have no entries in this regard—a sad testament to the plight of the *rélégue*.[13]

Once again, however, we see the outlines of a Foucauldian surveillance, as the *livret* represented the man's entire life, both before and after his arrival in the colony. With all of the documentation, whether pertaining to the *condamné* or the *rélégue*, there is a continuation of an earlier process of objectification in the metropole. The prisoner was now the subject of analysis, quantification, and normalization for penal colony authorities.

In their very formality and precise detail, such documents, while allowing the institution to operate in a coldly efficient and impersonal manner,
dehumanized the prisoner.

Given such detailed planning in terms of documentation, it is odd that
administrators gave so little thought to the "correctional" housing of prisoners, as there is no discussion in governmental literature or correspondence
over the relative merits of cellular isolation versus collective incarceration.
Indeed, officials simply modeled the layout of the primary penal camps or
depots after a typical military garrison. As such, prisoners were housed in
common barracks where they slept on individual wooden planks (although
with ever-increasing numbers these were eventually replaced with hammocks, which, while more appropriate to the local setting, allowed more
men to be crammed into narrow confines). Indeed, it was not uncommon
to have seventy-five to a hundred men housed in barracks originally designed for fifty. Poorly ventilated (having only small windows of .80 x .60
meters on either end) and with no inside plumbing, these buildings were
quite unsanitary. Aside from the barracks, all depots had separate buildings
that housed administrative offices, stables and blacksmith works, kitchens,
woodworking shops, and textile mills.[14]

Provided with their prison grays—a woolen shirt and pair of pants, a
hat, and wooden clogs—the *bagnards* began each day with reveille at 5:00
a.m. followed by inspection and breakfast. The men were marched every day
in military-style units to outlying areas to engage in jungle clearing, road
building, or agricultural cultivation between 6:00 and 10:00 a.m. Lunch was
provided at 10:30 a.m., followed by a short break at 2:00 p.m., and labor again
until 6:00 p.m., when they were led back to camp for dinner. According to
authorities, the daily repast consisted of "a half-loaf of bread for breakfast
and 183 grams of biscuit. For dinner, three times per week, fresh meat (250
grams) and wine (23 centiliters). On other days there are preserves of lard,
also soup and vegetables. Finally, each day for breakfast, one receives coffee,
and four times a week *tafia*" (a moonshine rum made from sugarcane).[15]

Those prisoners who refused to adhere to this regimen—the incorrigibles, or *incos*, as they were known—were placed in solitary confinement
in the *cachots* on either Île Royale or Île Saint-Joseph in French Guiana or
on Îlôt Brun in New Caledonia, as they were used as disciplinary establish-

ments after the mainland camps had been built. There the convict was kept in complete isolation in cells where the ceiling was replaced by a steel grate that allowed the guards, on permanent watch, to overlook the *cachots*. Each cell contained a wooden or metal plank for a bed and a bucket for waste, which was to be washed and disinfected every day. The *inco* could not speak and was not allowed any written materials. Regulations provided that he be allowed outside in the prison yard for half an hour in the morning and evening. A sentence to the *cachots* could last anywhere from fifteen to sixty days. If there was no improvement in the behavior of the prisoner (i.e., usually a willingness to work), the steel grates were covered by wooden boards to prevent daylight from penetrating into the cell, which forced the convict to live in total obscurity for periods of weeks, if not months, and sometimes even years.[16]

With the *cachots* we see another disjunction within the penal colony regime. Justification of such punishment was made on the same basis as separate cellular isolation in the metropole. This was a particular code of moralization based on the Philadelphia model of imprisonment developed in the United States and advanced by such notable penal theorists as Bentham and Tocqueville. In essence, the *cachots* provided the opportunity for the prisoner to reflect upon his misbehavior. Amid the silence and the dark he would reach into the parallel darkness of his own heart, his own soul, in search of metaphysical resolution for his punishment. In contrast to the communal atmosphere of the barracks, where individual circumspection was not possible, the prisoner's separation was also seen as necessary to prevent his obstinacy and misbehavior from spreading to his cohorts.

The other disciplinary alternative for local officials in the penal colonies was corporal punishment. The first governor of the penal colony of French Guiana, Sarda Garriga, decreed that the corporal punishments outlined by royal ordinance in September 1748 served as sufficient legal precedent for disciplinary actions taken by local authorities. The ordinance allowed for the lashing of prisoners guilty of disciplinary infractions (e.g., assaults or threats to officers, refusal to work) with the aid of a whip that—according to regulation—was 15 millimeters in diameter and 650 millimeters long.[17] Applied to the shoulders and back, twenty-five to fifty blows of the whip were permitted with approval from the governor, with additional blows allowed only after the camp physician had provided a certificate verifying the prisoner's health.[18]

Thus we see a blending of the modern and premodern elements of punishment that Foucault outlined in his study of the penitentiary. With its focus on separation and silence, the *cachots* had an almost monastic air about them, which is not surprising given that it was the Quakers who had initially developed the idea that a prisoner separated from his peers and left with nothing but time for reflection would inevitably see the errors of his ways. Yet with their reliance on the lash, the *bagnes* harkened back to premodern forms of punishment such as branding, punishment intended only to inflict discomfort and physical suffering. For local officials dealing with the recalcitrance of prisoners on a daily basis, corporal punishment—and perhaps more precisely its attendant pain—was a stimulus and a source of energy. In this context, the penal colony was a hybrid form of punishment that was different from, but not necessarily the inverse of, the penitentiary.

As in all prisons, however, there was a resistant and oppositional culture that existed beneath the surface. Indeed, many aspects of life were uncontrollable, went unnoticed, or were largely ignored by penal colony officials. The *bagne* was a cauldron of desperation, anger, bitterness, frustration, and resentment, all of which led to acts of resistance, defiance, and subversion. As such, the disciplinary power of the *bagne* was illusory at best.

In an effort to avoid the backbreaking work of deforestation or dredging swamps, prisoners discovered some rather sad, yet ingenious, ways to be removed from such grueling labor details. The practice, known as *maquillage* in penal colony slang, referred to any effort to feign illness in order to secure a transfer to a local hospital. In this regard, former convict Jean Carol recalled that a few of his cohorts in New Caledonia rubbed a variety of compounds, such as sand, phlegm, and even human and animal droppings, into their various scrapes to irritate, infect, and ulcerate small cuts and abrasions. Others smoked tobacco previously moistened in oil and then dried. Once it was smoked, according to Carol, the convict's complexion turned yellow, which some physicians mistook as jaundice. There were also prisoners who swallowed various liquid concoctions of soapy water mixed with human or animal detritus to contract dysentery, which sometimes necessitated their removal from work camps due to dehydration.[19]

The Dutch convict Aage Krarup-Nielsen knew of prisoners who rubbed ricinus (castor bean) seeds into cuts and abrasions to cause infections, although this practice sometimes inflamed limbs to the point that amputation was necessary.[20] Those suffering from tuberculosis often sold their sputum to healthy prisoners—for upwards of a dollar—who, when examined by the doctor, would produce the diseased sample as their own. The famed escapee René Belbenoit related the story of a prisoner by the name of Launay who purposely contracted erysipelas (a skin infection generally caused by streptococci that results in painful, ulcerated lesions) "by sticking a needle through his cheek and holding his hand over his mouth" and then "blow[ing] constantly and hard until soon he had the side of his head inflamed and very swollen." Other prisoners smoked quinine and "sulphur stalks" to "sham" fever and bronchitis.[21]

Administrators were aware that prisoners routinely faked illnesses in order to be removed from hard-labor details and reclassified to light work. In this vein, an inspector for the penitentiary administration in French Guiana charged: "The incorrigibles put their grand hope in the doctor so that they can escape hard labor . . . of the 167 men who visited the doctor in February, only one *transporté* was recognized as not sick, and he was not punished for missing work. It is truly incredible that in this entire lot there is only one lazy *forçat* who is feigning illness. These dangerous criminals should be classed as either sick or not sick, and the latter should be forced to do the most difficult work."[22]

New Caledonia's director of the penitentiary administration maintained that doctors detached to the penitentiary colonies "show evidence of the most grand indulgence . . . they are carried to recognize as sick all the *condamnés* who present themselves for a visit. . . . A simple examination of the visiting logs would be sufficient to recognize this. . . . I am struck by the ever-increasing number of *condamnés* classed to light work and maintained, because of this reclassification, in camps where they do nothing."[23] Convinced that this was a regular practice, the director issued a temporary order that reduced the ration for those engaged in light work and increased the ration for those employed in roadwork. As a result of this action, the director claimed, there was "an immediate diminution in the very notable proportion of those *condamnés* classified to light work. In other words, a great number of *condamnés*, around 25 percent, solicited or obtained from the doctor a reclassification to hard labor, which would allow them a greater ration."[24]

Camp physicians could not be blamed for being taken in by such ruses, however, for they treated the symptoms and not the cause of such ailments (although, as we shall see in chapter 5, some were sympathetic to the plight of the prisoner). Moreover, the convicts' desperate efforts to become ill typically resulted in a hospital stay of only a few days and did not bring about a permanent change in their sentences to hard labor. Such a reclassification required much more dramatic measures. The internal correspondence of some officials indicates that it was not an uncommon for prisoners to engage in various forms of self-mutilation in order to be permanently placed into lighter work details such as gardening or as domestic help.

As stipulated by regulation, convicts lacking a limb were excluded from hard labor. This reasonable policy generated much consternation from the director of the penal administration in New Caledonia, however, who remarked in a letter to the Ministry of the Marine that of the four *condamnés* who worked as gardeners at his place of residence, all had only one noticeable physical defect, a finger or thumb missing from a hand. The director noted the odd prevalence of such men in and around Nouméa and questioned whether such minor deformities were the result of premeditated acts on the part of the *bagnards*.[25]

The most highly sought-after position for prisoners, however, was to work as a *garçon de famille*, for it allowed the greatest degree of autonomy. Since much of his time was relatively unsupervised while his employer was at work, the convict was allowed to travel freely between homes or within the village or town within which he was employed. Charged with being "housemaid, cook, nurse, and washer-woman," the prisoner had plenty of opportunity to pilfer food, spirits, and other objects from the home that he could later sell to his fellow prisoners.[26] It was those convicts who were "young, smart, and adaptable" that were chosen to work in the homes of officials. Such a man, according to Krarup-Nielsen, "could steal on behalf of his mistress when he is out shopping; he must know how to buy on credit, and keep the creditors at arm's length. If a *garçon de famille* has all these attributes he will get on extremely well, and will eventually be employed by the very highest government families. . . . He will live comfortably, can have several children if he wants to, and can save enough for the day when he can stage a well-arranged escape."[27] Indeed, in a case uncovered by a ministerial inspection, one convict "was allowed his own sleeping quarters in the home, a pig, and a dog in order to guard it at night. . . . [H]e has also on many occasions procured spirits such as wine and absinthe from the home. In a word, this *condamné* was accorded nearly unlimited freedom."[28] In another instance, the same inspector found a *transporté* whose daily duties included cleaning the rifle of his employer.[29]

While such positions were granted to a select few and therefore had little impact on labor initiatives throughout the penal colonies, a problem that impinged directly on discipline and order in the camps was the prevalence of homosexuality. Given that authorities had established an open barracks system of housing in which there was no interior surveillance at night, this should not have been at all surprising. Nonetheless, outsiders to the colony, such as Dr. J. Tripot, a member of the Geographic Society of Paris, who happened to make a visit to the prison depot at St. Laurent before embarking on a scientific expedition of the two rivers that flow into the Maroni River, was shocked by what he termed the "Sodom and Gomorrah" of the prison barracks. "This is where the rut of pernicious instincts display themselves in all their perversity," he noted, "and where *condamnés* whose moral gangrene is such that they indulge in revolting displays of promiscuity without disgust, without nausea."[30] In his investigation of the penal colony in French Guiana, French journalist Albert Londres utilized the same "Sodom and Gomorrah" allusion when describing the barracks. "If one of the purposes of legislators when they established the penal colony in French Guiana was to improve the morality of the *forçat*," Londres wrote, "this has been a failure. What a farce, Mr. Legislator!"[31]

Even local officials such as Governor Rodier of Guiana were surprised by the "promiscuity that is practiced in the *bagne*, and which is an absolute obstacle to the moral regeneration of criminals. . . . At night the *condamnés* are grouped arbitrarily in rooms of fifty to sixty men, and left to their own devices. In these conditions, the most vicious, the braggarts of crime are allowed to influence those more timid, less perverse, the young, those who still have, in their souls, some good sentiment. From the point of view of

morality, there is in these quarters, the most abominable occurrences."[32]
This passage is noteworthy in that of the thousands of internal memoranda,
inspection reports, and bureaucratic correspondence, it is the only extended
examination of the behavior of prisoners at night—and this from a civilian
official. Indeed, there are no official statistics that demarcate rapes, assaults,
and murders in the communal barracks.

In a book that detailed their experiences while in the penitentiary administration in French Guiana, V. Darquitian and L. Le Boucher admitted
that there "have always been 'marriages' in the *bagne* . . . because nature,
imperious, always imposes its exigencies. . . . The cause of this lamentable
situation resides in the unfortunate promiscuity of the common barracks."
The barracks was an "agglomeration of males in which nature reclaims itself.
. . . The most shameful passions develop in a frightening fashion among
these beings who vegetate in a state where all bestialities exist. By their sad
practices of sodomy that are perpetrated almost daily there are no longer
any boundaries and their passion cannot be comprehended."[33]

Yet such condemnations only appear in the published recollections of
those outside the institution. The administrative silence in this regard points
to a marked ambivalence toward homosexuality and cases of rape and violence in the barracks. In part this attitude was born of necessity, as there
were never enough guards in the penal colonies, and most administrators
and metropolitan officials believed that their charges risked serious harm
if they patrolled inside the barracks at night. Moreover, the barracks themselves had originally been designed with metal bed frames that included
manacles for the prisoners' feet, thereby eliminating any freedom of movement. With an ever-increasing number of prisoners during the course of the
late nineteenth century, this device was gradually eliminated and replaced
with hammocks in order to house more men without having to resort to
new building construction. Thus the *bagnard* was free to move about the
barracks, and only one or two guards were stationed outside each building
to prevent escape.

It is also interesting to note the rhetorical recourse to "nature" in the
remarks of the two former administrators. One gets the impression that
such behavior—while certainly condemned by the two men—was seen as
inevitable. Indeed, Le Boucher remarked quite simply: "it [homosexual re-

lations] is an instinct that is aggravated by a lack of females."[34] Given the lack of attention paid to the matter by officials inside and outside the penal colony, this attitude also seems clear. Therefore, while there was certainly no institutional approval of homosexuality, its presence was tacitly accepted as an unfortunate but unavoidable by-product of imprisonment.

The biographies and autobiographies of former prisoners usually include a discussion of homosexuality (although, somewhat ironically, always involving inmates other than the author). For instance, Antoine Mesclon, a former convict in French Guiana who served fifteen years for attempted theft and murder, told the story of "Courtois," a male prostitute originally from Tunisia, who was arrested for theft in Marseille and sent to French Guiana to serve out his sentence. As a young man of slight build, he immediately became the "property" of Penne, "one of the terrors of the *bagne*." After being raped on two occasions by Penne, Courtois attacked his tormentor one night while he slept, killing him in the process. Although many of his fellow *bagnards* witnessed the act, none would testify against Courtois because of an unspoken "omerta" among all inmates (he was found not guilty of murder and was therefore released back into the regular prison population).[35]

This "code of silence" was a well-chronicled aspect of penal colony life. Roving reporter Gordon Sinclair referred to the "gangland rules" that operate in the *bagne*: "No squealers. Death to the squealer. Only two cases are on record of fellow convicts naming the executioner . . . for the Devil's Island telegraph spreads mercilessly around the world. The law is death to the squealer."[36] The adventurer Richard Halliburton noted during his visit to Guiana that murders in the barracks "are always done thoroughly, lest the victim squeal on the victor. Nobody else ever knows anything about it. To bear tales against another convict is unpardonably bad form. Half the murders in prison go unpunished. (The dead man is a good riddance, one less convict)."[37] If a prisoner was stabbed to death at night, the convicts were typically hustled out in the prison yard the following morning while guards searched each man for the weapon. They rarely, if ever, found such an item, according to Krarup-Nielsen, as "convicts had an extraordinary dexterity in making a knife disappear. They will pass them behind their backs from man to man until they reach the turnkey who stands at the end of each line, who will give it back for a suitable bribe."[38]

In return for sexual favors, older convicts formed relationships with those prisoners unable to fend for themselves. Krarup-Nielsen described a selection process that began "as soon as a convoy arrived. . . . The older and more experienced begin to pick out a succession of favorites among the younger and better-looking men."[39] The latter, according to Belbenoit, were referred to as " 'new blood' and 'sweet meat' every time a new cargo arrives!"[40] In the argot of the *bagne*, it was the job of the *fort-à-bras* (strong-armed man) to " 'keep house,' so to speak—to defend his young *môme* (wife) and make the money necessary for lavishing presents of tobacco, bonbons, and other gifts on his companion."[41] Such relationships were a way of easing the burdens of penal colony life for some *mômes*, as *forts-à-bras* "bribed bookkeepers and guards to give their pets easy jobs while protecting them in fights."[42] Others were gambled for over cards, however, as some convicts "had a whole harem of three, four, or five '*mômes*'" if they could afford it.[43]

While most had been bullied or bribed into accepting the role of "wife," there are also numerous accounts of *mômes* who, after lights out in the barracks, "willingly painted their lips, powdered their faces with chalk, and plucked their eyebrows."[44] Indeed, transvestism was a relatively open and common practice in the *bagnes*. George Seaton, an English convict imprisoned for theft in French Guiana, described "rosy-cheeked young men with clumsy movements and ugly voices whose voices assumed the plaintive homosexual whine. They pouted, swung their hips, painted their nails, and made pretty gestures."[45] Guards evinced little interest in this phenomenon, however, and no regulations explicitly forbade the practice. Indeed, historian Marcel Le Clère noted that officials in St. Laurent permitted the formation of a "transvestite ballet troupe, whose star dancer was a certain Coronella."[46] There were many famous "queens," known by such sobriquets as "la Marquise," "Mistinguet," "la Tigresse," "la Panthère," and "la Duchesse," who, according to anthropologist Richard Price, "flaunted their charms publicly."[47]

There was also little concern with the *affaires des moeurs* (sex dramas or crimes) that resulted from quarrels among jealous lovers. According to Krarup-Nielsen, a *fort-à-bras* never allowed his *môme* "to receive a cigarette or gift from another prisoner. If he does, this is enough to cause a bloody quarrel."[48] If a *môme* ever tried to break away from his *fort-à-bras*, he was often beaten or worse. In one case that was so well known it became part of penal colony lore, a *môme* decided to take his own lover. Upon hearing the news, his *fort-à-bras*, a man named Kleisser who had some thirty convictions for theft and robbery, dragged his *môme* out of the camp and into the bush, where he castrated him. His victim hanged himself a week later.[49]

Such violence was not limited to the actions of jealous lovers but extended to other activities that took place in the barracks as well. As all but the dim lamp in the center of the building was extinguished at 8:00 p.m. every evening, prisoners pulled out their empty cans of condensed milk from which they fashioned their own crude oil lamps. By the flickering light, groups of men would gather around the "rattling of a tin box filled with sous," as "its sound was the signal for *la Marseillaise* [a card game similar to modern-day blackjack or twenty-one], the favorite gambling game of the convicts."[50] With playing cards drawn on bits of paper and cardboard, the scene "could have been an etching by Dore or a drawing by Lautrec: a group of emaciated, unshaven jailbirds dressed in rags, grasping torn and greasy playing cards in their calloused hands, and casting grotesque shadows on the walls."[51] Others played poker, baccarat, and even checkers and dominoes "fashioned from kneaded bits of bread or lumps of sugar."[52] According to Felix Milani, a Corsican imprisoned in French Guiana, on some evenings "the *bagne* looked like a veritable casino, with all its drama and excitement."[53]

With a *fort-à-bras* acting as both dealer and banker—for which he usually took a 10 percent commission—prisoners collectively wagered between one hundred and five hundred francs per night.[54] This was not an inconsiderable sum, as prisoners earned only five to fifty centimes per day. Given the high stakes, disputes were common, as prisoners would "fly off the handle for nothing at all, and accuse one another of cheating."[55] If the dealer could not settle the matter and restore order, players often exchanged blows and engaged in knife fights. Old scores were also settled during the hours of sleep, as prisoners awoke to find one of their own stabbed to death in his hammock. As with the violence surrounding homosexual affairs, such activity generated little administrative interest, as "stock answers of 'self-defense' and 'unprovoked attacks' were accepted, and the killer would receive no worse punishment than thirty days cellular for carrying a knife."[56]

The ambivalence of authorities extended to tattooing, which was, after gambling and sex, the most popular activity in the common barracks. Utilizing sharpened bamboo splinters and ink, or vegetable dyes such as indigo, tattooing was "a favorite pastime" for those eager to distinguish themselves from their cohorts by commemorating their nefarious misdeeds or to express their utter sense of hopelessness on their bodies.[57] Although tattooing was forbidden by penal colony regulation, according to Auguste Liard-Courtois it was "extremely rare to encounter a *forçat* whose body is not covered by designs or mottos by the time he leaves the *bagne*."[58]

It was not the practice of tattooing that was surprising to observers—indeed, many men arrived in the *bagne* with some tattoos from earlier prison stints in the metropole or prior service in the Navy—but the appearance of etchings on the face. For instance, Londres encountered men "tattooed from head to toe. All the vocabulary of the unfortunate scoundrel is spread across the skin: 'Child of misery,' 'No chance,' 'No God nor master,' tattooed across the forehead. And some obscene inscriptions which one would only see in a street urinal."[59] Former prisoners such as George Batzler-Heim were also shocked "by men who often look as if the whole of their faces were painted black, to the horror of all who behold them outside the colony."[60] Seaton noted "faces turned into etching-blocks. Eyebrows transformed into writhing snakes . . . and foreheads with thick letters that read 'Innocent!' Either that or, in smaller letters: 'I came. I saw. I believed.'"[61] Krarup-Nielsen described foreheads with such phrases as "no hope," "no chance," and "death to traitors."[62] Others described men with blue lines around their necks with instructions that read "cut on the dotted line," or "cut here and be damned."[63] Belbenoit was fascinated by a convict known as "Le Masque, an old *fort-à-bras* given this name because his face is all blue, he has a red mustache on his upper lip, and his skull which is cropped like mine, is blue. He says that this tattooing is his hair! On each cheek he has an ace of spades and on his forehead an ace of clubs."[64] Felix Milani spoke of his own tattoos—already extensive because of his time in the navy—to which he added while in the *bagne*: "two stars on my cheekbones, and two smaller ones which twinkle in the corners of my eyes. On the eyelids, a line that looks just like makeup. My motto is written across my neck: 'Always the same.'"[65]

Although prisoners paid fellow inmates for such tattooing, there were many other ways to make money in the *bagne*. As in all prisons, convicts engaged in various forms of graft—or *débrouille* in the local argot. For those who possessed some sort of labor skill, such as metalworking, there were numerous opportunities to fashion a device known as the *plan*, a cylindrical aluminum tube approximately eight centimeters (three inches) long and about two centimeters (three-quarters of an inch) in diameter that convicts inserted into the rectum to safeguard their monies, papers, valuables, or other contraband.[66] The *plan* was crucial to one's survival and therefore highly sought-after on the black market. Indeed, the Dutch convict Krarup-Nielsen charged his fellow prisoners "a dollar and a quarter" for such a device. He also fashioned knives, razors, spoons, and forks that he sold—"with the help of the officers and wardens, who, of course, took their commission out of the transaction"—clandestinely.[67]

It was not just metalworkers who circumvented the basic pay scale established by authorities. Some carpenters made beautiful inlaid boxes, which were given to the guards, who, in turn, passed them on to their wives, who sold them to passengers on mail steamers passing through French Guiana.[68] Others built coffins with as few nails as possible in order to resell them to local merchants. Camp cooks traded in food and basic provisions for personal profit. Those who worked in the commissary had agreements with bookkeepers to cover up their thefts of clothing and blankets that they sold to other convicts or to the local Guianese. Prisoners employed in the medical dispensary had the greatest opportunity for profit, particularly for highly sought-after items such as quinine, a pound of which, "when sold privately," would bring "about one hundred twenty-five dollars" on the black market. According to Krarup-Nielsen, "no prisoner who has been lucky enough to hold such a position has made less than twelve hundred dollars a year."[69]

Another source of additional funds for convicts were their families back in France. Although all incoming mail for prisoners was censored and any currency contained therein confiscated, incoming mail for guards was not monitored by penal colony authorities. Thus prisoners arranged for their families to post money to local guards, who, "in return for a twenty-five to thirty percent commission for his 'services,'" would then pass along the remaining sum. Although there was always the possibility that the guard would simply take the money and run, "this graft was one thing over which the guards were usually honest." Because this practice was potentially so lucrative, most guards knew that if they "took all the money, word would soon get around and no other convict would have money sent through him." Only when a guard was near the end of his tour of duty did prisoners think twice about making such an arrangement.[70]

While in most cases such money was used as a means of survival, in others it was intended to fund an escape. To flee the *bagne* in either New Caledonia or French Guiana was a truly remarkable feat. In New Caledonia one had to somehow stow away on an outgoing cargo ship, usually bound for Australia. Those in French Guiana had two possible choices: brave the jungle on foot and head northeast to Surinam (which, unlike neighboring Brazil, British Guiana, and Venezuela, did not have a strict extradition policy), or float to the Dutch colony on a raft. Indeed, Michel Pierre estimates that throughout its entire history, fewer than one in six prisoners actually escaped the Guianese *bagne* without being recaptured by authorities.[71] Of those not recaptured, the governor of French Guiana once remarked rather ominously that "after a short time they are presumed dead, for the jungle constitutes a natural and nearly impenetrable barrier which few men can breach."[72]

Whether successful or not, any escape attempt required a ready supply of cash and some willing accomplices, all of whom demanded remuneration for their assistance. Horribly underpaid and overworked, penal colony guards were the ones most easily lured by the prospect of extra cash. In his autobiography, the escaped *bagnard* Belbenoit charged that "there is only one person through whom the convict can receive the money he needs for his escape—the guard!"[73] There are also numerous accounts of guards who, sent in pursuit of fugitives, released them after an early capture because the prisoners offered a sum larger than any reward the guards may have received from authorities.[74]

So what are we to make of life inside the penal colony? Certainly, we see various elements of a totalizing institution begin to take shape. With a regenerative vision of hard labor and of obedience inculcated through both violence and uniformity, the prisoner was part of a Kafkaesque penal colony machine.[75] Not coincidentally, this necessitated a new administrative apparatus. Transcendent power no longer resided in one administrator but was carefully spread out among a multiplicity of individuals, all of whose actions coalesced upon the literal and metaphoric being of the prisoner.

There seems to be a pervasive culture of prisoner resistance, or perhaps more precisely, adaptation. Although they rarely challenged penal authority, convicts subverted the regime by pilfering, feigning illness, conniving, escaping, and other tactics. In this regard the *bagnard* construed and constructed his own *bagne*. Prisoners co-opted those agents of the institution who were particularly vulnerable (i.e., guards) to suit their own particular needs. Indeed, it appears as though life in the penal colony was something of a cat-and-mouse game in which convict ingenuity undermined administrative imperatives, and vice versa.

Yet one must be careful to not attribute too much agency to the *bagnards*. Many of the activities they engaged in, such as homosexuality, transvestism, tattooing, and gambling, were of little interest to authorities. Indeed, there is something almost "carnivalesque"—as outlined by literary theorist Mikhail Bakhtin—about the ambivalence of officials to such behaviors.[76] One could argue that the "grotesque realism" of convict life—a world that inverted administrative hierarchies, structures, rules, and customs—was a means of social control in which the crude and immoral were contained and turned inward, finding expression in the narrow and unyielding space of the barracks. Nonetheless, Foucault's notion of power, which is entirely one-sided and total, must be reconsidered, for what existed in the penal colony was a combination of diffusion, accommodation, and containment.

Alignment of barracks in Bourail, New Caledonia (year unknown). Courtesy Services des archives de la Nouvelle-Calédonie (ANC Album Terres lointaines-8144).

Interior view of cellular quarter on Île Nou, New Caledonia (ca. 1875–1885). Courtesy Services des archives de la Nouvelle-Calédonie (ANC Album Nicolas Frédéric Hagen 1 Num 3-42).

Bagnards repairing a water line near Bourail, New Caledonia (year unknown). Courtesy Services des archives de la Nouvelle-Calédonie (ANC Album Max Shekleton 1 Num 10-30).

Bagnards who are ill await the arrival of a physician near Camp de Charvein, French Guiana (year unknown). Collection Roger-Viollet.

Bagnards board a boat leaving for Guiana (year unknown). Collection Roger-Viollet.

Devil's Island, Guiana, with the small white house where Alfred Dreyfus was held (year unknown). Collection Roger-Viollet.

4. The Lords of Discipline

The French Penal Colony Service

In her 1937 book *Bagne*, Parisian attorney Mireille Maroger found "the brutality, ignorance, and . . . dishonesty" of penal colony guards to be quite "obvious," but what impressed her most was "their villainy, their malicious hatreds, and the dread they inspire."[1] French poet and novelist Francis Carco characterized these men similarly: "Tanned, bilious, quick tempered and sarcastic, they swagger their gold banded uniforms in the cafés and court their prostitutes. They are devoid of any sort of good traits of character. Some of them stink of alcohol and cheap perfume. I don't envy anyone the misfortune of falling into the hands of these sinister individuals."[2] To many observers, such as adventure writer Hassoldt Davis, penal colony guards were not appreciably different in character from the prisoners themselves: "The question is moot as to whether the surveillants are brutalized by their association with inveterate thieves and murderers, or the other way around. Like husbands and wives, these two classes, supposedly contrary, have grown to resemble one another. . . . The making of pain was their trade and they are nourished by their product."[3]

Such considerations were neither new nor limited to literary luminaries or criminal theorists. Indeed, with the publication of newspaper reports in *Le petit national*, *Reveil social*, *Le citoyen*, and *Le temps*, a heretofore blithe French reading public was allowed inside the *bagne* for the first time. What they discovered was "true history in all its details, true-life accounts of suffering" by recently repatriated Communards who recounted "frequent whippings and the regular use of thumb screws" in New Caledonia.[4] One such article summarized prison life in the following manner: "If a guard finds your work unsatisfactory, you receive blows from the whip. If you march too quickly or too slowly, you receive blows from the whip. If you reply or attempt to deny any observation, you receive blows from the whip. For taking a piece of fruit along your daily route to work you receive blows from the whip. For no apparent reason, other than the enjoyment of the guards, you receive blows from the whip."[5] With growing public outrage, and with strident demands for an outside investigation coming from these newspapers, a parliamentary commission was convened to look into the matter in January 1880.[6]

In large measure, the vivid recollections of numerous former Communards supported the charges of abuse that had been put forth in the press. For instance, Alexandre Bauche testified that it was a "well-known fact that most *condamnés* received blows from the whip" and that he knew of a particular warden who "used to menace us by pulling out his revolver and pretending to shoot us."[7] Gaston Da Costa maintained that thumbscrews were frequently used as a means of interrogation and torture in the penal colony and that he had seen many prisoners sent to the hospital after having been "mutilated by these devices."[8] Perhaps the most dramatic point in the hearings came when Alphonse Humbert exclaimed: "There is nothing exaggerated in what has been reported. I have seen the thumbscrews and I can show the damage that these instruments can do!" He then raised his mangled hands to the committee.[9]

Although corporal punishment was allowed under penal colony regulation, the use of thumbscrews by guards was strictly forbidden by regulation. Indeed, officials referred to these rules in testimony and internal memoranda. For instance, Louis Le Gros, a retired penal colony commandant, testified that during his service in New Caledonia "the use of thumbscrews was not permitted by authority of the penitentiary. Never did a *condamné* complain of having been the victim of this instrument."[10] In a letter to the Ministry, the director of the penitentiary administration in New Caledonia admitted that corporal punishment was utilized, but only in "those exceptional cases that were to be determined by the administration in consultation with the governor." He concluded by saying that "that the whip is never used on the legs and rarely lasts more than one minute. It is repugnant that I have to respond to these accusations, since the state of punishment as mandated by the Ministry of the Marine has been followed with the utmost care."[11]

Obviously, such statements cannot be taken at face value, as they are simply attempts to deny culpability. As Alice Bullard has pointed out, penal colony authorities clearly employed violence against the Communards.[12] Moreover, such brutality was not limited to political prisoners but extended to common-law convicts as well. What makes the aforementioned denials noteworthy is that each deflects complicity to a higher authority: the guard to the administration, the administrator to the governor of the colony and the Ministry. In this manner, these individuals are not unlike the "banal" Nazi officials so aptly depicted by Hannah Arendt who simply vitiate their own action or inaction by dispersing responsibility amid a larger bureaucracy.[13]

Was the penal colony guard an automaton, a lowly instrument of state-sanctioned dominance and control, or was he a sadistic brute bent on the torture and abuse of those in his charge? As Primo Levi has observed, even ss guards whose "daily ration of slaughter was studded with arbitrary and capricious acts were not monoliths."[14] While neither absolving nor condoning such behavior, this chapter examines the institutional life and culture of the guard. Despite rhetoric that emphasized militarism as a means to ensure discipline and surveillance in the penal colonies, and despite a professional structure designed to fashion and instill a sense of pride and purpose, the corps never took on the air of a professional military service. A variety of obstacles, structural and individual, impeded its development as an effective disciplinary apparatus of the *bagnes*.

The guards who disembarked from the first prison transport ships onto Guianese soil in 1854 and New Caledonia in 1864—"a strong minority" of whom were Corsican by birth—soon came under withering criticism from local administrators displeased with their comportment.[15] One penal colony inspector in New Caledonia complained of "wardens who display a lack of energy, bad conduct, and a nearly continual drunkenness that makes them the object of contempt and scorn among most *transportés*." He maintained that such misconduct was pervasive and evidence of a "malaise that makes most wardens no better than those whom they guard."[16] Another such report noted that of those guards not returned to France for "their deplorable attitude and misconduct, most are debauched drunks who have succumbed to every vice imaginable, and are at this very moment a risk to security."[17] Statistics compiled by the penal administration seemed to support this general charge. Indeed, of the 561 individuals admitted to the penal colony corps in both French Guiana and New Caledonia between 1854 and 1867, nearly 23 percent, or 127 men, were returned to France for dereliction of duty, usually drunkenness.[18]

Those who evinced what Governor Guillain of New Caledonia termed a "moral gangrene" were former noncommissioned officers in the army and navy.[19] In a job that demanded vigilance, obedience, and a strict adherence to routine, prior military service had always been seen as an ideal training ground for prison guards in France. Penal colony officials were critical of this pattern of recruitment, however, for they believed that time spent "in civilian life after their departure from the service appears to have led to a weakening of the military esprit de corps and tradition that is so important for the maintenance of order in such rigorous and isolated surroundings."[20]

Another concern for the administration was the fact that these individuals had been culled from the staffs of the disreputable shipyard *bagnes*. Such prior employment was perceived not as invaluable preparation for service in the penal colonies but rather as an experience that "more or less taints one by the practices that operated there."[21] Indeed, corruption was rife in the shipyard *bagnes*, and guards routinely engaged in black marketeering, theft, and homosexual unions with prisoners.[22]

While such accusations were neither new nor solely limited to the *bagnes* of Toulon, Brest, and Rochefort—complaints of illicit activities among guards extended to the *maison centrales* and departmental prisons as well—the unsavory reputation of men who had worked in the dockyards preceded their arrival in the penal colonies. It is therefore not surprising that they received little respect from their counterparts in active military service. For instance, the frequent complaints of guards "who are constantly excluded from the dining table of the ship's officers while access is given to officials of the Church" led the governor of French Guiana to ask naval authorities to "inform these officers that their behavior vis-à-vis guards is disrespectful" and that they should "allow the wardens to join them for repasts" during their overseas voyage.[23] In relating the case of a warden who complained that a soldier refused to acknowledge his greeting, the governor of French

Guiana informed the Ministry that such "incidents are ever more common as the antagonism between the wardens and soldiers of other corps have become worse and worse, and even violent. The wardens have become increasingly sensitive to such displays of disrespect."[24] Indeed, as name-calling and brawling were not at all uncommon during the first years of settlement in French Guiana, guards frequently ran afoul of local gendarmes as well.

Officials were also convinced that the poor attitude and performance of their charges was the result of a malfunctioning career structure. Although guards were divided into three classes and pay scales and were to respect the authority of those warrant officers and assistant warrant officers in charge, there was no established hierarchy other than seniority based on years of experience, and thus no opportunity for meritorious advancement within the corps itself.[25] In what was a leitmotif during the early years of the *bagnes*, a commission established by the Ministry in 1856 to investigate the failure to attract and retain guards in French Guiana concluded that "it is important for the maintenance of order that the administration recognize the rude conditions these men face while serving in this most difficult and important task . . . and therefore endeavor to create a superiority of functions and the possibility of advancement based upon distinguished service and remarkable aptitude, so that the corps attracts elite subjects with legitimate ambitions in an honorable career."[26]

Such considerations were usually formulated within the framework of a direct comparison to the military. With the expansion of the army during the Second Empire, prospects for advancement improved for noncommissioned army officers but remained unchanged for French Guiana's wardens. By the outbreak of the Franco-Prussian War, nearly a million troops were either in active service, in the reserve, or in the National Guard.[27] The successive wars in the Crimea and Italy, as well as colonial campaigns in Indochina, China, Syria, Senegal, and Mexico, all demanded the creation of new posts for commissioned and noncommissioned officers, especially those with field promotions. This expansion probably made the prospect—however slight it might have been—of social advancement through a career in the military more appealing to many noncommissioned officers who might have otherwise considered serving in the penal colony corps.

There were other impediments to recruitment for service in the penal colonies as well. Concomitant with Napoleon III's coup d'état and subsequent policy of political repression—particularly in the provinces, where counterrevolutionary activity was quite high—was an extension of the gendarmerie in France, which reduced the number of noncommissioned officers available to recruit. As of 1853, according to historian Howard Payne, "461 new brigades were in uniform, bringing the gendarmerie's complement to four thousand men over that of 1847. About twenty-four thousand gendarmes now patrolled France."[28] Indeed, by 1866, three-quarters of all French communes employed a policeman: "67,000 in all, more than the number of teachers at the time." The number of municipal police also more than doubled during the Second Empire, from 5,000 to 12,150.[29]

With the expansion of the army and gendarmerie, and given French Guiana's insalubrious reputation, recruitment to the corps was nearly nonexistent. In 1861 there were 115 wardens for the 1,248 prisoners in French Guiana—approximately one guard for every eleven *condamnés*—well below the one-to-four ratio prescribed in the legislation that first established the penal colony in 1854. Even in the healthier climes of New Caledonia there were only 98 wardens for 1,100 prisoners in 1867.[30] Administrators complained that "surveillance has become nearly impossible in our establishments . . . as the number of wardens continues to decrease to levels below that permitted by the department."[31] Thus, officials in both colonies were forced to draw upon civil gendarmes to bolster security.

With the rapid turnover and indiscipline within the ranks, penal colony officials recognized that "the service of transportation, always executed in the open air, in which the warden is in constant contact with the *condamné* chain gangs, has nothing in common with the work of the prison guard, whose contact with the prisoner is contained within the walls of the prison."[32] This realization implied that the penal colony service had "a special need for men trained to obey and command, and who have not lost all the qualities of a good noncommissioned officer."[33] After years of relative inaction, the Ministry also came to this conclusion and determined that it was necessary to "replace the standing guard with a corps organized and animated by a zealousness of service similar to that which operates in a very special army corps."[34]

Making a call to regiments of the army and navy in November 1867, the Ministry invited all noncommissioned officers still in active military service to join the penal colony corps. Candidates had to be literate and between the ages of twenty-five and forty. A cursory examination—covering grammar and orthography, rudimentary arithmetic, regulations relative to the regime of transportation, and general principles of penitentiary jurisprudence—was given to all those interested in becoming a penal colony guard. After passing this examination, the guard signed a contract with the penitentiary administration that obliged him to serve four years in the penal colonies.[35]

In carrying out his assigned tasks, the guard was to adhere to a strict military code of conduct. His character was "to be one of exact discipline; wardens are to obey their superiors in totality and are to act on the basis of one single sentiment: duty." He was to exude authority by virtue of his carriage and dress, his bearing toward others within the hierarchy of the corps, and his attitude and demeanor toward the *transporté*. Attitude and bearing were seen as essential "in the battle against the bad instincts of those in his charge," as he was to "always maintain a strict discipline while assuring that the *transporté* does not escape and meets his obligation to work."[36] Adorned in military garb—cap, topcoat, vest, and lapels carrying grade insignias— guards were distinguished by ranks structured comparably to the army.[37]

At the top of the hierarchy was the principal warden, who in most cases was a former artillery guard, followed by chief wardens first and second class, who were usually former sergeants major, and finally wardens first and second class, who were previously sergeants. The lowest rank, warden third class, was roughly equivalent to that of corporal. Behavior signifying the men's place in the hierarchy was minutely detailed: "Each guard should salute with the right hand. If the warden is seated he should always get up and salute when his superior comes into view. The superior should then return the salute. Superiors are to address their inferiors by rank. The inferior is to address the superior by 'mon,' and then the grade of the officer. All guards are to speak to civil functionaries, without qualification, as 'sir.' "[38]

To guarantee that suitable subjects joined the newly formed corps, military superiors were to vouch for the good character of those interested in guard duty by signing a certificate that verified past good conduct and health. Upon the recommendation of the colonial governor and local commandant, candidates were approved by the Ministry. To ensure a prospect for advancement in the corps, the Ministry stipulated that all those serving one year in an inferior grade or class were eligible for promotion, upon the recommendation of a superior and conferral by the governor and the Ministry.

In addition, the 1867 decree stated that all guards were subject to a uniform gradation of punishment for acts of insubordination or indiscipline. A first infraction would result in a verbal reprimand from a superior. A second offense would lead to "an inscription in one's dossier." A third incident would bring about a demotion in class or a prolongation at the lowest rank before possible advancement. A fourth offense would be seen as sufficient grounds for dismissal from the corps. The recalcitrant guard would be returned to the army or navy, where he would finish his tour of duty.[39]

The decree also provided for a substantial increase in salary. The annual remuneration for the newly created position of warden principal was set at 3,700 to 4,000 francs, more than triple what the most experienced warden earned prior to 1867. The base pay for warden chiefs ranged from 3,000 to 3,500 francs, and the two highest classes of wardens earned between 2,000 and 2,500 francs per year. The salary for those first entering the corps nearly quadrupled, from 415 to 1,600 francs annually.[40] This compared favorably to salaries in the metropole, where earnings for an ordinary guard in a metropolitan prison were typically around 800 francs per year and a chief guard earned 1,600 to 1,800 francs.[41]

After twenty-five years of service, or at the age of fifty-six, the guard received a pension. In retirement, a warden principal would receive between 1,450 and 2,250 francs annually, depending upon time served. For chief wardens the range was 1,010 to 1,932 francs per year. The pensions for the three primary ranks of wardens ranged from a minimum of 600 to a maximum of 1,560 francs annually. Finally, the decree stipulated that all wardens be accorded a six-month paid vacation in Europe or France "to regain their strength through rest" at the completion of each tour of duty. Such vacations could not infringe, however, on the number of guards deployed in the penal colonies, which was to never drop below 4 percent of the total prisoner population.[42]

As a civil service employee of the Ministry of the Colonies, the guard was now a member of a distinct occupational group organized after the military's structure.[43] Designed to systematize the corps in order to improve its operation and function, the aforementioned measures were also fashioned to act on another level: the emphasis on discipline and decorum would imbue the guard with military virtues. The reconfigured guard would now be an obedient and reliable instrument of order in the *bagnes*.

Ministerial and local inspection reports indicate a high level of satisfaction with both the new recruits and those of the old corps who remained. One inspector remarked in 1875 that "military discipline has, little by little, forged the corps of wardens into a cohesive, homogenous force. . . . The governors, inspectors general, and directors of the penitentiary service have succeeded in developing and maintaining a military esprit de corps among the wardens. This has become an elite corps, which today renders a great service."[44] Governor Guillain of New Caledonia similarly noted observing "a great improvement from the first days of transportation. The military corps of surveillants is now generally well recruited. The corps is well composed. They now comprise some capable and meritorious subjects, who have a great interest in advancing in class whenever it is possible."[45] In a report to the Ministry, Guillain's successor, Governor de la Richerie, remarked that "the wardens are by all accounts excellent . . . they operate with the best intent and are viewed by the general population as not only guards in the *bagne*, but as an elite corps of noncommissioned officers."[46]

The efficacy of the reform measures seemed evident in the behavior of the prisoners themselves. Governor Guillain remarked that "discipline is very good. . . . Punishment for misbehavior among the *transportés* is rare, for the *condamné* now has a great respect for the warden."[47] A ministerial official was also impressed by "how a perfect propriety is rigorously enforced by the guards. . . . Discipline leaves nothing to be desired. There are few attempts at escape, and those are rarely if ever successful. The corps is now composed of military men who merit every confidence."[48] One local warden concluded that "the salutary influence of the new corps shows itself every day and in every circumstance among the *transportés*. . . . Experience demonstrates in an irrefutable manner that the military organization has given the wardens the moral influence necessary to conduct and lead themselves and the *transportés.*"⁴⁹

Following the horrifying and embarrassing press accounts of the Communards, however, this satisfaction was short-lived. The revelations of abuse prompted a reassessment—at least among ministerial officials—of the militarism embodied in the 1867 decree. Indeed, there was a move away from discipline and punishment as the modus operandi of the guards, toward a new emphasis on correctional and "rehabilitative" treatment. No longer bent on obtaining submission and obedience from his prisoners at any cost, the guard was to instead to see his task "as one of regeneration, moral reform, and rehabilitation. . . . At all times he must guard, guide, and supervise. It is necessary that a warden encourage the *transporté* to work through discernment and tact, rather than threat of punishment."⁵⁰

In this context, flogging and physical punishment in the *bagnes* was banned, and in their place a plethora of noncorporal punishments was instituted for recalcitrant *bagnards.* These included a reduction in the daily ration of wine or *tafia* for infractions such as laziness or rudeness toward a warden; cellular confinement at night for insubordination or drunkenness, for periods up to one month; cellular confinement day and night, for periods up to one month, for "grave acts of immorality," which included violence toward another *bagnard* or insulting a guard; and finally, the *cachot* for escape attempts or acts of violence against guards, for periods up to two months. For repeat offenses, successive sentences to hard labor were given to *condamnés.*⁵¹

This reorientation was not accepted without complaint, as local administrators were unhappy that sanctions could no longer be imposed unilaterally by guards. Instead, penalties were handed down by a disciplinary commission composed of the commandant of the camp and two functionaries in the employ of the penitentiary administration and appointed by the director of the penitentiary administration. Penal administrators also chafed at the requirement that guards charged with abuse or using their firearms against prisoners be tried before a council of war (a tribunal composed of various individuals from the Ministry and local colonial officials). The director of the penitentiary administration in French Guiana complained of the inconvenience surrounding a two-month-long trial that depleted the corps of a guard who was rarely replaced by another.[52]

If the guard in question was married, a prolonged hearing caused significant hardship for his family, as only the husband could collect the ration upon which the modestly paid penal employee depended. Thus, in the man's absence the wife was forced into debt in order to buy food. "Without the ration," the director remarked, "life is miserable." Nor were the circumstances improved if the family accompanied the guard to the trial's venue, as the state provided no expenses for a family's displacement. The director saw the prospect of debt as a "powerful motive that hinders the guard in the accomplishment of his work."[53]

To many it appeared as though the guard was no longer the pillar on which the disciplinary edifice of the *bagnes* rested. In a book entitled *La colonisation et le bagne*, one former colonial official asked: "And what of those charged with guarding these shameless mobs who are encouraged by these short-sighted regulations? What do we tell them? These are the men who are obliged to plead extenuating circumstances before tribunals when they are forced to defend themselves!"[54] In this same vein, an official complained about the low morale of guards and argued that this was the result of the new disciplinary regime "in which guards are subjected from morning until night to insults which cannot be dealt with by precise discipline because of an insufficient punishment. . . . It is much easier to be a guard in a *maison centrale* in France than in New Caledonia."[55]

Many believed that in the penal colonies—unlike in the metropolitan penitentiary, where discipline had shifted from the body to the soul of the prisoner—moralization justified and necessitated the continued use of violence. From his vantage point in Paris, attorney A. Rivière charged that "with the suppression of corporal punishment . . . the penal colony administration has not had at its disposal an effective and intimidating means of coercion."[56] Emile Laurent, an early-twentieth-century professor of law in Lyon, complained that "while prisoners who attempted to escape were given twenty-five blows with the whip on the backside by the commandant of the penitentiary, and in the presence of all the *transportés* . . . with the suppression of corporal punishment wardens lost the most persuasive means of coercion available to them."[57] As a result, according to metropolitan penal administrator M. James-Nattan, prisoners "laugh" at the authority of guards who are insufficiently protected by these regulations.[58]

In contrast to local officials, however, the Ministry was firmly convinced that what lay at the root of the problem was low pay, inadequate housing, alcoholism, and a stagnant career structure. Indeed, there was a growing realization that life in the penal colonies was difficult and that in order to foster a better demeanor and improve rapport with prisoners, the guards' working and living conditions had to be ameliorated. In this vein, an investigatory commission convened by the governor of New Caledonia to examine the corps of wardens in the wake of the Communard scandal concluded that although some guards performed their jobs well and ethically, others failed out of weakness or exhaustion. "Many, discouraged by the fatigue of service or lack of compensation, serve without vigor or display a real cruelty toward the *condamné*. Thus, what do we see daily? Regrettable scenes of disorder, indiscipline, and violence."[59]

A number of factors continued to inhibit the development of morale and performance and militated against establishing a professional self-image in the corps. First, the perquisites established in the decree of 1867 did not suffice to meet the exigencies of life in the penal colonies. In French Guiana, where the specter of illness and death was ever present, local officials urged the administration to provide "medical care for guards and their dependents."[60] Indeed, in the parliamentary debate surrounding the decision to transport criminal recidivists, politician René Bérenger contended that—based on a report made by Riou Kerengal, a doctor attached to the colony of Guiana for fifteen years—"mortality among personnel was as high as twenty percent."[61]

As no hospital care was provided to guards or their families free of charge, many had to seek monetary assistance from penal colony authorities. Local officials were inundated with written pleas from guards desperate to make ends meet. In one case, a warden second class wrote: "Since I have been in the hospital my wife and child have not had the five francs a day that I would normally earn. On my salary my means are very restricted, and now without it and with the great costs of hospitalization, my family is in a state of penury. I would like to obtain a reduction in these costs, which would be of great help to me and my family."[62]

The guard's family was also exposed to tropical disease. A warden third class by the name of Fouque sought "an exoneration of the costs of hospitalization incurred by myself and my family from January 1 to the current day." Poignant evidence of his plight can be found in the list he attached to his letter, which detailed the number of visits he and members of his family made to the hospital to receive treatment for malaria.

> Son 14 years old. Entered January 2 left January 6
> Daughter 10 years old. Entered January 2 left January 4
> Wife entered January 1 left January 6
> Wife entered January 23 left January 27
> Myself entered March 7 left March 13
> Son entered March 16 left April 2
> Daughter entered March 16 left April 2
> Wife entered March 16 left April 3
> Myself entered March 24 left April 7
> Wife entered April 9 left April 14
> Son entered April 9 left April 14
> Total 89 days at 2.40 per day = 213.60 francs[63]

Given that the annual salary for a warden third class was only 1,300 francs, this bill for treatment was no inconsiderable sum. Although requests for debt forgiveness were heard on a case-by-case basis—in this instance the amount to be repaid was lowered by 115 francs—the Ministry's long-standing policy had been not to provide free hospital care to guards.

One also gains a sense of the precarious financial situation guards faced when examining the documents surrounding the admission of children into military boarding schools. Such schools were separate from those provided by the state in that they were free and available only to those who had previously served in the military. For those guards who had not, however, tuition and room and board were charged. As such fees were typically beyond his means, however, the guard had to petition the administration for a waiver or reduction to gain admittance for his child. Aside from basic information (rank, location of posting, length of service, etc.), these records also contain an assessment of the guard's general living situation, as the administration had to make a determination based on financial need. Although this practice became something of a moot point with the increasing emphasis on prior military service in guard recruitment during the late nineteenth century, such records nevertheless provide a glimpse into the guard's family life.

It is apparent from these documents that those with larger families had a distinct advantage in obtaining admittance for their children. Not coincidentally, these same individuals had the greatest pecuniary interest in having the child removed from the household and placed in the financial hands of the military. In this context, Guard Third Class Rolland submitted a request for his son Adrien, age seventeen. The administration determined that Guard Rolland, the father of four other children, was "in a most precarious financial situation with needs and debts beyond his means." Given this determination, and with his father's record of good service, Adrien was admitted. In contrast, however, Guard Second Class Marty had only two children, and while he was a "reliable server" from a "very dignified family," the administration decided that his financial situation did not merit such an action, although "it might demand more study in the future" (i.e., if there were additional children). As Guard Second Class Charpiat had but one child and "has lived with relative ease on his salary," his request was denied.[64]

Like prison guards in the metropole, penal colony wardens were quartered in barracks on prison grounds. Those who were married, however, were required to live outside prison with their families. These individuals were forced to maintain a separate household without salary compensation. In a report forwarded to the Ministry, the inspector general of French Guiana remarked that "the married wardens third class live in the most absolute distress; all are for the most part lacking the necessary resources to live. ... Their salary is insufficient for their needs."[65] In a missive to the Ministry, an investigatory commission characterized the situation of a guard third class with a family as "without dignity. ... These unfortunates are obliged to live by shameful expedients. While the majority remain honest, others resort to illegal activities."[66]

Official reports are replete with complaints against wardens "who, because of their economic situation, permit their wives to sell themselves, which is the cause of even more scandalous behavior and grave disorder. ... The husbands who engage in such a commerce are as guilty as the wives, and we should redouble our efforts to discover these agents, who merit severe punishment from their superiors."[67] It was a relatively common practice among guards to marry women from the dockyard brothels of Brest and Toulon and then arrange for their transport overseas, where they would engage in prostitution, thereby supplementing the income of the husband.[68]

This concern with the continued impropriety of the guards led officials to acknowledge that "although the Ministerial Decree of 1867 contained many excellent dispositions . . . its application was deficient."[69] Thus, authorities attempted to rehabilitate the guard in the same manner as the convict. In 1881 the Ministry decreed that all married wardens be provided lodging (i.e., a private home) adjacent to land suitable for a garden. In addition, each guard with three or more children was entitled to a supplementary ration, excluding wine and *tafia*. Finally, the decree established free medical care for the guard and his family. Such an effort would encourage the settlement of "honest and courageous families" in the penal colonies.

Although the decree of 1881 was intended, at least in part, to improve the standard of living for married guards, complaints persisted. Five years later, for instance, the director of the penal administration in French Guiana observed that newly arrived guards could find no acceptable housing for their families, as the administration had done too little to install or locate affordable living accommodations. If the government wanted these noncommissioned officers to display goodwill and devotion to a difficult job, he noted, "it must provide them with a decent standard of living."[70]

Although inadequate housing was a significant problem for penal colony personnel, the abuse of alcohol was perhaps the greatest impediment to professionalism and posed the most serious threat to security in the *bagnes*. Indeed, drinking seemed to be the besetting sin of the warden and the means by which he staved off the isolation and boredom of life in the penal colonies. Disciplinary reports testify to the pervasive and pernicious hold that alcohol had upon not only the life of the guard but the daily operation of the penal colony as well. A physician in French Guiana noted the sad case of Guard First Class Octeau, who was admitted to the hospital in St. Laurent after "falling off his horse dead-drunk!" Indeed, after a period of nearly fifteen hours in the hospital the guard was still inebriated. In his report to the administration, the physician mentioned that he had seen Octeau three times in a two-month period for such behavior, and he believed it was "his duty to make it known that this agent should not be allowed to carry a weapon," as Octeau posed a "real danger to public security."[71] In his remarks to the Ministry, the governor of French Guiana agreed that Octeau was a "habitual drunk" who had continued to drink to excess despite the "strongest admonitions of his superiors." Indeed, Octeau had served 128 days in jail since April 1904 and had spent 24 days consigned to his room for five other occasions of drunkenness. Despite such a desultory record of behavior, however, the governor—in consultation with the penal colony administration—simply demoted Octeau to the second class.[72]

Such behavior and relatively minor disciplinary sanctions were neither rare nor limited to those guards serving in French Guiana. In an examination of hundreds of individual dossiers, one uncovers many incidents not unlike that involving Guard Second Class Reydellet and Guard Third Class Rully, both of whom, after an extended and very public drinking binge on the Île des Pins in 1895, passed out. Upon awakening, Rully believed Reydellet to be dead and frantically informed the commandant of the camp, who, along with the chief physician, found the latter to be in various states of undress and gesticulating wildly amid a large group of convicts. In the investigation that followed, it was noted that these men "always appear to be in a constant state of drunkenness" and that "the convicts in their care are often subject to brutalities while they were in this scandalous state." For their actions, both men were demoted to third class.[73]

In examining Reydellet's personnel file one finds a desultory career path that was all too typical. A thirty-eight-year-old single man from Lyon, Joseph Marius Reydellet had an unremarkable stint in the navy as a noncommissioned officer before heading to French Guiana, where he served for over ten years prior to his demotion in 1896. As we have seen, advancement in rank was always difficult for penal colony guards, but Reydellet's record reflects an individual unconcerned by such matters, despite the fact that in his long tenure he had been promoted only once. In the year preceding his public drunkenness, the chief guard remarked that Reydellet "is a very ordinary server inclined to intemperance." The local commandant was harsher and more personal in his assessment, declaring Reydellet "a backbiter who disparages others." Reydellet finished his four-year term of service as a warden third class and returned to France in 1897.

Jean-Marie Rully followed a similar path in that he had served in the military, albeit as an noncommissioned artillery officer, before joining the penal colony corps and being shipped to New Caledonia. A thirty-six-year-old single man from the Isère, Rully was promoted to second class in 1891. Interestingly, however, his file reflects a relatively reliable and dignified service in the colony, as his conduct and "morality" were always rated as "good" by his commandant. Nearly a year after his demotion, however, Rully was found dead of natural causes on June 21, 1897, although it was reported that he had been extremely drunk the preceding evening.[74]

Alcohol was also utilized as a justification for or defense of homosexual unions. One such case involved Wardens Third Class Ferdinand Rouge and Emile Vidal, who were surprised by their comrades while in bed "committing an act of pederasty." In a report on the affair, both explained that their actions were the result of their mutual drunkenness. Both men also offered to be "demoted as recognition for the indignity they have brought to the uniform of all military wardens." Instead, the camp commandant immediately placed the guards in the prison on the Île Nou. Although he admitted that Rouge and Vidal were "just two of what seems to be an entire corps of inveterate drunks . . . we cannot lose consideration and all dignity. The presence of such individuals in the colony should no longer be tolerated."[75] As both men had their commissions revoked and were returned to France, it is clear that administrators perceived homosexuality among guards as a far more serious offense than drunkenness.

Authorities were incapable, despite the pernicious and pervasive nature of alcoholism, of devoting anything more than lip service to the problem. In this regard, remarks such as those offered by General Borgnis-Desbordes in his investigation of the New Caledonian penal colony were typical: "The corps is filled with incorrigible drunkards . . . the Inspector General has recommended that the chief wardens and principal wardens act with much greater rigor vis-à-vis drunkenness. . . . Not a single drunk should remain in the corps of surveillants."[76] Aside from trying individual wardens before disciplinary panels when determining punishments for such behavior—typically time served in a civil prison or, for repeat offenses, revocation from the corps—no coherent policy initiative concerning alcohol was ever enacted by penal colony authorities.

There was also long-standing discontent over the fact that after the first wave of appointments following the reorganization of the corps in 1867, the rate of promotion once again began to stagnate. As early as 1872, a governor's commission noted that "experience demonstrates that advancement is still not very rapid, which discourages and impairs the spirit of guards who dream of a better future. They are often tempted to resign, even though they have not yet finished their service, and this idea, even when they do not act upon it, adversely affects their conduct."[77] Of all the wardens third class in French Guiana, none were advanced during a period of nearly five years between 1890 and 1895, and more than half of the twenty-seven men promoted to second class had languished in the third-class rank for over six years.[78] The governor of New Caledonia complained that while he had nominated many guards for promotions, the Ministry had not acted on his recommendations. In this vein, he complained that

> for a long time, there have not been any promotions in the de-
> tachment at New Caledonia, which has produced, I must argue,
> a real discouragement that is growing each day among the sur-
> veillants. This discouragement has manifested itself in a decreas-
> ing sense of zealousness and a growing desire to leave or retire
> from the corps . . . many are demanding leaves or a change in
> location where they believe nominations will be more rapid. It
> is important to advance in class with only a brief delay. For ex-
> ample, among the oldest surveillants second class, one can count
> two who have more than nine years of service; eleven who have
> more than eight years of service; and four who have more than
> seven years of service. Among surveillants third class there are
> five who have more than nine years of service; thirteen who have
> more than eight years of service; and thirty-one who have more
> than seven years. One must recognize that of this number, most
> have never been demoted and are deserving of advancement, and
> many are also the head of families.[79]

Perhaps the greatest barrier to the development of a professional self-image among penal colony wardens was their pay. Indeed, the pay scale established by the decree of 1867, while generous in comparison to what the metropolitan prison guard received, was still lower than that provided by the military.

Principal guard 4,500 vs. Warden principal 4,000
Guard first class 3,850 vs. Warden chief first class 3,500
Guard second class 3,400 vs. Warden chief second class 3,000
Cavalry sergeant 2,502 vs. Warden first class 2,400
Infantry officer 2,202 vs. Warden second class 2,000
Noncommissioned officer 2,002 vs. Warden third class 1,600[80]

Thus, the recruitment of guards was poor. In many minds, the penal colony guard ranked no higher than a common soldier in terms of social status. Certainly, a warden's pay was no better. Inspector General Bourget remarked: "During the course of my inspection, I have noticed that guards earn less than noncommissioned officers in the army. This situation is to the disadvantage of the service. . . . If this is not ameliorated, recruitment to the guard corps will remain difficult, if not unrealizable."[81] The governor of French Guiana also observed that recruitment was difficult and good applicants rare. "At the beginning," he added, "some noncommissioned officers of good caliber, lured by the prospect of rank, entered the guard corps, but today the noncommissioned officers of the army are sufficiently recompensed, while our situation of employment is difficult and insufficiently remunerated."[82] In French Guiana in 1894 there were only 75 guards for the nearly 1,300 convicts in the colony, and only 32 for the 1,000 convicts on the Îles du Salut, neither of which met the 4 percent guard-to-prisoner ratio established with the 1867 decree.[83] The situation was no different in New Caledonia, where an 1881 inspection noted that the corps was "insufficient in all aspects."[84]

Not surprisingly, such a limited contingent of guards made prisoner escapes easier. This problem was exacerbated by the implementation of a new work regime in which prisoners were no longer remanded only to large-scale public works projects but dispersed throughout the colonies in small work crews. Originated in 1883 at the behest of Governor Pallu du Barrière of New Caledonia as an effort to hasten colonization efforts, this initiative came under fire from local administrators, who maintained that it was "inhumane to allow a guard, for a period of three or four months, to be in the middle of the jungle in the company of prisoners."[85] Another local official remarked: "The dissemination of numerous work crews to various points throughout the colony makes it extremely difficult service for those who must act as guards. As a result of a lack of wardens, the administration is often forced to concentrate work in a single spot, where there are too many convicts employed for the necessary task at hand. . . . Discipline has suffered, as it is impossible to effectively supervise a work crew of seventy to eighty prisoners."[86]

Figures compiled by General Borgnis-Desbordes in his investigation of the penal colony in New Caledonia seem to support this general claim. For instance, during the first year of operation the number of escape attempts nearly tripled, from 394 in 1882 to 986 in 1883, without a corresponding increase in the overall number of prisoners.[87] There was even a story "of half of fifty convicts at a mining camp who disappeared in one day" outside Bourail, New Caledonia, in 1885.[88]

The work initiative engendered consternation not only among those local officials charged with guarding the prisoners but also from emissaries of neighboring countries who complained that escapees were appearing with greater regularity on their soil. This was certainly the case in Surinam, where an official communiqué with the colonial government in French Guiana noted that "the cause of the numerous escapes of deportees . . . is the fact that there are usually around twenty guards for 500 deportees in the jungle camps near our border."[89] In another letter to the governor, the Dutch ambassador complained about the increasing number of escapes:

> During the last month officials of this government have arrested six escapees who were attempting to reach British Guiana through Surinam. That same day we received a letter from you stating that a dozen fugitives had escaped and were presumed headed toward our border. During the last week another French fugitive has been arrested in the act of committing a burglary in

Berbice. We request that the government of the French Republic
have the goodness to consider whether more effective measures
could not be taken to prevent the influx of escaped convicts from
French Guiana into our colony.[90]

Although the work initiative clearly taxed the guards, the most obvious
indication of a breakdown are those cases in which guards were complicit
in the escapes of prisoners. For instance, guards were interested in obtaining portions of the reward money offered by the colonial government for
information leading to the recapture of escaped prisoners. For every escaped
prisoner captured within the boundaries of the penal colony there was a
reward of ten francs, but this was raised to thirty-five francs if the prisoner
was captured on the Maroni River, and to fifty francs if overtaken at sea. As
only free citizens could collect this reward money, however, some guards
made arrangements with either locals or citizens in neighboring countries,
providing information as to the identity, time, location, and probable where-
abouts of the recent escapee in exchange for a split of the proceeds.

Although quantitative information in this regard is scattered and insub-
stantial, officials within the penal colony administration were inundated
with missives from diplomats, particularly in Surinam, who complained
that "as there is a reward accorded for each escapee from French Guiana,
this results in guards who have an interest in facilitating escapes in the cer-
titude that such an individual will be arrested in Surinam and repatriated to
French Guiana, at which time he will inherit the reward."[91] The Dutch also
charged that guards in the more isolated jungle camps "reclaim from the
penitentiary administration in the case of an escaped convict, the complement of that individual's month-long ration.... Thus one sees many escapes
occur during the first days of the month [before it was entirely consumed
by the prisoner]. The guards have an immediate interest in allowing such
escapes, and thus it is natural for them to carry out their duties with a very
marked complacency."[92]

Aside from a seemingly ever-increasing number of escapes, it appears
that acts of violence against prisoners continued. In one report, an inspector noted: "It is clear that grave acts of brutality are still being committed
by guards on *condamnés*.... Following an investigation, I do not hesitate to

ask of the Ministry to make a severe example of those who continue to act in this manner."[93] Governor Rodier of French Guiana characterized guards as having "no ability to reason or ability to convey any sense of moral persuasion" and that as a result "they are too often are carried to exert strong force, which leads to abusive punishments." He spoke of seeing "*condamnés*, who are not bad workers, punished to days and sometimes months in the *cachot* for chattering or having a smoke while at work. And for smoking what? The butts of cigarettes thrown to the ground by guards."[94]

Penal colony authorities never put into place a program of practical training for guards that might have established a better sense of decorum toward the prisoner, despite the fact that a special school for the training of guards in metropolitan jails operated between 1893 and 1934.[95] Indeed, guards in the metropole who were interested in a career in prison administration could be sent to the École supérieure des gardiens at the Conciergerie prison in Paris, after which they could be considered for advancement to chief guard and eventually to prison director.[96] Although in the early 1930s some officials discussed the possibility of an extended *cours* in which guards would be instructed by a coterie of penal colony administrators and camp directors on general rules of comportment and elemental penal and juridical codes pertaining to transportation and the rights of prisoners, this never came to fruition. Indeed, one report noted that "most young surveillants do not appear to be instructed in the tasks which they are to accomplish. I fear that they are even ignorant, for the most part, of the fundamental regulations of transportation and relegation." Thus the training of guards remained the province of individual camp commandants, which meant, for all practical purposes, that it was nonexistent.[97]

The only effort made in regard to training was a short-lived experiment that began in 1900 in which the Ministry paid guards to attend the renowned École d'agriculture in Valabre, where for three months they were trained in the latest scientific methods in agriculture and charged with imparting their knowledge to prison concessionaires upon their return. Under the supervision of agricultural agents, the wardens were established as landed proprietors and provided with "a residence and farming equipment" with which to instruct prisoners in the ways of "colonial agriculture."[98] The school, which was originally established for children between the ages of thirteen and eighteen, provided instruction in three core courses: general notions of agriculture, general notions of horticulture, and general notions of botanical agriculture. Not surprisingly, the school had limited success. In a final report to the administration that marked the official end of the program in 1908, the headmaster noted that "we have attempted to teach these functionaries the principal fundamentals of agricultural operation . . . but they are not accustomed to the habits of study and have not assimilated this material."[99]

To many it appeared as though the penal colony corps was beyond repair. In this regard one local inspector concluded rather ominously: "For many, many years the number of guards has been insufficient, as evident in the yearly reports, which have never ceased to express to the Ministry this shortage of personnel and how this is connected to their often dire circumstances. . . . As the number of agents continues to diminish, those who remain are increasingly overworked and overburdened. In these conditions, the progress of the service has never been and will never be assured."[100]

In conclusion, the attempt by administrators to militarize the corps was continually undermined by ad hoc measures that failed to address the significant problems guards faced every day, such as low pay, inadequate housing, alcoholism, and a stagnant career structure, all of which inhibited the development of any sense of professionalism and military decorum among the rank and file. In addition, as no training or education was ever provided, the militarism of the corps was essentially aesthetic and therefore insufficient in steeling the guard for the rigors of penal colony duty. Thus the guard did not act as a soldier but instead remained the simple turnkey so loathed by administrators and prisoners alike.

In his study of Police Battalion 101, a unit composed of non-career military men who participated in the murder of Polish Jews in World War II, Christopher Browning cited a Stanford University prison experiment in which a "normal" (based upon earlier psychological profiling) test group assumed roles as guards and prisoners in a simulated prison. While corporal punishment was obviously not available as a means of coercion for the test subjects, it was discovered that "within six days the inherent structure of prison life—in which guards operating on three-man shifts had to devise ways of controlling the more numerous prisoner population—had produced rapidly escalating brutality, humiliation, and dehumanization." It was the "prison situation," and not the individual personality, that produced "the anti-social behavior."[101]

This is relevant in understanding the behavior of the guards. With fewer and fewer recruits and the extreme nature of life in the penal colonies—with its isolation, material deprivations, and endemic disease—it is not surprising that guards employed violence and abused disciplinary practices such as cellular isolation. The increasing demands placed upon the corps and the changing nature of the penal colonies facilitated such behavior. The corps was the pillar upon which the disciplinary edifice of the penal colonies rested, and their low morale and indiscipline clearly impinged upon the institutional regime itself. The result was that guards found themselves to be the subject of surveillance, control, and frequent accusations of failure from those both inside and outside the institution. Like the prisoners they guarded, they too were exiles. Both prisoner and guard alike were subject to the same daily routine, the same food, even the same diseases. As we shall see in the next chapter, however, the entire operation was threatened not only by the failure to professionalize the guard but also by the inability of local officials and physicians to coordinate their administrative efforts.

5. The Battle over the *Bagnard*

Tropical Medicine in the Bagne

According to Foucault, power is dispersed throughout modern society by various processes of surveillance, discipline, individualization, and normalization. Not coincidentally, these processes are integral to the practice of medicine. At the close of the eighteenth century Foucault sees the birth of a medical discourse that was part and parcel of a "disciplinary strategy that extended control over the minutiae of conditions of life and conduct."[1] Within this context, the physician was "the great advisor and expert" in all aspects of life, even in that "darkest region in the apparatus of justice," the prison.[2] Indeed, Foucault argues that the prison was the quintessential laboratory in which the advice and expertise of the medical profession was highly valued and esteemed because it aimed to reintegrate the confined back into "normal" society. In essence, medicine took its place alongside psychology and criminology in normalizing the malfeasant.

Such a role for the physician was concomitant with the notion of "total care"—the idea that the institution must provide for all the prisoner's daily needs—that emerged in the early nineteenth century. As we saw in chapter 1, prison reformers believed that inmates had to be isolated from their unsanitary social milieu if they were to be reformed. This was based, as both O'Brien and Zinoman have pointed out, on the idea that a deleterious physical milieu fostered criminal propensities.[3] In the reformed prison, the physician was to constantly monitor the physical environment and make certain that inmates were provided with adequate nourishment so that the unhealthy influence "of family, friends and peddlers"—all of whom were resources for survival in premodern jails—were not necessary and no longer a source of distraction from the mission at hand, which was of course rehabilitation.[4] As we shall see, however, the penal colony was not a site of hygienic and normalizing intervention for medical authorities.

Indeed, the internal memoranda and correspondence of those physicians of the Corps de santé des colonies et des pays de protectorat—split from the navy by ministerial decree in 1890 and charged with overseeing public health initiatives for civilian populations in the colonies—who were charged with the care and hygiene of prisoners and personnel in the *bagnes* reveal a medical service severely limited in its therapeutic reach.[5] Among the many causes for this was the medical corps's discordant relationship with penal colony administrators. Physicians tried to disentangle the convict from the prevailing prison structure and reintegrate him within a morally and physically hygienic environment in which they would play a more significant role as normalizing agents. Their effort was hindered, however, by the intransigence of an administration that viewed the medical corps and its various attempts to intervene in the operation of the *bagnes* as a threat to their institutional autonomy and mission. Caught between the perceived imperatives of security and the exercise of medical conscience, prisoner health was abysmal—despite advances in the clinical treatment and prophylaxis of tropical disease—well into the twentieth century.

Penal colony doctors considered the European frame to be uniquely unsuited for the tropical environment. Although such opinions were widely shared by metropolitan physicians at midcentury, one sees a general move away from environmental explanations of disease causation and a move toward—with advances in cytology (microscopy)—a better understanding of parasitism, germs, and disease vectors by 1900. Although his discovery was initially rejected by the medical community, Alfonse Laveran identified the parasite in human blood cells that causes malaria in 1880. In the late 1890s, William Gorgas and Ronald Ross, respectively, discovered that mosquitoes are the principal vectors of yellow fever and malaria.[6] Indeed, during the last quarter of the nineteenth century the various microbial agents of dysentery, leprosy, and the plague were also identified, as was the tsetse fly.[7]

It is not coincidental that these discoveries coincided with the "Age of Imperialism," and that "tropical medicine" emerged as a specific field of medical enquiry. Its development in various medical schools and institutes met the needs of European imperial states that sought to better protect its citizens and soldiers from the deadly environs they were attempting to conquer. In France this role was fulfilled by the École du Pharo, which was established in Marseille in 1906 and would for all practical purposes become the preeminent training ground for students interested in tropical medicine, superseding the smattering of courses on the subject offered at the naval *écoles* and even the army medical school at Val-de-Grâce. Indeed, from 1906 to 1980, all personnel of the newly formed Corps de santé des colonies—some 4,813 doctors, 386 pharmacists, and 93 officers of administration—participated in the program of study offered at the Pharo.[8]

Thus, after the completion of their traditional medical training, those who wished to practice medicine in the tropics completed an additional eight-month intensive course of study that focused on a diverse array of subjects, such as tropical illnesses, army surgical techniques, bacteriology and parasitology, hygiene and tropical disease prophylaxis, police sanitation, and principles of legal medicine and administrative health service in the colonies.[9] Armed with their newfound knowledge and training, these practitioners were convinced that the etiological riddles of diseases such as malaria and yellow fever were nearly solved and that, with proper precautions, Europeans could withstand the rigors of the tropics. Despite the fact that these physicians were an autonomous corps, they often found themselves at odds with local officials, which many believed seriously undermined their ability to treat the sick.[10]

At the head of the medical hierarchy was the chief of the health service. Chosen by the Ministry of the Marine from among surgeons first class in active service, he had under his direct command all other medical personnel employed in penal colonial hospitals and infirmaries. It was his responsibility to visit and inspect each penal colonial establishment once a week and to provide the commandant of the penitentiary with a summary report that detailed the prognosis of those free and condemned men in the hospital. At the end of each month he was also to forward to the Ministry a report on sanitary conditions inside the various penal establishments and to offer suggestions and advice on how they might be ameliorated.[11]

Beneath the chief of the health service was the chief physician, who was to have the ostensible authority of a *commandant supérieur* concerning the service of the hospitals (one in Cayenne, one in St. Laurent, and one in Nouméa), their interior function, and matters dealing with the medical care of troops and prisoners.[12] All requests for supplies or additional medical personnel came under the purview of a military quartermaster, who determined if requisitions were possible within the confines of the budget established each year by the Ministry and the governor. As a result, the plaintive cries of physicians for additional materials and manpower were frequently heard. The implication of such a policy was clear, at least to local doctors. It was not the attending physician, or even the chief physician, but the quartermaster who—by virtue of his control over personnel and provisions—was the ultimate arbiter in managing the hospital and determining patient care.

In an undated report forwarded to the Ministry (likely from 1890 to 1900), the chief physician in French Guiana complained that the system which had established relations between the health service and the Ministry of the Marine was ill-conceived and that when "the chief physician finds himself in immediate contact with the sick, he knows better than an accountant, a stranger to medical science, how best to enact hygienic and hospital measures."[13] Such complaints were heard in New Caledonia as well, where the chief physician remarked on what he saw as the absurdity of putting a physician in charge but denying him the authority to order necessary supplies: "Knowing nothing of medicine, the quartermaster commits errors whose consequences are incalculable. . . . When one believes that he has prescribed a regimen of milk for a typhus patient, the quartermaster instead delivers dry bread . . . the doctor always encounters the shackle of the quartermaster and often his outright opposition."[14]

Given this state of affairs, local doctors believed that their professional prerogatives were infringed upon by the budgetary concerns of the quartermaster. Physicians called upon the administration to allow them more control in making hospital appointments as well as formally removing "all rights to control the delivery of rations and medicines" from the quartermaster and putting them in the hands of the chief physician. The administration believed, however, that such a move was "beyond reason" and denied the request.[15]

The lack of cooperation between the two services extended to the process of deciding where camps were located. Although the miasmatic theory of disease—associated with the inhalation of "humid air and putrid swamps"[16] and the "upturning" of soil in locales where the diseases had earlier been present[17]—had fallen into some scientific disrepute by the late nineteenth century, it was still of some practical value for "prompting the relocation of human habitations away from malarial sites."[18] Local doctors took very seriously their consultative role: they were to advise penal administrators as to the "orientation, elevation off the ground, circulation of air, and inclination for the drainage of rain water" during construction of new encampments.[19] In this context, there was great consternation when a *médecin major,* upon visiting an interior camp in French Guiana, discovered that it lay on the same spot where a cemetery containing the bodies of men who had died during an earlier outbreak of yellow fever had been buried.[20]

Although it may have been of little medical import, the vitriolic dialogue between the two services points to the larger issue of administrative autonomy. In a strongly worded communiqué to the director of the penitentiary administration, the chief physician demanded that the local commandant "be made aware of his impudence in ignoring the consequences of his actions, because he knows of the hygienic dangers he has raised."[21] In a memorandum to the director of the penitentiary administration, however, the commandant maintained that he had known the site was a cemetery, but since the remains were more than thirty years old, the excavation "would not expose Maroni to an epidemic of yellow fever as the doctor himself well knows." He also argued that the issue was not "purely a medical question to which I am refused all competence, but a matter of the administration's rights, which supersede [those of] a specialist such as the doctor."[22] In a later missive the physician in question charged that all penitentiary commanders were "ignorant" of hygiene—an attitude that "has seeped down among all personnel . . . has hampered the progress of the medical service and poses a serious threat to health."[23]

Although the relationship between the medical corps and the penal colony administration was severely strained, it would be a mistake to place the blame entirely on local officials. As there had been only a very modest improvement in the health of prisoners since the decision to stop sending metropolitan convicts to French Guiana in 1871—largely attributable to the change of locale to New Caledonia, and certainly not due to any particular health initiatives—physicians had yet to display any particular ability to manage and effectively control illness and disease in the *bagnes.* Despite their long-standing ineffectiveness, however, physicians were nonetheless adamant that penal colony officials accord them the authority and hegemony to which they believed themselves entitled.

This is evident in the numerous complaints of local officials who maintained that physicians treated the prison hospital as their private preserve, outside the purview of the penal colony administration. Indeed, it was not uncommon for physicians to refuse to allow authorities to question prisoners in their care. In one such case, the head of the penitentiary administration angrily chided the chief of the health service: "The penitentiary hospitals are annexes of the *bagne,* and the doctors who are detached there should accomplish their mission without taking moral charge and only formulate prescriptions appropriate to the nature of each illness. The doctor is a man of art; he does not possess the right to designate who the Commandant of the penitentiary is allowed to visit, regardless of their illness, if they pose a risk to security."[24] The chief physician, however, strongly disagreed with this assessment: "In all other colonies doctors are allowed the habit of professional independence, and hence there is no conflict. When functionaries of the penitentiary administration stop intruding on our authority, there will be, without doubt, in the execution of service, a desirable moderation and a conciliatory spirit. . . . The penitentiary hospitals are not, in sum, annexes of the *bagne,* and the doctor who is detached there cannot accomplish his technical mission without taking a moral stance in formulating the appropriate prescriptions with regard to each malady."[25]

Also troubling to officials was the fact that some physicians countermanded orders to punish recalcitrant prisoners by reducing or withholding their rations while hospitalized. In one such case a physician in St. Laurent refused to reduce the ration—despite being ordered to do so by the director of the penitentiary administration—of water given to a prisoner in his care who had attempted escape on a number of occasions and had just been recaptured by local guards. It was noted in a letter from the governor to the undersecretary of the marine that a formal complaint had been lodged against a Dr. Ricard and forwarded to the chief of the health service for disobeying the order of the director of the penitentiary administration in French Guiana.[26] After convening a meeting of a council of physicians to determine Ricard's punishment, it was decided that he had not engaged in any form of disobedience but acted under his own authority and within the context of standard medical proscriptions of health and hygiene. "By prescribing a hygienic ration of water to this man, Ricard did not in any fashion impose or engage in disobedience," the commission concluded. "Medical prescriptions are executed by law. Ricard is not a turnkey: he has the authority to prescribe in his own medical opinion what is necessary. This is not a forced interpretation of events."[27]

The director of the penitentiary administration was quick to complain that no disciplinary action had been taken against this physician, and he went on to explain in a letter to the governor that such behavior was not atypical: "There have been many incidents between the penitentiary administration and individuals of the medical corps. In a spirit of appeasement, I have ignored many such incidents. However, Ricard and other doctors have claimed it is they who should exercise policing and discipline with regard to prisoners in the hospital."[28] In an inspection report two years later, it was similarly noted that "there are frequent difficulties between the penitentiary administration and the service of health. This state of things is very harmful, and its nature compromises our operation. . . . It is necessary to recognize that the officers of the health corps are not always of the most conciliatory spirit in their battles, and often do not show the desirable degree of moderation that is necessary to maintain harmony between the services."[29] Unfortunately for Ricard, the governor of French Guiana agreed with the assessments provided by penal colony officials and—as the chief judicial and military authority in the colony—sentenced the doctor to nine days in jail.[30]

Later that same year, a Dr. Mariot not only refused to allow a warden first class by the name of Jarry to visit two *transportés* suspected of fomenting a prison riot but also would not release them from the hospital so that they could begin serving their thirty-day sentences in the *cachots*. In these small cells, which had little ventilation and no outside light, prisoners suffered from bouts of anemia and hookworm, usually from a lack of medical attention and proper diet.[31] In a deposition, the guard who presented himself at the hospital to deliver the prisoners to the *cachots* claimed that Dr. Mariot said the men were still too ill for such punishment and, when told that this was irrelevant, reportedly screamed, "You are a pig without a soul, you represent a band of pigs, you are a coward."[32] He also began to sign all of his reports to the penal administration as "Dr. Mariot, man of art charged with service to the *bagne*," a mocking and insulting reference aimed directly at the commandant's earlier characterization of penal colony physicians.[33]

What the director failed, or perhaps chose, not to understand was that most *condamnés*, particularly those residing in the *cachots*, were in a constant state of near starvation. Thus, obtaining a reclassification to hard labor in order to receive an extra ration of food was not so much an indication of the gullibility of physicians as a testament to the desperate plight the convict faced. The diet of the *bagnard* ostensibly consisted of "three meals per day; a half-loaf of bread for breakfast and 183 grams of biscuit. For dinner, three times per week, fresh meat (250 grams) and wine (23 centiliters)." On other days, preserves of lard, soup, and vegetables were provided. Finally, each day for breakfast the convict was allowed coffee, and four times a week he received *tafia* (a moonshine rum made from sugarcane).[34] This regimen represented a substantial caloric intake of 2,475 per day, which local doctors nonetheless considered insufficient to meet the rigors of hard labor.[35]

Moreover, given the general insufficiency of food, problems of procurement, and poor preparation, such quantities rarely made it to the convict.[36] In an autobiography that detailed his term of service in French Guiana, Louis Rousseau, a former penal colony physician, noted that a convict "never touched a ration of meat greater than 115 grams, and he is lucky to receive 90 grams at the most. . . . The flour is usually filled with parasites . . . and I saw many *condamnés* throw their bread away in disgust . . . only to be picked up by guards who used it to feed their chickens."[37]

In 1902 the chief physician in French Guiana noted: "If we demand of the *condamné* an appreciable work necessary for colonial exploitation and development, a healthy ration is absolutely necessary."[38] A later inspection report also contained such remarks, concluding that "the sickness and death resulting from malnutrition justifies the aphorism that is currently employed here: 'one convoy simply replaces the other.' "[39] Indeed, there was a near consensus among local physicians that the climate was less murderous than the process of transportation itself.[40] In a medical report from 1918, the life of the *bagnard* was characterized as "based essentially on hunger . . . the ration is not only insufficient, but it regularly fails inspection . . . with the result that men are morally broken by the *bagne*."[41]

Many convicts were stricken with diseases of nutritional deficiency such as beriberi, which is caused by a lack of vitamin B. Characterized by neuritis, muscle atrophy, poor coordination, heart failure, paralysis, and even death, beriberi was endemic in the penal camps. The condition was traditionally seen as having a bacterial origin and was therefore considered contagious. Although some medical authorities had posited a vague but possible link between nutrition and beriberi during the nineteenth century, it was not until 1895 that the Dutch physician E. Vonderman, in his two-year study of health conditions inside the prisons of Java—which held more than 250,000 men—provided solid evidence for such a connection. Through an exhaustive statistical compilation of rates of mortality, Vonderman discovered that in those prisons in which detainees subsisted on a diet that consisted primarily of polished (white) rice, cases of beriberi were 300 percent higher than in those establishments in which milled (red) rice was provided. With an appreciation for the nutritional import of vitamins, Vonderman—and the medical inquiries that followed—argued that, although polished rice did not "cause" beriberi, its presence as a dietary staple coincided with the appearance of the disease.[42]

This linkage had a particular relevance for physicians in the French penal colonies, as the typical prisoner diet, so lacking in fresh vegetables and meat, was often supplemented only with polished rice, which lacked the essential vitamin. This was also the case in the prisons of Indochina (e.g., in the prison at Poulo-Condore, 89 percent of the deaths reported in 1906 were the result of beriberi),[43] and it was in this part of the colonial empire that French research focused. In his study of French colonial prisons in Vietnam, Peter Zinoman also discusses beriberi, noting that "24 of the 48 deaths in Hanoi Central Prison were owing to beriberi" and that "between 1902 and 1913, beriberi accounted for 83 out of the 856 deaths that occurred throughout the provincial prison system in Cochin China."[44] Despite Vonderman's discovery, initial efforts in the prison focused on the elimination of "microbial parasites" through the sterilization of beds, walls, and floors. Only after such measures failed to stem the tide of the disease raging in Poulo-Condore did prison physician A. Thereze distribute red rice to the sick on August 9, 1906, and then to the rest of the prisoner population on August 14. The results were nearly immediate, as the last new case of beriberi was reported on August 20, and in those already afflicted, "little by little . . . the paralysis of their limbs seemed to diminish. . . . The substitution of the red rice for the white rice, with no other medication made available, had in a very short time, played a curative role superior to all antiseptic treatments employed previously." With another outbreak of beriberi in the civil prison in Hanoi—in which 75 of the 472 detainees were afflicted with the disease in 1909—a similar policy was followed, and upon the substitution of milled for polished rice the epidemic was halted in fifteen days. This new understanding of beriberi was soon supported by various proclamations from the Congress of Tropical Medicine held in Manila in 1910, the Société de pathologie exotique held in Paris in 1911, and again at the Congress of Tropical Medicine in Saigon in 1914.[45]

Despite the findings in Indochina, the proclamations of tropical physicians throughout the world, and the long-standing complaints of penal colony doctors, efforts to improve the diet of the *bagnard* were frustratingly slow and insignificant. This was not the result of local or even metropolitan ignorance of the issue. Indeed, the Institut colonial français explicitly mentioned the disease in a letter to the Ministry in which it remarked that "the absence of necessary vitamins clearly explains the cases of beriberi and the increasing number of hospitalizations that we see in the *bagnes*. . . . [T]his opinion is common among all doctors who have served in the medical service of the penitentiaries."[46]

Unlike physicians, however, penal administrators had no professional interest in the nutrition of their prisoners; indeed, they were keenly aware of—and sensitive to—critics in the metropole who charged that the penal colony regimen was too soft. As David Arnold has pointed out with regard to colonial prisons in India, penal administrators' primary interest was making certain that living conditions in no way exceeded those of the poorest classes outside the institution, and this was certainly no different in the *bagnes*.[47] This is clearly evident in the words of attorney Emile Clairin, who knew "of many honest *colons* who would volunteer for a similar regimen. Most *colons* in New Caledonia are reduced to a life of labor more painful than that of the *transportés*, and [they] never get to enjoy a taste of wine."[48] Fellow attorney Maurice Pain argued that it was a mistake to assure the *transporté* "a prison mess-tray with provisions better than our most loyal soldiers receive."[49] Other jurists advocated that the condemned be provided only a daily ration of bread and water and be forced to earn extra provisions through hard labor and good conduct.[50]

The cavalier attitude toward hygiene among local administrators was also apparent in the main penal colony establishments. In a letter to the chief physician in French Guiana, A. Duvigneau, a physician stationed in St. Jean, believed that prisoners would be more effective laborers if they were housed in a more hygienic manner: "Lodgings are crowded, latrines are in general improperly installed and so few in number that many dispose of their waste in the weeds that grow several meters high at the outskirts of the camps, which threatens health, for human waste is a breeding ground for disease."[51]

Indeed, dysentery—a disease of the large intestine characterized by the frequent passage of small, watery stools containing blood, accompanied by severe abdominal cramping, dehydration, and in severe cases, death—afflicted thousands of *bagnards* and personnel. Caused by various parasites, dysentery is most commonly spread through contaminated water or by flies that carry disease-producing bacteria and amoebas from infected feces to food.[52] As camps grew more crowded with the addition of the recidivist *rélégues* after 1885, and with no concomitant expansion in the number of latrines, dysentery was chronic and acute by the turn of the century.

This was certainly the case at the camp of St. Jean, where it was noted that "dysentery and diarrhea have become very common afflictions since 1888, and have caused 409 deaths, a number which represents two-thirds of the total sick population."[53] Although local physicians were well aware that dysentery was transmitted through fecal contamination and infected water supplies, they had little power to implement hygienic measures (see table 5.1). Frustration over their limited province in dealing with dysentery in the camps is evident in a medical report on the St. Jean camp: "Defective and crowded lodgings, and impure drinking water are the etiological

Table 5.1. Cases of Dysentery and Diarrhea in St. Jean,
French Guiana, 1888–1891.

Year	Cases of dysentery/deaths	Cases of diarrhea/deaths
1888	139/62	25/6
1889	366/110	116/9
1890	250/18	195/32
1891	199/47	138/30

Source: *Duvigneau Report*, 1892, carton H2013, AOM.

forces behind this sickness. . . . I do not pretend that the sanitary state will ever become excellent . . . but I am certain that the sanitary state can be improved to a point that penal labor can be effectively utilized if we were allowed to resolutely apply and maintain the laws of hygiene in the camps. Otherwise, this administration must strongly fear and anticipate that its mission will fail."[54]

The practical effect of the seemingly irrevocable split between administrators and physicians was nowhere more apparent than in the long, torturous effort to link St. Laurent and Cayenne by road. Initiated as a means to enhance trade between French Guiana and its neighbors Brazil and Surinam, construction of "Colonial Route 1" commenced in 1906. Traversing bottomless swampland and impenetrable jungle, work on the 160-mile road resulted in an incalculable number of prisoner deaths (estimates range as high as seventeen thousand).[55]

Physicians were displeased with many aspects of hygiene along the colonial route. They complained that convicts were housed in lean-tos with no mosquito netting, were fed an "insufficient ration of meat that spoils quickly and can only be distributed for a day or two," were clad in hats that "do little to protect them from the sun," and were "provided no spare clothes, despite the fact that regulations address this point."[56] Also troubling was the fact that prisoners frequently worked barefoot (disdaining the uncomfortable and impractical prison-issue wooden clogs), which needlessly exposed them to the ankylostomiasis parasite (hookworm), which enters the body by burrowing through the sole of the exposed foot and eventually gestates in the small intestine of its victim, leading to skin lesions, anemia, and sometimes death.[57] Indeed, the Institut colonial français estimated that 75 percent of all road-crew convicts were "carriers of ankylosteme eggs."[58]

The penal colony administration remained unconcerned about the ramifications of bad hygiene, poor nutrition, and improper clothing along not only Colonial Route 1 but throughout the *bagnes*. This mentality was largely guided by a general belief that the *bagnes* were to serve as a deterrent to crime and that by ameliorating conditions—through diet and general improvements in living standards—deterrence would be vitiated. The divide between the two services can also be attributed to the lowly status accorded medical opinion and the limited influence of physicians over how the *bagnes* were run. In essence, administrators ignored medical advice and drew their own unscientific conclusions about prison conditions.[59]

The character of the relationship between the medical corps and the local administration began to show signs of change during the 1920s. To a degree, this stemmed from a larger trend in French military medicine granting physicians greater freedom in the field of battle. Following the "medical disaster" of the Crimean War, in which there was a profound shortage of trained physicians to treat battlefield wounded, and then the Franco-Prussian War, where medical supply lines were ill-conceived and failed to meet the demands of surgeons in the field, the French medical corps was reconfigured. With support coming from an international congress on military medicine in 1878 and a government commission appointed to investigate the issue four years later, the army medical corps was made completely autonomous in 1889.[60]

Of more immediate impact, however, was the separation of the Ministry of the Colonies from the Ministry of the Marine in March 1894. Intended to more effectively meet the bureaucratic needs of a seemingly ever-expanding empire in Africa, this new Ministry soon embarked on its own path to secure improved public health in the colonies. At the instigation of Eugene Etienne, then undersecretary of state to the colonies and a strong supporter of the colonial movement, the Ministry decreed in August 1903 that all territorial holdings were to have their own health service. As such, the Service de santé des troupes coloniales was created for each colony and was soon entirely composed of physicians who had passed through the school of tropical medicine in Marseille. Although the navy was responsible for the general discipline and order of this corps, physicians were to implement various efforts to prevent and halt the spread of disease on their own accord.[61] As historian Marc Michel has pointed out, however, the recruitment of civilian doctors into this new corps was nearly impossible, as few were attracted to a career that offered few advantages, was sometimes dangerous, and was almost always unappreciated.[62] Of those civilian physicians who did make their way to the insalubrious climes of French Guiana, many worked at the Institut d'hygiène et du prophylaxis in Cayenne, which was established in 1914 as both a research institution and a treatment center for a paying clientele.[63]

As the *bagnes* offered no such remunerative advantages, responsibility for the prison hospital in St. Laurent and the prisoner ward in Cayenne still fell to the naval physicians and personnel assigned there. Like their brethren in other colonies, however, penal colony doctors now operated under a slightly different command structure in which they could, at least in theory, engage in health initiatives independently of prison officials. Moreover, an increasing number of these naval physicians had also passed through training in tropical medicine while in Marseille.

As we shall see in chapter 7, however, it was only with the increased public scrutiny that was largely the result of a journalistic campaign led by Albert Londres that significant attempts to improve conditions in the *bagnes* were made in the mid- to late 1920s. Nonetheless, the Ministry of the Colonies did make some efforts during this same period to improve administrative "cohesion." Given that doctors worked not under a single hospital chief but under three authorities (the penitentiary commandant, the quartermaster, and the chief physician, who had little power to order necessary sanitary measures), the Ministry granted greater autonomy to hospital administrators, expanded the responsibilities of the chief physician, and ordered that the administration of the penitentiary hospitals be limited to doctors.[64]

Officials also recognized that military wardens had neglected basic principles of disease prevention, particularly in the prophylactic use of quinine. Consequently, French Guiana's guards were ordered to administer a daily dose of quinine to the prisoners, disguising the bitter taste in wine. Penitentiary commanders were to keep an eye on those "careless" guards who, "despite the frequent counsel and advice they received from doctors who visited the camps," had neglected to distribute quinine effectively in the past. Once again, the Ministry argued that this was not a humanitarian measure per se but an issue of cost-effectiveness, given that "malaria has put so many men out of commission and led to numerous trips to the hospital." Guards were also to monitor the illicit sale of clothing among prisoners (usually in exchange for *tafia*) so that they would always have a hat and clothes to protect them from the heat and sun. Similarly, the Ministry did away with the uncomfortable work clogs, which were usually discarded by the men, and instead provided basic work boots.[65]

Finally, the penal administration established a far-reaching plan to improve sanitation practices and ordered penitentiary administrators to cooperate with the medical authorities. In addition to obligatory prophylaxis with quinine, the director ordered that stagnant water near the camps be reduced or sterilized, that wells be covered, and that all water sources be checked daily for signs of mosquito larvae.[66] To implement these measures, four-man teams were organized to visit roadwork and permanent penal camps weekly. Their job was to clear vegetation in and around the encampments, seal wells and reservoirs, and remove all receptacles that could collect water and breed mosquitoes. They burned dead animals, garbage, fecal matter, and other debris and spread disinfectant over surfaces likely to harbor microbes.[67]

If physicians of the mid- to late nineteenth century believed that the Guianese *bagne* would never function effectively because of health concerns, their successors in the medical corps during the 1920s and 1930s were much more favorably inclined. This attitude toward the viability of penal colonization is evident in a report forwarded by the chief physician to the Ministry: "The work of deforestation, agriculture, and hard labor, are they possible in French Guiana? Our predecessors said 'no,' for they believed that every European who moved to the tropics dug his own grave. But since, preventive colonial medicine has made great progress. We know the etiology of malaria. We know that the terrain has nothing to do with the hatching of mosquitoes as a vector of this illness. We know that preventative treatments for this affliction are recognized around the world as the most effective."[68] This opinion extended back to the metropole, where the Institut colonial français characterized the newfound hygienic effort as "indispensable": "Such measures permitted the Americans the means to build the Panama Canal, and they are the same means that will allow penal labor to succeed in providing French Guiana with important economic development. . . . [We must] renounce the errors of the past; if we have no success in French Guiana, if we still cannot build roads and railroads there, it will only be because we have not given preventive medicine and hygiene the capital importance that they must have for any such colonial enterprise to succeed."[69]

Such attitudes reflect a broader set of ideas that had great currency in the 1920s and 1930s and can be loosely labeled *mise en valeur*, a term that historian Alice Conklin has translated as "rational economic development." According to Conklin, the colonial orientation of the French had changed from the outright expropriation and unlimited expansion that characterized the late nineteenth century to a policy of rationality, progress, and conservation by the early twentieth century. This reorientation demanded that greater attention be paid to issues of public health, as the human resources of the colonies, both European and indigenous, had not been adequately tapped. To transmit ideas of French civilization abroad necessitated a "mastery, not of other peoples . . . but a mastery of nature, including the human body and what might be called 'social behavior.' "[70] Thus we see throughout the empire an efflorescence of scientific laboratories and modern sanitation and health facilities as the French state began to take a more active role in public health measures.

Yet in the years immediately following the implementation of the new hygienic regimen, rates of morbidity and mortality seemed to belie this confidence. Figures compiled by the medical service show that in the four penal camps still in operation in French Guiana, the number of those afflicted with malaria rose from 1,672 to 2,123 and the number of those who died from the disease climbed from 203 to 321 from 1926 to 1928.[71] Mortality rose as well. If one includes the 1,553 *relégués* in these figures, mortality in 1927 exceeded 11.45 percent, with 178 additional deaths that year (see table 5.2).

Not until the early 1930s did hygiene and sanitation begin to improve significantly in the *bagnes*. Consequently, the numbers of those dead and hospitalized with malaria show their first decline in 1930 and 1931, a trend that continued throughout the decade. As of 1938—by which time the Daladier government had decided to halt all shipments of prisoners to French Guiana amid continued public and political criticism of incarceration practices at home and abroad—the annual rate of mortality among prisoners had

Table 5.2. Mortality in French Guiana, 1924–1927.

Year	Prison population	Deaths/Rates
1924	6,243	485/7.85%
1925	5,758	352/6.14%
1926	6,113	461/7.54%
1927	5,592	566/10.30%

Source: *Rousseau, Un médecin au bagne*, 355.

dropped to an unprecedented low of 2.6 percent, a figure that the medical corps maintained "shows the progress accomplished in the amelioration in the condition of the *bagnard*."[72] Although mortality rates would again reach horrifying levels following the onset of World War II, this was a temporary occurrence largely due to the deprivation of food and supplies stemming from the Atlantic blockade, not the result of any internal strife or limitations placed on the health corps by the penal administration, as had been the case throughout the nineteenth and early twentieth centuries. Indeed, the rupture in shipping "caused the value of imports from France to Guyane to drop from 49 million francs in 1939 to 4 million in 1941 and zero in 1942 and 1943." Not surprisingly, mortality rose concomitantly, as "more than half of the prisoner population" died between 1940 and 1943.[73]

It is apparent that during the long life of the penal colonies, an institutional culture of mistrust prevailed between physicians and local administrators. Determined to maintain their autonomy in the face of what they perceived to be a Trojan horse of health and hygiene that doctors used to impose their institutional will to power, officials ignored, hampered, and sometimes directly subverted efforts designed to make the penal colonies more salubrious. This stance, along with a general ignorance of routine health precautions among penal colony guards, cost untold numbers of lives, for convicts would not benefit from advances in medical knowledge until shortly before the permanent closure of the *bagnes*.

This is not to suggest, however, that physicians shared no complicity in legitimating the institution. Local doctors did not evince any moral qualms about penal colonization per se; they desired only that the practice be made more efficacious by adherence to their medical proscriptions. Indeed, once they were granted more autonomy within the administrative apparatus of the *bagne* in the late 1920s, physicians believed that penal colonization was still a viable alternative to imprisonment in the metropole.

As we saw in chapter 3, prison labor was tied to medical authority in the penal colonies, and therefore it became the site of a guerrilla war between prison doctors and prisoners. While the former tried to use their powers of diagnosis to determine convicts' capacity for work, and to keep them healthy in order that they might continue to work, the latter endeavored to prove their sickness. Thus, prisoners' health became a source of tension between medical authorities and penal colony authorities.

What we have seen here is a battle over the *bagnard*: administrators engaged because their task was to discipline him; physicians engaged because the health and survival of the *bagnard* was the touchstone of their art, testimony to their professional competence. For both, the prisoner was the locus of a contest for authority and control. As a result of this internal struggle, however, the health of the convict languished. The tropical environment of the *bagne* was not administered, managed, and controlled through the intervention of modern medicine; instead, it served as an institutional site of death and disease for those unfortunate enough to be within its confines. As we shall see, however, what drew the attention of criminologists in the metropole was not outrage over disease but rather the supposed attractiveness of convict life in the penal colonies.

6. The Not-So-Fatal Shore

The Criminological Conception of the Fin de Siècle Bagne

In his doctoral thesis, Édouard Teisseire, a Toulouse attorney, described what he believed to be the major shortcoming of the overseas *bagnes* of French Guiana and New Caledonia. According to Teisseire, although "the general public believes that men condemned to the colonies are in leg irons, under the constant watch of guards, engaged in the most painful work, and pass hours and days in incredible suffering . . . this is a false idea and far from the truth." These individuals' "adventurous spirit is pleased by the prospect of exile in a far-away land under an unknown sky, and thus the idea of punishment disappears and is replaced by a passage across the seas . . . they leave without regret a country where they have no material interests to hold them, no bonds of family, for a land where they lie about in hammocks . . . and nap in the cool shade. When they do work, they have a daily lunch hour, where they smoke and drink their wine and *tafia*." Thus, "transportation is a very sweet punishment that has attracted the interest of our worst criminals. . . . All want a new life at the expense of the state."[1]

Many of Teisseire's colleagues held similar opinions.[2] For instance, Henri Joly, an esteemed member of the law faculty at Paris, characterized those sentenced to French Guiana as "living like foxes in a henhouse. One begins to be convinced that transportation is a penalty that punishes little but is very expensive for those of us who pay to inflict it."[3] Famed jurist and social theorist Gabriel Tarde agreed: "The penal colony is an Eldorado for the worst criminals. In sum, it will not intimidate any more than prolonged incarceration in the metropole."[4] Even the prominent penitentiary reformer Charles Lucas believed that the prospect of a lifetime spent in the penal colonies was "attractive to the adventurous spirit of the condemned. . . . Transportation produces an envy of sorts . . . because it provides the conditions of material well-being in *transportés*."[5]

As there was always an element of rumor and legend surrounding the *bagnes*, it was believed that news of these carceral utopias traveled by word of mouth among criminals. According to Paul Dislère, a former director of the colonies: "While I would like to say that there is a salutary fear of being sent to the penal colonies, it is not a subject of fear for those condemned. . . . The *rélégues* and *transportés* know, because they have heard it from others, that the punishment of hard labor and the regimen of relegation does not have to be hard."[6] This also seemed evident to commentators dismayed by the statements criminals purportedly made after their overseas sentences were announced. Teisseire told the story of "a criminal named Delbarry, who, after being convicted to eight years of hard labor exclaimed . . . 'Ah well, so much the better! I will be going to tame the Kanaks' [the indigenous peoples of New Caledonia]." In another case, he described "a bandit by the name of Altmayer," who, after being sentenced to twelve years' hard labor, supposedly told the court: "I am going to New Caledonia, and it does not displease me; I prefer an agreeable voyage to internment in a cell; it is more enjoyable, and I can escape more easily."[7]

Given that the unhealthy living conditions in the overseas colonies had long been known[8] and that a sentence to hard labor in such an establishment was considered the most serious punishment after the death penalty in the French penal code, why were Tarde and other jurists so critical of the penal colony regime? What came to be the criminological understanding of the penal colonies cannot be disentangled from local officials' coterminous complaints that there had been a general and ill-advised attenuation of punishment in the *bagnes* during the late nineteenth century. Indeed, at many points the criminological critiques of the overseas *bagnes* converge and coalesce with those inscribed in the internal memoranda and correspondence of local administrators and inspectors of the Ministry of the Marine, which oversaw the operation.

As we shall see, these points of congruence are not testament to the fact that the *bagnes* were a tropical paradise; rather, they speak to the conflicted nature at the epistemological core of penal colonization. Indeed, penal trans-

portation was a hotly contested issue in fin de siècle France, drawing into its
nexus a host of ideological oppositions—reform versus deterrence; colonization versus punishment; retribution versus rehabilitation—from which
contemporaries fashioned their various positions on the *bagnes*. These competing and often conflicting demands fostered depictions of the penal colonies as places of rest and relaxation for the *bagnards* and ultimately led officials to fundamentally redefine and reconfigure the practice by the close
of the nineteenth century.

The perception of the *bagne* as tropical paradise can be traced to a series
of reforms implemented during the early 1880s that dramatically altered
the penal colony regime. The first of these measures came at the behest of
Pallu du Barrière, governor of New Caledonia,[9] who—displeased with the
slow pace of colonization yet firmly convinced of the island's potential as
a penal colony settlement—prevailed upon the Ministry to approve a plan
in January 1882 whereby convicts were placed on parcels of land (ranging
from two to six hectares, depending upon the size of a convict's family) before their sentences were fully served.[10] Those who displayed good conduct
would receive their provisional concessions, and, as long as the land was
kept under cultivation, these grants would become permanent upon completion of their sentence.

To enable the convict to succeed as a colonist, he—along with his wife
and children—was also entitled to free supplies, clothing, hospital care for
a period of up to thirty months, a moratorium on the payment of rent, and
an indemnity of 150 to 300 francs. The wife's trousseau included such items
as a mattress, bedframe, blanket, two sets of cotton drapes, two meters of
fabric, two head scarves, two neck scarves, two handkerchiefs, and two pairs
of stockings.[11] Provisional concessions were also awarded in French Guiana.
There, married prisoners received four hectares of land, and if the prisoner
had two or more children he was awarded six hectares. With the implementation of this plan, the number of *condamné* concessionaires increased dramatically. For instance, while only 382 grants of land were awarded in New
Caledonia from 1869 to 1880, 548 convicts received concessions during 1883
and 1884 alone.[12] The total number of concessionaires and their families on
the island thus jumped from 206 in January 1879 to 1,288 in January 1884.[13]

The early reports of penal colonial inspectors who visited the convict concessions were favorable. For instance, an 1883 report described an idyllic scene in which two former convicts, "now married, each with three children, tend to their coffee beans while their wives are occupied with the children and animals. They each live in a very proper and respectable home. . . . [B]ecause we have given these individuals our grace and the freedom to work this land, they now have a taste for ownership."[14] Another inspector was "pleased" with the concessionaires he visited and commented that "the institution itself appears to me to be the best means of bringing about the most serious amelioration in the spirit of the *condamné.*"[15]

This initial euphoria was short-lived, however. Indeed, as the penal administration availed itself of nearly 110,000 hectares of land, making it the largest landholder on the island,[16] the *bagne* soon became "an object of jealousy, scorn, disparagement, and the focal point of discontent" for critics in both New Caledonia and France.[17] Highlighting one obvious injustice, Parisian attorney Augustin Delvincourt complained that it was unjust to "reward" a convict a concession of land that was often already cleared by local authorities when "the free *colon* generally arrives without resources and lives in an uncomfortable hovel, or works land of inferior quality."[18] One local political official ruminated that it was "immoral" to award land to a convict still serving his punishment, fearing that the convicts were "rapidly and fatally overrunning the colony."[19] The metropolitan social theorist Charles Lemire asked, "After reserving 110,000 hectares of the best land, what is left for the free *colon*? Absolutely nothing."[20]

In its assessment of the provisional concessions, the local press was also critical. A series of editorials appearing in the *Neo-Calédonien* excoriated the logic of the policy,[21] as did the Caledonian newspaper *La lanterne*, which described concessionaires as "more happy than our countrymen in France . . . with their free plots of land and the tools furnished by the administration, they can sell their products at an advantage!"[22] In an open letter to its readers, the newspaper *La libération* characterized the plan as "sacrificing the free element to the penal element. Everything is given to the latter, nothing to the former. . . . It is not us who are absorbing the penal element, but it is they who are absorbing us."[23] This 1883 complaint was prescient, as by

1894 New Caledonia had a free-settler population of 12,576 inhabitants and a penal population of 12,539.[24]

As cattle ranching was the most prevalent industry on the island among free settlers, they too had a seemingly insatiable appetite for land, which brought them into conflict with penal colony officials. Indeed, in 1859 the first thousand head of cattle arrived from Australia, and by 1878 there were more than eighty thousand head wreaking untold havoc on local fauna. Before the arrival of settlers there were no pasture animals on the island. The French adopted what they knew as the Australian style of pasturage, which meant large-scale, unfenced grazing of an extensive rather than an intensive nature.[25]

What free settlers also failed to mention in their complaints about the concession policy—perhaps because they were also guilty of the charge—was that both groups were encroaching upon land belonging to the Kanaks.[26] Unlike French Guiana's indigenous peoples, who tended to retreat to the jungle upon the arrival of the French, those of New Caledonia attempted to maintain tribal claims to their land. For the Kanaks, the soil was the very foundation of their society, whose different clans were designated by the name of their original dwelling site. In principle, the land belonged to the first established clan that worked it, whose origins were so distant that it was often believed to have sprung from the very soil it owned. Only a small portion of the soil was cultivated at a time by the Kanaks, however, and their system of land rotation—by which gardening areas would often lie fallow for several years or longer—led on occasion to parallel shifts of dwelling place.[27]

The colonial government had declared as of 1855 that New Caledonia belonged to France and that France had the right to purchase lands occupied by the Kanaks.[28] Although there was a tacit recognition of the Kanaks' right of ownership over occupied lands, all claims to those not actually occupied were thrust aside.[29] This worked to the disadvantage of the Kanaks, who practiced crop rotation and were semi-nomadic in nature. As a result, French authorities appropriated all vacant or fallow land and granted much of it to convicts.

With the increasing number of convict concessionaires, tribal reserves were created in 1868. Under the reserve law, the French governor could define tribal territory and regulate Kanak affairs concerning land.[30] As a result, the Kanaks were increasingly herded onto overcrowded and infertile reserves where imported diseases such as smallpox, leprosy, and tuberculosis took a huge toll. Thus, the native population, which was estimated at 42,000 in 1887, shrank to an all-time low of 27,768 in 1901.[31] Indeed, one contemporary observer described the native population as "in the process of disappearing. . . . One can predict that their race will be extinct within the next thirty years."[32] While the Kanaks rebelled at the continued appropriation of their land, attacking colonists and penal colony settlements at La Foa and Boulonparis in 1878, this was swiftly and brutally put down by the French military.[33] Any village suspected of supporting the revolt was burned to the ground, and more than six hundred rebels were deported to neighboring islands.[34]

Even with the Kanak threat diminished, the fact remained that the concessions were failing. For instance, while there were only 173 repossessions of land by penal colonial authorities (due to insufficient development or abandonment) among 1,150 concessionaires between 1869 and 1885, 82 of these occurred in the two years immediately following implementation of the early provisional concessions (i.e., 1883–84).[35] More distressing was that of the 2,680 total concessions granted in New Caledonia between 1869 and 1910, 1,400 were repossessed by penal authorities.[36] One early-twentieth-century account confessed: "The attempts at penal colonization have been crowned with little success in New Caledonia. The rural grants have failed on an average of two out of three. . . . No serious industry, no profitable cultivation has been created."[37] In French Guiana the results were even more disastrous. Of the 1,659 individual concessions awarded between 1852 and 1900, 1,466 were repossessed during the same period.[38]

Officials attributed such poor results, at least in part, to unrepentant convict concessionaires. Typical was the following inspection report forwarded to the director of the penitentiary administration in French Guiana: "There is little gratitude for the concession. When [the freed convict] attaches a small price to something that he has done nothing to deserve and must work incessantly to maintain . . . it is not surprising that the concession fails. . . . A day in the camps is not as difficult as maintaining a concession, for one is obliged to work less, yet still receives a guaranteed ration. . . . We must recognize that delivering these concessions was a bad idea."[39] Social theorist Pierre Lallier argued: "It is easy to see the results of the early concessions; *forçats* improvised as cultivators without having ever before spent any time working the earth, without ever having the necessary desire or goodwill to put it into cultivation; and because of the disorder, the laziness, and the debauchery of concessionaires they usually will have squandered their thirty months of supplies in just a few weeks."[40] Similarly, in a letter to the governor of French Guiana, the undersecretary of the Ministry of the Marine argued: "Most of the concessionaires, whose vice and lazy behavior have been the bane of the police, have never worked in prisons in the metropole, or have skills that cannot be utilized in the colonies, and are thus ill-prepared for their existence. . . . [O]ne should not be surprised that these concessions around St. Jean have not been very satisfactory."[41]

It appears as though a poorly conceived system of cultivation had as much, if not more, to do with the failure of the concessions than lazy and improvident prisoners. Indeed, historian Alain Saussol has characterized the agricultural effort in New Caledonia as "primitive in the extreme." Moreover, according to Saussol, land was overworked: "At the very best, the land lay fallow one year in four. At the exhausting rate of two crops a year, without fertilizer or any restitution of organic matter—river flooding was relied on to regenerate soil—land could hardly grow poorer. The result was a constant reduction in productivity that contributed to the economic failure of the small penal concessions."[42]

The placement of convicts on land concessions before their sentences were fully served also brought into focus a fundamental question: Was the *bagne* to serve the needs of colonization or of punishment? This ambiguity is apparent in a series of internal dispatches in which the policy of early land concessions was castigated by ministerial officials for its failure to take into account the fact that "transportation is to work both in the direction of the metropole and the colony. Transportation is not simply the removal of the criminal from the metropole in order to help the colony profit in its development. It is indispensable that the *condamné* be subjected to a regimen which is not too sweet . . . to be inculcated with habits for life."[43] In the same dispatch, Noël Pardon, Pallu du Barrière's successor as governor, was asked "if transportation had become in reality, a favor for convicts" because of this "indulgence." Pardon replied: "While *condamnés* sentenced to short punishments, less than eight years, rapidly become *libérés*, I believe it is equitable to accord land to them. Transportation is the favor; liberation is a much heavier charge."[44]

These exchanges illustrate that while local colonial administrators held out hope that the *bagnards* could be rehabilitated by living as colonists— a salient point, not coincidentally, to officials whose motive was to further the work of colonial expansion and economic progress in New Caledonia and French Guiana—those within the Ministry were less enamored with the idea. In this regard, Félix Faure, then undersecretary of the colonies in Jules Ferry's ministry, remarked: "It is important that the *transporté* pass through three very distinct periods . . . repression, amendment, and reward. The first two periods should be sufficiently prolonged, in order that public vindictiveness is satisfied and for the *condamné* to give certain signs of his repentance and his will to be better in the future . . . this is no longer the case as the law currently stands."[45]

As it became apparent that the concessions were failing, the Ministry adopted the position that a sentence to the *bagne* was no longer a sufficient deterrent to crime and that the regenerative force of colonial life and labor upon the concessionaires was negligible at best. Governor Pardon, however, questioned the effectiveness of suffering as a means of deterrence by maintaining that "cruel laws guarantee only cruel morals. . . . The tilling of the soil is the most powerful rehabilitative force, because it is the most direct and reveals most clearly the moral effect of the land upon the man serving a sentence."[46]

While Pardon preferred to expatiate on the futility of deterrence, local penal administrators persistently complained that the new land policy was an enticement to criminals in France. For instance, in a report to the governor of French Guiana, the director of the penitentiary administration noted: "To my mind it is the exclusive right of society to submit the *condamné* to a special regulation in harmony with his tendencies and capabilities, and thus oblige him to suffer. If one considers the sacrifices the honest worker makes to provide bread for his family, one is astonished to see the convict enjoy a well-being that he otherwise could not procure. The *condamné* is exempt from the cares of the day and mocks the society that has given him free reign to pursue his bad instincts."[47] Theorists in the metropole were similarly critical. For instance, jurist M. Francis Brouilhet complained:

> Punishment to hard labor should inspire serious terror. But, by an incomprehensible aberration, the penitentiary administration has softened punishment in every measure. . . . Why do we allow such feebleness for people who do not merit it? Why do we allow them to walk around in the fresh air, why do we place them as landed proprietors, and in a word establish a penal regimen that is in their favor? The truth, the real truth, is that the *bagne* is not a place of torture, but a place of rural relaxation. . . . Transportation is neither intimidating nor repressive, and the punishment of hard labor, as it currently stands, constitutes an attraction for criminals on the continent.[48]

A. Riviére, an attorney, agreed: "The punishment of hard labor is neither moral nor inflictive nor exemplary: the prospect of an overseas voyage, on the contrary, seduces the criminal. He knows that he will find there an enchanting climate, an admirable nature, healthy and abundant nourishment, health care in case of sickness; and as long as he works, even just a little, he will receive, if he so desires, a free concession of land."[49]

Those already dubious of the rehabilitative power of penal colony life and labor were made more uneasy with a corollary to the land policy, that is, the employment of convicts at tasks other than agriculture or public works. Traditionally, upon their arrival at Bourail in New Caledonia or at the offshore island outposts in French Guiana, convicts were placed in heavy or light work details. In an effort to deal with a chronic shortage of labor in the colonies, however, the penal colony administration instituted a new work regime, once again at the behest of Pallu du Barrière, in which prisoners were not simply remanded to large-scale public works projects from their communal camp dormitories but dispersed throughout the colonies in small work crews or employed in a variety of tasks for free colonists or colonial officials. Indeed, as of 1888, 1,988 *bagnards* were employed as miners for companies exploiting nickel reserves in New Caledonia, 806 in the service of other various private enterprises, and 306 in the homes of *colons*.

Thus, of 5,011 convicts on the island, 3,100 were employed outside the auspices of the prison itself.[50]

This practice encountered stiff resistance from those who believed it vitiated the original intent of the 1854 law, which specified that convicts were to be utilized in the most painful aspects of colonization. In a dispatch to the Governor Pardon, a ministerial official cited this provision and added that it was often violated: "The most intelligent *transportés*, those who are at the same time the most dangerous, find themselves too easily, upon their arrival in the colony, employed as clerks, orderlies, and servants. . . . They only work eight hours a day, and receive gratifications for labor that is accomplished without any fatigue or profit for the colony.[51] "Pay and rewards are in general too easily obtained," according to attorney Edmond Henri, "when *transportés* work as gardeners, bakers, telegraphists, cooks, or nurses."[52]

As with the early land concessions, this seemed to violate the perceived transformative character of the *bagne*. Based upon the Christian notion of atonement, penal colony work was not to be an end in itself but rather a means toward the rehabilitation of the prisoner's character, personality, and identity. One could not undergo such a profound change, however, without experiencing the redemptive value of suffering as tied to hard labor. Only through such adversity would the moral virtues of a well-regulated and disciplined life crystallize in the mind of the *condamné*, which is perhaps why in all the complaints formulated about convict labor no one condemned the utilization of the *bagnard* in the backbreaking work of nickel mining.

There was particular consternation over the minority of *bagnards* employed as *garçons de famille*. Such employment, according to attorney Maurice Pain, was "in complete disagreement with the spirit of the 1854 law."[53] In this same vein, attorney Emile Clairin maintained that "the *transporté* should be condemned to public work, not work as a domestic: he should build roads and bridges, and in a word, pay his debt to society, the debt for his crime. . . . He has not been sent to the *bagne* to polish shoes, wash dirty clothes, or watch over the children of functionaries."[54] Officials within the Ministry were similarly troubled by the practice of employing convicts at tasks other than manual labor. For instance, the minister of the marine remarked: "I have been informed that a considerable number of *condamnés* are employed as servants in the homes of military and civilian functionaries; this state of things is contrary to the spirit of penal law, and by weakening punishment in this manner, one makes *condamnés* the object of envy for prisoners in France."[55]

Officials were also troubled because the selection of *condamnés* for employment in the homes of officials had an ad hoc quality that was open to abuse. Concern with the practice is evident in an 1883 inspection report in which the employment of *condamnés* as *garçons de famille* was characterized as "an abuse of power by the administration."[56] Penal colony administrators were portrayed in criminological texts as highly susceptible to the entreaties of a convict intent on becoming a *garçon de famille*. For instance, Clairin maintained that "if the condemned is just a little intelligent, he can manipulate his wardens; if he is obsequious to his bosses, he can create a very comfortable situation for himself, with pay and gratuities; civil servants will turn them into cooks, gardeners, even domestics and baby-sitters."[57] According to social critic Jean Carol, "Most *bagnards* hide their true thoughts in a humble and obsequious attitude. The *bagne*, a fountain for all cultural vices, is a great school of hypocrisy. One goes through all the motions, even those of repentance. The eyes of the most ardent criminal become cunning and fleeting . . . they know that if they appear submissive, they will find themselves rewarded with many advantages, favors, and rewards whose sum will constitute the envy of all honest and irreproachable workers."[58] He added, somewhat facetiously: "In France you give chase to burglars: here we install them as domestics in our homes. . . . But, complaints from employers are rare. . . . To get an excellent domestic one must always take a certain risk."[59]

Amid such criticisms, the Ministry instituted a series of conditions that obliged those officials who employed convicts as domestics to reimburse the penitentiary administration for the cost of their daily ration, to pay each *transporté* they employed a sum of ten francs in salary a day,[60] and to pick up their *garçon de famille* by no later than six in the morning and escort him back to his penitentiary camp by five in the evening.[61] These requirements, designed to dissuade officers from employing convicts in their homes, fostered much resentment among local functionaries. In an angry letter to the director of the penitentiary administration, the chief of the health service complained:

The tariff to which we are henceforth obligated to pay in order to employ *transportés* makes it impossible for us to use them. It is unnecessary that an officer escort his domestic to and from the prison, or provide him with rations. It is particularly unacceptable that he be returned to camp by five in the evening, just at the moment when his presence is indispensable in the kitchen and nearly two hours before the time he must be present to serve dinner in the evening. Thus, officers are in fact denied *garçons de famille*. This is an injustice without precedent. In such a situation what is an officer to do? He should always have the right to have a convict at his service. . . . I must conclude that the dignity of all officers and functionaries residing in French Guiana is threatened by the application of this dispatch.[62]

The director forwarded a similar complaint to the governor and asked for "a delay long enough to permit those employing *transportés* to take measures to obtain the necessary personnel from among the natives in the French Antilles. . . . You cannot ignore the difficulty that all functionaries face in procuring the necessary servers for the daily operation of their homes."[63] His request for such a delay, however, was denied.

Despite this effort to restrict the employment of convicts as domestic help, the application of the work regimen in the colonies continued to evoke criticism—not only for its perceived failure to punish, but also for its "failure to sufficiently supervise the labor of the *condamné*."[64] For instance, there was also widespread disapproval of *transportés* in the employ of engineers and land surveyors who would travel throughout the colony. "It is not rare," according to Clairin, "to encounter two or three *transportés* detached to engineers, allowed to travel alone for long distances while in their service . . . and enjoying the most absolute freedom, with their flasks of wine and *tafia* by their side."[65] A New Caledonia newspaper asked: "How is it that we have received many reports of *condamné* C . . . supposedly interred on the Ile of Ducos where he is serving a sentence of ten years in prison, in plain view, at eight in the evening, circulating freely on Solferieno Street where he visits his ex-wife? The surveillance of these laborers is poorly managed and racked with too much complacency."[66]

The prohibition on colonial governors—by virtue of the same ministerial decree in 1880 that restricted the use of corporal punishment—to order prisoners' execution also drew the ire of commentators. Anyone condemned to death for the murder of a civilian, guard, or other inmate by the maritime tribunals (Tribunal Maritime Spécial) in charge of administering justice in the penal colonies could appeal the verdict to the president of France.[67] This resulted in a lengthy appeals process and often led to a commutation. Indeed, during 1884 and 1885, of the fifty-six *transportés* condemned to death in New Caledonia, only four were executed. In French Guiana, of the seventeen death sentences between 1877 and 1885, there were only two executions.[68] Overall, Marcel Le Clère has estimated that there was an "average of seven to eight executions per year in the penal colonies from 1830 to 1925."[69]

"Capital punishment is no longer a deterrent in the penal colonies," complained H. Denys, a former director of the penitentiary administration in New Caledonia, "because everyone knows that it is rarely put into effect."[70] Within the standard syllogism of deterrence, critics such as J. Bernier, a New Caledonian journalist, charged that the chief executive had lost all sense of the moral value of atonement, a condition he blamed on "a philanthropy which reigns today in France, and especially among our politicians . . . it is a sickness whose effects are very dangerous, a nervousness that affects the intelligence of people and obliterates their moral sense."[71]

Many contemporaries in the metropole, however, were similarly dismayed. Theorists such as Pain lamented that "the death penalty is rarely applied, because the right to decide capital executions has been given to President Grévy, who usually commutes the sentence."[72] Clairin was dismayed by the sight of "convicts condemned to death for a new crime, only to be pardoned and simply returned to the punishment to which they had previously been condemned."[73]

Officials within the Ministry as well as metropolitan criminologists were critical of the successive sentences to hard labor given to *transportés* found guilty of infractions committed while in the penal colony. For instance, in a ministerial dispatch directed to the governor of French Guiana, Undersecretary of the Marine E. Etienne remarked that convicts often accumulated additional sentences of as much as two hundred years at hard labor.[74]

Clairin's testimony confirmed this: "We can cite numerous cases where individuals who were already sentenced to perpetuity are condemned to another twenty to forty years of hard labor!"[75] Such absurd sentences, in the opinion of attorney Henri Cor, "foster a sense of impunity for all the misdeeds committed by *transportés* in the *bagne*."[76]

Once a prisoner was brought before the Tribunal Maritime Spécial, however, such sentences were handed down quite quickly. In his memoir of his life as a prisoner in the *bagne*, René Belbenoit depicted a court procedure in which the president first questions the convict, the prosecutor follows with the presentation of his case, and the defense counsel ("usually a guard that has no facility for speaking in public") concludes not by questioning witnesses but rather by simply asking for the court's "indulgence for his client." It was not atypical for the Tribunal Maritime Spécial in French Guiana during the 1920s to hear and pass judgment on twenty cases in four hours.[77]

Governors often found themselves responding—via their correspondence with both inspectors and officials within the Ministry—to their critics in the metropole. To lend credence to a complaint, functionaries employed the exegesis of criminologists in their reports. For instance, in an 1889 dispatch on the functioning of the penal colonies, Inspector General Espeut conveyed his displeasure with the current regimen by directly citing the work of Jules Leveillé,[78] who had written a treatise condemning what he saw as a failure on the part of the local administration in French Guiana to effectively punish its prisoners.[79]

Similarly, in an unsigned report from Cayenne, one inspector compared the penitentiary administration to an anchorless ship, and in asking for more autonomy he invoked Leveillé's call for "a penitentiary administration that is autonomous, independent, and disengaged from all surrounding daily activity . . . under the general direction of the metropole but still allowed the greatest latitude in adopting and implementing its program."[80] In a letter to the governor of French Guiana, Undersecretary Etienne spoke of "criminalists" who "for many years have discussed the merits of different penitentiary systems. In their opinion (and the facts in this regard seem to support them) transportation has in no way made efficient use of penal labor; it is too mild for perverse natures; in a certain measure it is an incitation to commit crime; and it is to all points an inversion in the order of punishment."[81]

Stung by these criticisms, Governor Pardon of New Caledonia denied claims that "*condamnés*, despite what certain individuals allege, are not subject to any regulations, that they are allowed to grow their beards and hair as they want . . . and that they are placed on land concessions so favorable that they can easily attain success there."[82] Moreover, he expressed his displeasure with "the presumption that I supply for your approval a considerable group of reforms based upon the sincere, respected, and profound theories of legal science." Based on his long experience, Pardon believed no significant changes in the 1854 regimen were necessary. It was a mistake, he argued, to base decisions not on past experience but on "abstract speculations, despite the great works and parliamentary debates."[83]

As has already been noted, a ministerial group appointed to investigate the operation of the penal colonies, led by General Borgnis-Desbordes, was dispatched to New Caledonia in 1888. Desbordes was no less critical of the policy by which early concessions of land were granted to convicts than he had been toward the elimination of corporal punishment. He remarked that the law worked poorly because it unacceptably attenuated the offender's punishment and because it stretched the capabilities of penal colony authorities by increasing the number of concessions to oversee. Desbordes noted that it was inequitable to allow

> the prisoner to become a farmer who does not pay any rent, and whose efforts not only allow him an immediate profit but assure him of a prosperity from land which is still in usury. Because of the privileged situation that he occupies there is not enough time to appreciate and judge if his conduct merits such an award. Here is an excessive indulgence by an administration that has forgotten that they must first ensure the execution of the original punishment. They seem dominated by the notion that by making him a proprietor, a father of a family, even a citizen, the *condamné* will somehow be moralized.[84]

Borgnis-Desbordes's 1888 investigation marked a key point in the history of the French penal colonies: an official repudiation of any reformative intent. In doing so, it laid the ideological and political groundwork for the implementation of a much more severe regimen in the *bagnes*. Toward this end, metropolitan criminologists, in tandem with local penal administrators, fundamentally reshaped the penal colonies through their participation in the ministerial-sponsored Dislère Commission of 1889–91. Headed by Paul Dislère and charged with "discarding the excessively humanitarian ideas that were dominant when the decree of 1880 was issued,"[85] the commission based its work on the idea that the real purpose of punishment was expiation, with rehabilitation "a doubtful second goal."[86]

With this proviso, the commission put an immediate end to the practice of awarding land concessions to *transportés* before their sentences were fully served. This was followed by a decree in 1895 that not only reduced the entitlements the *condamné* concessionaire received but made the transfer of legal title much more difficult to obtain. The moratorium on the payment of rent was reduced from thirty to six months; the cost of tools, clothing, and bedding was to be reimbursed; and medical care was no longer free. Moreover, to gain legal possession of his holding, the concessionaire had not only to keep his parcel of land under cultivation but also to build a house and accumulate a nest egg of one hundred francs. If these conditions were not met within five years, the *condamné* was dispossessed of the land and any money he may have saved.[87]

The commission also determined that the practice of automatically trying guards before a military tribunal for firing their weapons at prisoners "presents a serious advantage to those convicts considering escape, as the agents of surveillance find themselves in a situation whose formalities and rigors do not allow them to act."[88] It therefore placed the fate of the guard in the hands of the governor, who, after an investigation and in consultation with the penitentiary administration, would determine whether the guard should be tried.

In addition, three basic punishments were stipulated for *transportés*: cellular imprisonment for six months to five years or longer; cellular reclusion for periods of at least six months to five years or longer; and the death penalty for "grave" crimes such as the murder of a warden.[89] Those in cellular isolation were attached to a shackle that was affixed to their cots and were allowed bread and water every two days. The practice of additional sentences to hard labor was also suspended, and the power to order executions was returned to colonial officials, thereby eliminating the recourse to presidential clemency.

The same logic of "expiation" governed the decree of September 4, 1891. Now the *transporté* could not advance in class for at least two years, and to pass into the first class, thereby escaping hard labor, he would have to serve at least half his penalty, or in the case of those sentenced to perpetuity, ten years. This would ensure that convicts spend a requisite amount of time engaged in "the most painful work of colonization," as outlined in the Relegation Law of 1854. Furthermore, all movement between the classes had to be approved by the Ministry, on the recommendation of a commission composed of representatives from the penal administration. Thus, colonial officials were no longer allowed to unilaterally determine how convicts were to be employed. Finally, the daily diet for the convict was reduced to a guarantee of only bread and water, with the promise that daily provisions of meat, vegetables, and coffee would be provided if his efforts at work were judged sufficient by penal authorities.[90]

Clearly, these "reforms" do not represent what has traditionally been identified as the slow but steady progress of the rational and humane in the incarceration of criminals.[91] In the eyes of the Dislère Commission, regenerative work and independence had superseded retribution and punishment in the penal colonies. The decrees of 1889 and 1891 attempted to redress this imbalance, and—as Gordon Wright has noted—officially marked "the end of the humanitarian decade," in which local colonial officials tried to ameliorate conditions in the colonies.[92]

The fin de siècle *bagne* had a complicated and ever-changing complexion, and it is from this ambiguous history that its incongruous image as a paradise for convicts derived. Because of this ambiguity, it was an ideological battleground on which criminologists, penal administrators, and colonial governors fought over whether its primary mission was incarceration, reformation, or colonization. Consequently, there is a persistent tension between the regenerative penal colony envisioned by colonial officials and the more strictly punitive regimen favored by local penal administrators. By the close of the nineteenth century, however, the delicate balance between these competing institutional ideals shifted as colonial governors came to be associated, fairly or unfairly, with a failed policy initiative. Faced with the complaints of local functionaries and criminologists in the metropole, the Ministry placed the fate of the penal colonial effort squarely in the hands of local officials. In this regard, 180,000 hectares of land surrounding the main penal site of St. Laurent were ceded to the penitentiary administration. They would "no longer be under the direct jurisdiction of the colony of French Guiana" but rather under the direct authority of a council composed of penal colony officials.[93]

This epistemological and administrative shift also culminated in the eventual cessation of transportation to New Caledonia in 1897, amid continued charges that the island was still too attractive "for rascals maintained at public expense."[94] In its place, the territory's first civilian governor, Paul Feillet, embarked upon an active propaganda campaign to attract more free settlers to the area. Although he used the same totems of "property" and "family" in convincing legislators to approve his plan of offering land and financial incentives to landless and impoverished French peasants, he was critical of similar efforts on behalf of the convict.[95]

The romanticized vision of the regenerative moral power of colonial life and labor had given way to a new vision of the *bagne* as a quixotic attempt to redeem the 21,600 convicts—unable or unwilling to participate in a bygone way of life—transported to New Caledonia between 1864 and 1897.[96] By the turn of the century, the Pacific island was no longer the imagined land where

> men clear trees, women take care of the household, and children play in doorways . . . with boutiques in town with signs that read "Lascombe, Coiffeur," "Falconette, Shoemaker." In France these men would have never found work, and would have fallen back into their lives of disorder, their hunger and their misery leading them back to their previous lives of crime; here they live honestly, they are gay, they are happy. In the evenings, when the shops close, the husbands return from cultivation, and the children return from school, a well-garnished table awaits them. An hour later, the sweet and soothing voices of mothers singing their

children to sleep can be heard throughout the countryside just as if one was in a French village.[97]

As we shall see in the next chapter, the basic imagining that was the impetus for this change—the *bagne* as tropical paradise—was subsumed by a new center of power and knowledge as the penal colony would become a point of journalistic and literary mass consumption by the turn of the century.

7. The *Bagne* Obscura

Representational Crisis and the Twentieth Century

Traditionally the intellectual province of French criminologists and legal theorists, the *bagne* became the imaginative preoccupation of a worldwide audience during the 1920s and 1930s. Indeed, with the rise of what we today would call "investigative journalism"—along with a spate of mass-market memoirs and novels—the French penal colonies moved out of professional journals and into the public consciousness. In examining this literature, one discovers another metaphorical shift: a move away from the conceptualization of the *bagne* as a tropical paradise toward a new understanding of the institution as the "dry guillotine."[1] This chapter explores those leitmotifs that gave the increasingly transnational dialogue about the penal colony such discursive and cultural weight, as well as the attempt and ultimate failure of French officials to craft alternative public imaginings of the *bagne*.

As literacy spread from Paris to rural areas throughout France during the nineteenth century, long-standing oral traditions gave way to a new vehicle of information exchange: the mass-circulation newspaper. With the efflorescence of literacy, the newspaper industry expanded concomitantly. By 1880, Paris alone supported sixty-seven newspapers, with a circulation of slightly more than two million.[2] While a few of these papers, such as *Le temps* and *Le journal des débats*, blended news and opinion into what would come to be accepted as a traditional journalistic format, others had a much different focus. Collectively known as the *quatre grands*,[3] *Le petit journal*, *Le petit parisien* (both founded in 1876), *Le matin* (founded in 1884), and *Le journal* (founded in 1892) were the foremost exemplars of a brand of journalism much less concerned with political happenings or world events than with

"scandal, sensation, and disruptions of the norm."[4] In particular, crime—
and the lurid circumstances surrounding criminal trials—was the preeminent domain of the *fait divers* (sensationalist true-crime stories that appeared in regular columns).[5]

Stories dealing with crime and punishment resonated powerfully with a
public accustomed to the moralistic tales of good versus evil long evident in
oral culture or depicted in the *canards*. Indeed, the *fait divers* had their immediate origins in these broadsheets of the first half of the nineteenth century, which—in a very condensed format—contained details of extraordinary crimes or scandalous or curious events. As simplification had always
been a necessary hallmark of the *canards*—this was, after all, a reading public only a generation or two removed from illiteracy—journalists of the *fait
divers* were steeped in a writing style that relied upon anecdote and stereo-
type. Hence their stories were replete with "sensational personalities, particularly those who could be pictured in the most diabolic manner possible."[6]
With a low price (one sou) and appealing rhetorical style, these journals were
enormously popular with readers. *Le petit journal* was the first French paper
to sell over one million copies, and *Le petit parisien* became the world's largest newspaper, with 1.5 million copies sold on the eve of World War I.[7]

The primary innovation of the *fait divers* that attracted such a vast read-
ership was a new reportorial practice. Rather than simply recounting findings on a daily basis, individual staff correspondents were assigned to "make
an investigation or *enquête* of a subject at home or abroad,"[8] extending over
long periods and culminating in a special series of articles on the subject.
These often led to their republication in book form. No longer dependent
on the events of the day, this practice (referred to as *grand rapportage*) allowed for the "creation" of news. Thus, journalists could expand their rep-
ertoire—moving beyond the basic linguistic and conceptual binary at the
heart of their crime stories—by stimulating a "variety of unconscious fears
and impulses which activate the collective imagination and bring into play
various forms of projection and identification."[9]

Fin de siècle journalists were for the most part uninterested in the overseas penal colonies. While metropolitan and local colonial journalists discussed the *bagne* as a news event—particularly following the decision to
halt additional shipments of prisoners to New Caledonia in 1897—they sel-

dom appeared on the pages of the *fait divers*. When the *bagne* did appear, however, it was within the same basic trope of "tropical paradise" utilized by criminologists of the day. It was in this vein that the journalist Jacques Dhur wrote the first extended series of articles on the subject for *Le journal* in July and August 1907.

With titles such as *"Forçat* Proprietors: A Challenge to Honest People," "The *Bagne*: The Dream of Criminals," "The *Bagne* and Its Sweetness," and "The *Forçats* Have Domestics," one gains a clear and palpable sense of Dhur's use of hyperbole concerning the *bagne*. More diatribe than objective journalism, Dhur's various narratives made no attempt at balance, relying instead upon the standard rhetorical conventions of the *fait divers*. Thus his stories were replete with anecdotes of unrepentant convicts mocking penal colony authority by prospering at the expense of the system. "Take Yeghene, for example. He is an old *colon*. He is president of a municipal commission, and was even mayor for a short time. Today he does not have a home. He leases a room on top of a bar owned by a *bagnard* named Degaus, for whom he now works as an employee. . . . The free population is reduced to misery. They must hire themselves out to convicts such as Degaus; to become the domestics of these criminals. . . . This is monstrous."[10]

As in criminological descriptions, Dhur characterized the *bagne* as "weak and a mistake. I repeat: the prospect of a sentence to the *bagne* does not frighten the guilty. On the contrary, it seduces; it exerts a sort of attraction." In addition, Dhur appropriated the same story that Borgnis-Desbordes had included in his inspection report on the penal colonies nearly twenty years earlier, while failing to acknowledge (unlike the general) its apocryphal provenance. Thus, Dhur relayed the tale of the concessionaire near Bourail who, when asked by the governor how his farming was going, replied: "Very well. If I had known it would be like this, I would have committed my crime ten years earlier."[11]

What is striking is not the substance of Dhur's claims—as previously mentioned, such charges were neither new nor particularly novel—but that it is entirely unclear whether the author actually stepped foot in New Caledonia. Despite frequent allusions to having seen things with his "own eyes," there is a level of generality in Dhur's depictions that calls such a claim into question. This ultimately undermined the raison d'être of the series, which,

in the tradition of the *fait divers*, was to provide the reader with a sense of
verisimilitude: a narrative designed to elicit a visceral response.

While this explains why there was little public reaction to Dhur's articles, his writings did not escape the attention of penal colony officials. As
evidenced in internal memoranda, there was a keen awareness of how the
bagne was being portrayed in the press. One missive noted: "In the series
of articles published by *Le journal*, Jacques Dhur has developed certain al-
legations that are manifestly erroneous. . . . He has tried to establish a parallel between the situation of free *colons* and that of *forçat* concessionaires.
There is no possible connection to make between these two categories."[12]
Another memorandum questioned Dhur's veracity: "The information contained in his articles refers to the practice of awarding concessions which
was completely abrogated years ago. . . . It is important to note that the penal element has diminished with each passing day from New Caledonia,
with the transfer of prisoners to French Guiana having begun in 1897. . . .
[G]iven the situation described by Dhur, one must ask if he has even truly
seen New Caledonia."[13] While officials in the metropole believed that a formal response was unnecessary, the governor of New Caledonia wrote a letter to a colonial newspaper that read, in part:

> New Caledonia has long been misunderstood. One misunder-
> standing that seems to persist is that it remains a *bagne*. I recently
> had the occasion to read the writings of Jacques Dhur in *Le jour-
> nal* describing New Caledonia as "the dream of criminals." Our
> compatriot described the insufficiency of punishment in the *ba-
> gne* with much documentation and the supposed testimony of
> personnel. But this campaign perplexes me. Has Dhur some-
> how forgotten that since 1897, New Caledonia is a paradise lost
> for the *forçat*? New Caledonia is no longer the fiefdom of the *ba-
> gne*. It is the beautiful free colony where nickel is king. But that,
> as they say, is another story.[14]

As its penal population steadily shrank during the first two decades of the
twentieth century, New Caledonia was slowly transformed into a free colony. Indeed, by 1929 the penal administration withdrew the last of its personnel from the island and turned over custody of the few remaining pris-

oners to local police.[15] This left the Guianese *bagne* to attract the attention of journalist Albert Londres. While working as a reporter for newspapers such as *Le matin*, *Le petit journal*, and the socialist paper *Le quotidien*, Londres had made a considerable reputation as "a crusader for the underdog and something of a muckraker," but it was his investigation into the penal colonies that made his career.[16] Why and how he gained such access to the *bagne* remains unclear, as "all those persons not directly employed by the penitentiary administration, or those whose functions do not require them to reside in penitentiary establishments," were not allowed "entry without the permission of the penitentiary administration and the Ministry."[17] Although some have speculated that in association with left-leaning forces in the Ministry, Londres embarked upon the idea to embarrass the right-wing Republican government of Raymond Poincaré, the impetus for the series remains unclear.[18] Whatever the genesis, however, the articles were pivotal to the fortunes of the penal colony.

In a simple prose style, Londres's twenty-seven-day series in August and September 1923 fostered contradictory yet compelling impulses in his readers: a simultaneous fascination with and revulsion for the *bagne* as an institution, and conflicted feelings of disdain and sympathy for those trapped within its confines. In part, this can be attributed to his vivid descriptions of penal colony life. Indeed, Londres provided a veritable travelogue of his tour. Thus, we are taken aboard the prison transport ship, *Le Martinière*. "I descended into the bowels of the ship. What had been the hold now held the *forçats*. Around me were the cages. The cages were somber. One could see the men behind the bars in front, but not those in the back. It was a confused swarm of men. . . . It was as if I had entered a can of sardines with the sardines still inside. The odor was overwhelming. I believe that this hold could maybe contain 100 men. Yet this boat held 672 men! Minus, of course, all those who died on the voyage."[19] The journalist also visited the infamous "Colonial Route 1," or as Londres deemed it, "colonial route zero, as it leads to nowhere."

> When we arrive at kilometer twenty-four of the road, it is at the
> end of the world. And now, for the first time, I see the *bagne*!
> There are one hundred men, all sick to their stomachs. Those

who are standing can barely lift a pick. Those who are lying on
the ground moan like dogs. The bush is in front of them like a
wall, but it is not they who will cut down this wall, it is the wall
that will cut them down. This is not a work camp, but a hidden
well where we throw men who will never crawl out.[20]

To understand a world that was completely alien—a world where the laws
and mores of civil society did not apply—such rich detail was absolutely essential for the reader.

The *libérés*—those ex-convicts required to reside in French Guiana for a
term equal to their original sentence, or for life under the law of *doublage*—
also made their way into Londres's cavalcade. The *libéré* had a particularly
hopeless condition in the penal colony as—unless he had a useful trade,
such as mechanic—he could find no work, since potential employers had a
ready and ample supply of cheap convict labor at their disposal. As such, he
was usually reduced to a life of homelessness, alcoholism, begging, and petty
thievery on the streets of St. Laurent (*libérés* were forbidden to live and work
in Cayenne). "We touch here upon a grave error of the *bagne*," Londres continued. "It is the law, but the law is wrong. . . . What we have here is a hag-
gard herd of debased men shuffling about the cruel streets of St. Laurent:
2,448 men without shelter, without clothes, without land, without work,
and without hope. All are hungry. They are like dogs without an owner.
. . . Their punishment is complete. They have paid. Do we have the right to
condemn a man twice for the same mistake?"[21]

Londres concluded his series with an open letter to Albert Sarraut, minister of the colonies. Londres did not recommend the permanent closure of
the *bagne*; indeed, he held firm to the belief that French Guiana was a veritable treasure trove of natural resources waiting to be exploited, and so he
encouraged the minister to embark upon a program of reform. The problem was not the principle of penal colonization but rather the cruelty and
ineffectiveness of its execution. For Londres, French Guiana was "an Eldorado, but you would think that we landed there yesterday. For sixty years
we have been turning this shell that contains a treasure around and around,
and yet we dare not open the shell."[22]

The journalist maintained that prisoners could be made to assist in the
exploitation "of this vast natural wealth: gold, wood, and all sorts of materi-

als which France in her present distress so desperately needs," but only if they were treated more humanely. In this regard he recommended that *transportés* be given better clothing; that quinine be made more readily available; that rations be increased and improved; and that the sentence of *doublage* and perpetual residence in the colony be eliminated. Londres concluded: "During this month I have seen hundreds of spectacles from Hell, and now it is the *bagnards* who stare back at me. . . . Each and every day, I dream of them staring at me, imploring me. 'Assassins, thieves, traitors, you have made your fate,' I scream, but your fate is terrible. Justice! You are only a memory. Happy are all the souls of France, certain that these wretches are deserving of this punishment. . . . My conscience, however, is less clear."[23]

Londres's series was remarkable, not necessarily as an example of great literature or even great journalism, but for its formidable power to stimulate political action. In the wake of his press campaign, shipments of prisoners to French Guiana were temporarily suspended and an inter-ministerial commission of "experts"—which included members of the judiciary, two colonial governors, officials from the Ministry of Justice, as well as one journalist, Pierre Mille—was appointed on January 17, 1924, to investigate conditions in the *bagne*.[24] This diverse group presented a report to President Alexandre Millerand which determined that "it appears necessary that the system of transportation be reformed" and advised that shipments of prisoners be temporarily halted for a period of one year.[25] Acting upon the recommendations of this commission, Parlement enacted legislation that eliminated the *cachots*, forbade the use of the ball and chain, and limited the time spent in solitary confinement to sixty days. In addition, the Salvation Army—under the stewardship of Major Charles Péan[26]—was allowed to establish itself in French Guiana and act as a relief agency for the *libérés*.[27]

The diet of the prisoner was also reassessed as an issue of economic expediency, if not necessarily humanitarian considerations. A more varied, nutritious, and substantial diet would support a healthier prisoner population that would be more effective laborers, particularly those working along Colonial Route 1. As such, the Ministry ordered that, whenever possible, the daily 100 grams of rice be replaced with 500 grams of fresh vegetables. Convicts also saw their daily rations of bread and beef increase by

125 and 100 grams, respectively.[28] A healthy ration was no longer seen as inimical to criminal deterrence or discipline within the *bagnes* but rather as a vital correlative for institutional progress and survival.

Operating within the rhetorical framework of the *fait divers*,[29] Londres's *rapportage* stands alone: a catalog of horrors whose very existence is its own explanation, whose very appeal is based upon a secret relief in the reader that the *bagnard* is someone else. As the aforementioned excerpts suggest, however, Londres appeared to be searching for "a specific image, illustration, anecdote, or event that illustrates his point . . . without presenting the abstract argument."[30] Indeed, what is decidedly absent and somewhat at variance with the genre is a sustained focus upon an individual, someone who—by virtue of strength of will or nefarious character—seemed larger than life and was a favorite topic of literary consumption. In 1927, three years after his first series on the *bagnes*, Londres found such a picaresque character in the *bagnard* Eugene Dieudonné and constructed a second series of articles that engaged the intellect and imagination of not only the French reading public but an international audience.

Dieudonné had been a cabinetmaker and fellow traveler of the "Bonnot gang," an anarchist group that engaged in a number of bank robberies in Paris between 1911 and 1912. After a robbery followed by a bloody shootout with police (two policeman were killed), all known associates of the gang were arrested. Despite the protestations of members that Dieudonné had neither planned nor participated in any of the crimes, he was identified by an eyewitness to the shooting, convicted, and sentenced in April 1913 to penal servitude for life in French Guiana. Although Dieudonné's case was notorious in France, his attempts at escape made him a legendary figure of the *bagne*. To escape the Guianese penal colony was, indeed, an extraordinary feat, as one had to either brave the jungle and head northeast on foot to Surinam—which, unlike Brazil, British French Guiana, and Venezuela, had no strict extradition policy—or float to the Dutch colony on a raft.[31] While serving a sentence on Île Royale for a previous escape attempt, Dieudonné chose the latter method for a second prison break. Over a long period, he built a raft of banana leaves, which he lashed together with some rope. With no equipment or supplies, he spent three days and nights drifting at sea before his crude vessel ran aground. Unaware of his location,

Dieudonné made his way through the jungle until he had the misfortune of stumbling upon the timber camp at Charvein (about twenty miles from St. Laurent), where he was promptly captured and sentenced to two years' solitary confinement.

The case would become something of a cause célèbre once the bystander in the original trial contradicted and later recanted his testimony. Many lawyers and journalists (including Londres) petitioned the Ministry of Justice to obtain Dieudonné's release. In 1927 he was pardoned by the French government but was ordered to serve the remaining three years of his sentence for his prior escape attempt.

Despondent over the prospect of three more years in French Guiana, Dieudonné embarked upon one final escape, this time actually reaching Brazil. He was soon arrested, however, and the French government demanded his immediate return to French Guiana. But, as the case began to garner the intense scrutiny of the international press, Brazilian officials hesitated about holding what would normally be a swift extradition proceeding.

Londres moved to the forefront, championing Dieudonné's cause by traveling to Brazil and writing a series of articles that appeared in *Le petit parisien* between November 6 and November 26, 1927 (later republished as a book entitled *L'homme qui s'évada*). In daily installments, readers learned how Dieudonné, along with a few other convicts, had first set sail in a stolen and fragile *pirogue* (canoe) along the coast to the Oyapock River, which serves as the boundary between French Guiana and Brazil. Because the craft was not made for the open seas, it soon ran aground. It is at this juncture where the reader encounters the florid prose of a narrative that reads like an adventure tale: "Gliding beside a forest of mangroves, sinister trees stretch their meager arms upward and dip their exposed roots in the millennial mud: a forest none but shipwrecked persons would attempt to penetrate. In spite of their efforts, they become stuck in the mud again. The three weakest begin to moan, fearing the death that flies above this Dantesque place."[32]

When the others decided to turn themselves in, Dieudonné took refuge in the jungle with no food or supplies. After several days he came across a local bushman who agreed to transport him to Brazil aboard his own vessel. Dieudonné eventually made his way to the town of Pará on the Amazon

River, where he took on a new identity (Michel Daniel) and began work as a carpenter before being discovered. Between Brazilian intransigence and the renewed public outcry in France, Dieudonné was officially pardoned and allowed to return home in December 1927. Afterward, Londres's readers see Dieudonné embracing his wife and child upon his arrival in Marseille; the concluding chapter of the drama has the former *bagnard* declare: "I like the elms better than the mangroves."[33]

With news agencies such as Havas, Reuters, Wolff Büro, the Associated Press, and United Press International proliferating during the early twentieth century,[34] Dieudonné's story was grist for not only *Le petit parisien* but for daily newspapers around the world. Wire service reports from Rio de Janeiro and Paris evinced little interest in the horrors of the *bagne*, however, instead focusing upon the escape itself. Even in articles intended, at least ostensibly, to describe the diplomatic maneuvers and extradition proceedings surrounding the case, there was always an homage to Dieudonné's "harrowing adventure, which has caused a stir throughout the world."[35] Indeed, with headlines such as "Jungle Prison Could Not Hold This Convict" and "The Man Who Cheated Two Guillotines," the *New York Times* was positively breathless as it followed the affair.

In this context, Dieudonné's importance is twofold. First, his escape was the event by which a transnational—particularly American—audience was first introduced to the *bagne*. This scrutiny was to become increasingly nettlesome to penal colony officials. Given the compelling nature of the story, it was only natural that public interest was catalyzed. Indeed, on the heels of Dieudonné's escape a profusion of articles appeared in the *New York Times* detailing other escape attempts. Under a screaming headline—"200 Convicts Flee French Guiana Lumber Camp"—one article began: "A thrilling story of the escape of 200 convicts from a forestry camp in French Guiana has just been reported."[36] (The fact that they were almost immediately recaptured was not reported in the American press.) Another story in September 1928 reported: "A Havas dispatch from Cayenne, French Guiana, says that Dr. Pierre Bougrat, the well-known physician of Marseilles convicted of murder, has made good on his dramatic boast during his trial that he would escape French Guiana. . . . The details, which are sure to be absorbing, are still lacking."[37]

For the public at large, the prisoner escape provided an entrée into the *bagne*. Escapees would become not only the dramatis personae of the institution—"signs" whose very existence was a condemnation of the penal colonial regime—but also a point of cultural consumption. I am utilizing "sign" and "cultural consumption" in the same manner as Jean Baudrillard, who has argued that "the generalized consumption of images, of facts, of information, aims to conjure away the real with the signs of the real, to conjure away history with the signs of change."[38] In this regard, Dieudonné was the first of several escaped *bagnards* to write of their exploits in published autobiographies that appeared during the 1930s, the 1940s, and well after the closure of the *bagne* in 1952.[39]

On the surface, Dieudonné's story bears a resemblance to that of Capt. Alfred Dreyfus, the most famous resident of Devil's Island. Wrongfully accused and convicted of high treason, Dreyfus—with the aid of literary luminaries such as Émile Zola, Anatole France, and Joseph Reinach, among others—was eventually set free amid a veritable torrent of publicity and was allowed to return to his long-suffering family and once again set foot on French soil.[40] Finally, and as with Dieudonné, Dreyfus would write of his nearly five years of suffering, and upon his release he published his anguished recollections.

The differences between the two cases far outweigh the similarities, however, and they are notable in the larger context of the history of the Guianese *bagne*. Dreyfus was the first prisoner on Devil's Island, which had previously been a leper colony. The island was connected by a series of cables to Île Royale and Île St. Joseph, and provisions of food and water were delivered daily along these lines and brought to the prisoner's hut by his jailers, who were forbidden to speak with him. He was also allowed his own books and writing materials and had free reign of the island during the daytime.

Dreyfus's suffering was one of complete and utter isolation. There were neither the various personal degradations associated with life among a convict population nor the specter of rampant disease and death that hovered over the mainland *bagne*. One gains a sense of this difference in the following two passages. In the first, Dieudonné speaks to Londres of the *bagne*: "But what is much worse is the infernal milieu of the *bagne*. The morals are scandalous. What they have done is transport the convict to a world where immorality is the law. How does one stand up to this? One must expend all his energy to avoid this sickness."[41] In the second passage, Dreyfus tells his wife of life on Devil's Island, where he feels like a "Trappist Monk, in my profound isolation, a prey to sad thoughts on a lonely rock, sustaining myself by the force of duty. . . . My days, my hours, slip by monotonously in this agonizing, enervating waiting for the discovery of truth."[42] There are no *plans*, *fort-à-bras*, or *cachots* in Dreyfus's milieu, only the abject horror of his own loneliness.

Dreyfus's memoirs are those of political exile. There is no opportunity of escape from Devil's Island or salacious details of prison life to captivate readers, only the painful memories of an Alsatian Jew wrongly convicted. His anguished prose is that of a well-educated and rather prosperous army officer, and certainly not that of a humble cabinetmaker writing in the style of the *fait divers*.

Given the penal colonies' growing notoriety in the mid- to late 1920s, it is not altogether surprising that a whole series of penal colony exposés were written and published during roughly the same period of time as Londres's series on Dieudonné. For instance, a reporter by the name of Blair Niles, an American woman who traveled to French Guiana, wrote a four-part series of articles on the *bagne* for the *Sunday New York Times Magazine* in 1927. Previously married to the American naturalist, scientist, and author William Beebe, Niles had first learned of the penal colonies while acting as Beebe's research assistant on his many travels to South America. After their divorce in 1913, she traveled to French Guiana and visited the *bagne* with her second husband, architect William Niles, who acted as a photographer on the journey.

As with Londres's first series for *Le petit parisien*, Niles presented an overview of the penal colony system: its history, its physical and geographical milieu, and the general indignities and cruelties suffered by the *bagnards*. At variance with Londres, however, is her use of anonymous, picaresque characters to illustrate how the *bagne*'s failure to make moral distinctions between prisoners led to the excessive, unnecessary, and counterproductive cruelties imposed on those less depraved. For instance, we meet a young man imprisoned for desertion during World War I: "a drummer boy, too young to go to the front, and still living with his parents. . . . Condemned to life in the 'dry guillotine' he will spend the few francs he earns unloading the monthly cargo steamer on rum in an effort to forget how he will starve between boats."[43] The reader is also introduced to a war hero who, upon returning from the front, confronts his wife in flagrante delicto:

> And in that dark, horrible moment which has haunted him ever since, struck her by throwing a bauble with a deadly precision so usual at those times when the conscious mind has temporarily gone down before the subconscious. . . . So in cases of unpremeditated murder the most unlikely weapon hurled without conscious aim goes straight to its deadly mark. And then, if one happens to be a Frenchman, and if one is granted a commutation of the death penalty, one goes to French Guiana for hard labor and exile "en perpétuité." And the world may never be the same. For him, French Guiana is both the end and the dreadful beginning.[44]

Significant in these passages is an inherent criticism of the *bagne*'s institutional inability to differentiate between petty criminals or those guilty of a "crime of passion" from the common run of malfeasants. First offenders led astray by circumstance or a momentary lapse in judgment are subject to the same ignominy of permanent exile as the deliberate, "professional" lawbreaker. By virtue of their age or life story, the "anonymous" *bagnards* of Niles's story are living monuments to suffering and a direct challenge to the moral universe of the penal colony system.

Some two years after her return from French Guiana, Niles fictionalized her research by penning a novel entitled *Condemned to Devil's Island*. Based upon the life of the pseudonymous convict "Michel" (in actuality René Belbenoit), the book was wildly successful. Social-scientific authorities such as Harry Elmer Barnes considered its publication a veritable "international event. No other book in any language presents such an adequate picture of life in the convict colony." Literary critic Percy Hutchinson, in the *New York Times*, declared it "amazing. Not to be duplicated anywhere. Fathoms the psychology of the convict with uncanny accuracy. An epic of the living dead." Novelist Ellen Glasgow called Niles's work "remarkable" and "profoundly moving."[45]

As evidenced by the publication of *Hell's Outpost: The True Story of Devil's Island*, it was not only such luminaries who were moved by Niles's work. After reading *Condemned to Devil's Island*, merchant mariner W. E. Allison-Booth decided to jump ship in order to conduct his own investigation of the *bagne*. Unlike Niles, who had the permission of French authorities to visit the penal colony, Allison-Booth believed that the "surest way to see conditions as they actually exist would be to go there as a member of the crew of a ship, as the authorities would scarcely expect a sailor to undertake a self-imposed exile."[46] Therefore, the author purposely stranded himself for two months—until the arrival of the next cargo ship—in St. Laurent.

During his stay, Allison-Booth met a *libéré* by the name of Paul Lamont, an elderly Belgian professor of languages at "London University" who had spent nearly his entire adult life in French Guiana. Witty, urbane, and charming, Lamont was wrongly charged and convicted of forgery some forty years prior, never again to see the young wife and son he was forced to leave behind. As with the anonymous "drummer boy" and mournful soldier of Niles's work, the reader discovers another innocent martyr amid the downtrodden *bagnards*. Booth writes of Lamont: "During our conversation he would often emphasize his remarks with quotations from Greek and Latin. The irony of it was appalling—that a scholar should suffer this life in a man-made hell where even the harmless recreation of reading the books his intelligent mind craved was denied him. I lost my temper and fell to cursing the French authorities who deliberately kept a man at St. Laurent for forty years and then, after draining the very life from his body, refuse to return their victim to his native land to die in peace."[47] Of course, the other standard leitmotif of escape also appeared, albeit with a bit of a twist: Allison-Booth would be imprisoned by authorities on suspicion of fomenting a plan for Lamont's escape. Thus, he was held in the dreaded *cachots* (this despite the fact that they had been eliminated as a means of punishment five years prior) where at night he was "as surely a prisoner as was any convict who had ever been condemned to this spot." After his release, Allison-Booth begged Lamont to stow away on board the cargo ship that would take both to Surinam, but he refused, saying that he was "too old for such adventures." The author promised Lamont that he would write of Devil's Island in order to let the public know of "this grim place." As the ship pulls out of port and Allison-Booth waves good-bye to a weeping Lamont, the author laments: "If the manhood of France could understand only a part of the suffering that is being inflicted on some of her patriots, they would never again rest until Devil's Island and its associated penal colonies were but a nightmare of the past."[48]

The publication of Allison-Booth's book created a sensation in both the United States and Great Britain. Indeed, it generated not only surprisingly favorable reviews but also cries of indignation. For instance, one reviewer remarked: "Do the majority of French people really know what happens on Devil's Island and the other penal settlements in French Guiana? If they did, would there not be a national outcry against them? These are the questions that will inevitably occur to readers of this amazing book."[49] There was also great concern among readers about the fate of "Paul Lamont." According to the publisher of Allison-Booth's tome, American readers pledged $300,000 to help free the former professor.[50] An anonymous member of the British National Committee on Prisons and Prison Labor offered to pay for Lamont's passage to Belgium.[51] The French government also received many angry letters from readers such as Paul Kingston, "a retired insurance executive" from Memphis, Tennessee, who noted that he had enclosed "a clipping which was taken from our Saturday afternoon paper . . . that contains the story of Paul Lamont which I believe you should investigate. . . . This story is no doubt appearing in each and every newspaper in the United States. Certainly it will not redound to the credit of France to have the citizens of this country realize that such penalties could be inflicted upon poor human beings who are unable to protect themselves."[52]

As evidenced by secret administrative correspondence, French officials did investigate the situation surrounding the professor. However, there were no records of such an individual ever being transported to French Guiana. In a letter to the minister of foreign affairs, the minister of the colonies noted that "despite repeated searches there does not exist any *transporté* who answers to that name. It is therefore safe to assume that Booth's account is pure fiction."[53] It was in this vein that the Ministry sent to the outraged Kingston a reply which simply stated that there was "no *condamné* by the name of Paul Lamont who Booth describes as a Belgian professor who has been in prison for forty years."[54]

Although the old Belgian professor may have been the product of Booth's imagination, such images altered the mental landscape, making the image of the *bagne* more problematic, a source of discomfort for ministerial and local authorities. Even diplomatic functionaries in neighboring countries were concerned about the negative publicity surrounding the Guianese penal colony. Excerpts of a wire-service article in the *Journal do Brasil* that described the departure of the prison ship *La Martinière* from Saint-Martin de Ré (the island off the coast of northern France from La Rochelle where deportees were held before being transported overseas) were translated by the French ambassador to Brazil for officials in the Ministry and read as follows: "One could hear the terrible cries of despair fill the air as the men receive blows as they are thrown below and the boat lifts anchor for South America . . . many prisoners prefer suicide rather than suffer the heat and disease of French Guiana." In a sharply worded missive that accompanied the translation, the ambassador complained: "It seems to me that if this American agency (United Press International) cannot find something disagreeable about our country to publish, it will invent something. We must have our representatives in Paris prevail upon this agency to stop printing such falsehoods about the *bagne*."[55]

This single article engendered a voluminous exchange of correspondence among penal colony functionaries, all variously denying the charges and castigating the media. For instance, the chief warden on board *La Martinière* maintained: "I can affirm in the most formal fashion that there were no beatings, threats, or blasphemies leveled at the prisoners as expressed in the United Press article, and I maintain that the author has shown in his falsehoods a disdain for the truth that has never been equaled in the press of any country."[56] "Given that the facts advanced by the American agency are inexact," the minister responded, "we should formulate some kind of a written protest."[57]

As historian Robert Young has noted, such concerns among officials about the image of France in the United States—particularly in the wake of French delays in paying war loans—were quite pervasive in the interwar period. Indeed, the Service des oeuvres françaises l'étranger—founded in 1920, and in close cooperation with officials at the Quai d'Orsay—had as its primary function "to monitor and analyze foreign press coverage of

France, with a view to ensuring informed ministerial decision making in Paris." As a "pioneer in the field of subtle and inoffensive propaganda," this organization—with the assistance of local embassies and consulates—regularly employed Francophile "academics, lawyers, journalists, and financiers" to counteract negative images of France in the popular press and forestall the development of any postwar sympathy for Germany in the United States.[58]

It is in this context that French officials embarked on their own press campaign to create a more benign image of the *bagne* through what internal memoranda termed "an active counter-propaganda campaign." The primary instrument of this effort was Alexander MacGowan, journalist and editor of the *Trinidad Guardian* newspaper. Officials in Trinidad had long been publicly critical of the *bagne*, and in 1931 they put an end to the extradition of escaped prisoners to French Guiana, making it a safe haven for those escapees fortunate enough to reach its shores. Indeed, Trinidadian officials typically allowed all convicts who arrived from French Guiana to rest and recover from their escape before being given supplies to continue their journey.[59] Thus there was a profound local interest in the penal colony and its denizens, which local newspapers were happy to fulfill.

Evidence of MacGowan's role in the "counter-propaganda" effort of the French can be gleaned from a letter from the Ministry of the Colonies to the governor of French Guiana, which read, in part: "Mr. MacGowan, well known for his Francophile sentiments, has recently been commissioned by the *New York Times* to write a 2,500 word article on the *bagne*. Upon the advice of this department, I request that Mr. MacGowan be awarded a sum of 5,000 francs and that his wife, Anne, a journalist who is writing her own article for the *Trinidad Guardian*, be accorded any request she might have upon arrival. . . . I know that it has not escaped your attention that there is a need to counterbalance the vile propaganda against the *bagne*."[60]

As indicated in the aforementioned memo, this "campaign" was to be waged in both the regional and international media. It was initiated by a dispatch sent to the *Trinidad Guardian* from a mysterious Maj. M. B. Blake, ostensibly a retired British army officer in the employ of the "French Guiana Rivers Syndicate Company," which was mining gold in both Peru and the Venezuelan frontier at the time. Blake noted in his "unsolicited dispatch" to the *Guardian*:

> While gathering information as to the prospects for the gold industry in French Guiana, the one thing that struck me very much was that everything I have hitherto read in the newspapers about French Guiana and the treatment of prisoners is utterly misleading twaddle. I should say that prisoners in French Guiana have a better time than anywhere else in the world. It does not matter what a man's crime is, if he has the sense to behave well, he can be promoted in a few months and then hire himself out to work, his employer paying the government a certain amount and the balance to the prisoner. . . . I spoke to several convicts outside the jail and no one had any complaints to make of the food or the treatment accorded him.[61]

Given the sensational nature of such claims, the dispatch was picked up by the international wire services. Indeed, it appeared verbatim on page 1 of the *New York Times* under a headline that read: "Tales of French Guiana Penal Cruelty Are Called Twaddle by Briton."[62]

What is surprising, however—given that Blair Niles's excoriation of the *bagne* had appeared in the *New York Times Magazine* a scant four years previous—was that Blake's veracity was unquestioned. His wire story nevertheless laid the foundation for MacGowan's front-page piece in the *Times*, which appeared the following day. Under the headline "Convicts in French Guiana Build New Riviera," MacGowan described the *bagne* as a place where, "amid tropic palms, Turneresque sunrises and gorgeous butterflies of many hues . . . the chief complaint of convicts is the monotony of tropical life." Interestingly, we hear penal colony officials criticize their administrative predecessors for their "inhumanity" and "neglect" and actively propagate the notion—so antithetical to fin de siècle officials—that a rather "luxurious situation has developed here in recent years." Thus, we learn from Colonel Prevel, the director of the *bagne* at St. Laurent, that the hospital now serves the sick four-course meals that include champagne, hors d'oeuvres, and salads. In addition, MacGowan describes the X-ray machines of the hospital and its "huge store room that is lined with hundreds of shelves bearing every medical requirement, like a great New York hospital." The city of St. Laurent itself is depicted as a peaceful hamlet where "fewer policemen need patrol the streets than in an average civilized city." Clearly, the image that the reader is to take away from the article is that the " 'Capital of Crime' has emerged from the chrysalis of its lurid past."[63] Bearing this message to the world, MacGowan's story circulated transnationally via wire-service reports. Thus, readers of the *London Evening News* and the *London Times* learned of this "new Riviera," as well.[64]

Back in Trinidad, MacGowan's wife, Anne—also, as we have seen, targeted by the French government to be a mouthpiece for its public relations campaign—painted a portrait of the *bagne* as a tropical paradise. The *Trinidad Guardian* announced her series with a prologue alluding to "the amazing claims of Major Blake . . . which have been met with incredulity, amazement, surprise, and frank disbelief. . . . It is in this atmosphere of 'whitewash' that Mrs. Gault MacGowan—travel writer and journalist, will be the first British woman reporter to visit the notorious convict colony and relate her experiences. She will not be browbeaten by officialdom or overwhelmed by bureaucratic explanations. She will see the penitentiary through a woman's eye and bring to the investigation a woman's sympathy and understanding. She will keep nothing back from the public." Readers were also gently reminded that "edition after edition with such exclusive news will be sold out. The best way to prevent disappointment is to register your name as a regular subscriber today!"[65] The series was thus doubly profitable, at least for the MacGowans: immediate remuneration by the French government, followed by increased newspaper sales.

In her first installment, MacGowan alluded to her familiarity with the charges of her journalistic predecessors: "I must tell you that my literary diet over the past few weeks has been spicy fare. I have been working up an honest-to-goodness state of righteous wrath over the *bagne*."[66] Her unbiased view established, MacGowan went about refuting earlier claims. Her second installment focused on the treatment accorded to convict stevedores, which, not surprisingly, she found to be quite humane.[67] The next installment covered a tour of the various prison barracks in St. Laurent, where MacGowan "discovered" that prisoners "preferred communal living." One prisoner was quoted as saying: "I am of Paris, I like companionship, I like to be sociable.

For me, I would rather be here than shut up alone to pace the narrow limits of a cell and do nothing but think, think, think until my brain gave way."[68]

In the third installment of the series, MacGowan toured the hospital in St. Laurent, where—just as her husband reported in the *Times*—she found the storerooms to be a "revelation. Every conceivable medical necessity is there. Everything bears the stamp of good French firms. And medical comforts include champagne, if you please! Also, good red wine, which is the blood of any Frenchman be he ill or well." She added that those convicts stricken with malaria were most likely "malingerers who pour their daily dose of quinine down the drain rather than their throats. . . . Why not get malaria, as it means a rest in this wonderful hospital?"[69]

On the heels of MacGowan's series, the *Guardian* published a letter from Major Blake commending them on their journalistic integrity.

> The editor of the *Trinidad Guardian* on reading my interview obviously regarded the statements contained therein to be completely untrue, but before exposing me, he took the prudent course of sending a special correspondent to obtain the facts. He specially selected a distinguished lady journalist of wide experience . . . Mrs. MacGowan, whom I have never had the pleasure of meeting. . . . As was inevitable in the case of any honest, fair-minded person capable of assimilating evidence and forming a judgment thereon, she corroborated my statements at every point. Had she flatly denied them her evidence would have been accepted as conclusive, but by her corroboration she has become suspect to many who reject the truth as poison. . . . At a time when everything possible should be done to foster good relations between nations, it is deplorable that the English newspaper press should continue to publish untrue fabrications about barbarous treatment in French Guiana, which a pathetically gullible public avidly swallows.[70]

Aside from their Francophilic sensibilities, it seems that the press campaign of the MacGowans was motivated by venality or, perhaps more charitably, naïveté. If there was no monetary quid pro quo for their stories (aside from the aforementioned memo in which a sum of money was mentioned, there is no additional evidence in this regard), then it is possible that they were players in a Potemkin-style charade put on by penal colony officials. Apparently the English novelist Somerset Maugham was the unwitting victim of such an effort. After visiting French Guiana, he sent a telegram to the governor that read, in part: "I would like to offer my thanks for my reception in your colony. With the courtesy of Monsieur Valmont and the Commandant, I have seen the camps in all their details and have come away impressed, and with my curiosities satisfied. . . . I left St. Laurent with the conviction that everything is done humanely to make life more tolerable for deportees."[71] Indeed, it was not uncommon for prisoners—derisively referred to as the *marchand de pomades*—to supply journalists with bromides about the relative pleasures of the *bagne* in return for certain privileges such as additional rations.[72]

It is also clear from internal memoranda that officials closely monitored the visits of journalists. For instance, when French journalist Henri Danjou arrived in French Guiana in 1934, his movements and conversations were relayed to administrators. In a letter, an Arab interpreter who accompanied Danjou and his wife on a visit to the Îles du Salut remarked: "You have asked me to detail my discussions with Mr. Henri Danjou and his wife. . . . [N]o critique was formulated as to the organization of the penitentiary, which appeared to please both the journalist and his wife. They had, however, in my humble opinion, the very distinct belief that they were being tricked and that the penitentiary administration was showing the *bagne* in only its best light. I assured them, however, that they were being given every freedom in their visit."[73] In a report from the guard who accompanied the Danjous on their visit to the hospital in St. Laurent it was noted that "they seem to have a favorable impression of the military organization of the infirmary and the quality of food the kitchen serves. . . . To my knowledge, they formulated no objections against the medical service."[74] Finally, in a missive to the governor, the director of the penitentiary administration remarked that upon accompanying the Danjous on their return trip to Trinidad the journalist thanked him for the "total freedom he received in conducting his investigation" and that "while he had expected to see a Hell on earth, he had instead found that the administration treated the *condamnés* well." The director closed his memo by assuring the governor that Danjou's reporting would illustrate an "institution that is repressive, but also humane and just."[75]

Tellingly, it was the penitentiary director who personally thanked the Ministry for allowing the Danjous to visit French Guiana. He believed that "in an administration such as mine, when one closes the door, many people are inclined to believe that we manhandle, torture, and kill."[76] Statements such as this could lead one to believe that ministerial officials did, in fact, play a role in facilitating Londres's visit years earlier. Unfortunately for the director, however, his assessment of this latest tour was overly optimistic, as Danjou was publicly critical of living conditions in the *bagne*.[77]

While no surviving memoranda or letters detail the MacGowans' visit— a fact that is perhaps suggestive about their complicity in a "counter-propaganda" scheme—local officials were quite pleased with their reporting. The language of these documents is even more suggestive, indicating almost beyond doubt that the MacGowans were not naive pawns but active collaborators. In a letter to the Ministry, Governor Bouge remarked that the "articles of Mr. and Mrs. MacGowan represent a great success in our counter-propaganda. The first page of the *New York Times* is rarely conceded and carries with it the great attention of the American public. . . . It seems certain that our efforts at counter-propaganda have born fruit and have effectively counteracted the untruths leveled against our penitentiary establishments in French Guiana." The governor included with his letter translations of Anne MacGowan's articles, which, he admitted, "occasionally border on fantasy. . . . [T]he obligation to combat our detractors at their own game may have influenced some of the precision and exactitude of her descriptions, but in order to interest a public habituated to sensational accounts, an exact and rigorous description is not sufficient." Bouge concluded by commending "our consul in Trinidad for bringing Mr. and Mrs. MacGowan to our attention and aiding us in representing our work abroad. These two are defenders of the French cause who merit a high degree of gratitude on the part of the government."[78]

The counter-propaganda efforts of penal colony authorities also included travel and adventure writers. Indeed, from the 1930s through the 1950s there was a steady stream of popular literature on the subject. Not unlike the stories of journalists, these tales were enormously popular with readers. Relying on anecdote, narrated in the first person, and containing many of the same melodramatic and sentimental elements of sensational journalism, these stories did not contain information as to awful conditions but instead portrayed the *bagne* in a positive light.

Before embarking on a nearly forty-year career as a nationally known radio and television broadcaster in Canada, Gordon Sinclair was a roving reporter for the *Toronto Daily Star*. As part of publisher Farrar Rinehart's "Books of Adventure in Far Places" series, he visited Devil's Island "to write about prison conditions in this so-called cesspool of civilization." Unlike Danjou, however, Sinclair was much less skeptical of penal colony authorities and much more willing to accept their claims at face value, particularly regarding the health and well-being of prisoners. For instance, he recounted a conversation he had with the governor of French Guiana during his visit: "Observe that man. . . . He killed his wife, not his wife, but his mistress. Throttled her to death. Observe him. Regard him. Is he ill-treated? Is he flogged or beaten? Does he look like a walking skeleton wracked with coughs and fevers? . . . Remember that the outside world is eager and anxious to accept wild exaggerated descriptions of suffering, of debauchery and of death. Most of it is highly coloured nonsense."[79] While dining with a penitentiary administrator at a restaurant in Cayenne, the British adventure writer Nicol Smith took notice of their waiter:

> A white man, youngish, pleasant of countenance, with the shoulders of a varsity football player and the waist of West Point cadet. He moved like an athlete, and looked as though he never missed three square meals in all his life. When this Gene Tunney of a fellow had gone off to fetch our drinks, Blalock said: "Now there's an interesting example, of what this country can do for a man. That's Marcel. He recently finished a term of seven years as a convict. Now that he's a *libéré* he's got this job as a waiter. Just look at his physique! You're always hearing stories, you know, about the convicts dying off here like flies, because of starvation? Does Marcel look as though he has ever been starved? . . . Don't ever tell me they starve 'em in French Guiana. Not if Marcel is a sample. Why, he looks as strong as an ox! They ought to advertise this place. Come to Devil's Island for a rest cure. Put on weight."[80]

In this same vein, the adventurer and travel writer Hassoldt Davis toured what was left of the penal colony in 1951 and remarked that he "had not the slightest doubt that the so-called Devil's Island colony had been grossly libeled in the Sunday supplements, that horror and torture were no worse here than in the jails of Cambridge, Mass, after the sophomores, including me, had dropped—for some reason which escapes me now—water-filled balloons or whatnot on the heads of passing policemen." Upon touring Dreyfus's shack on Devil's Island—and ignoring the fact that he suffered unimaginable loneliness on the island—Ruth Staudinger, Davis's wife, exclaimed: "In its day it must have been a handsome villa." "House hunters in Westchester would pay a fortune for that little estate if it could be transplanted. . . . Were it not for the barred windows and the rusty bolts on the doors you would have thought it an enviable winter resort."[81]

This attempt on the part of officials to turn back the clock, to recall the imagined bucolic *bagne* of yesteryear—which had been anathema to their predecessors—was a failure. Indeed, the governor was correct in his assessment that readers were "habituated" to the horrors of the *bagne*. The flood of newspaper exposés would never again allow the public to be so easily swayed. Once officials recognized that public-relations efforts were futile, the *bagne* was effectively closed to the prying eyes of journalists. In a September 1938 letter to the governor of French Guiana, the minister of the colonies stated that "in light of the press campaign against our regime of transportation . . . access to the penitentiaries will be rigorously forbidden except to those individuals with the special authorization of this department."[82] In response, the governor "regretfully acknowledged . . . that not all of the people admitted to the different camps of *condamnés* have been of a goodwill and abstained from criticism. They were often inconsiderate of our penal regime. . . . In the metropole, access to the *maison centrales*, prisons, etc., is not permitted except for those who have an interest in conducting a serious study such as penologists. The same rule should be applied here in the colony."[83]

Although the attention of journalists shifted with the approach of war in Europe, the die had been cast. Through the sensational accounts of the *fait divers* and the international press, a worldwide audience was introduced to the *plan* and the escapee. What was once unknowable was now suddenly knowable through the employment of such synecdoches: totems standing for the whole confused chaos of penal colony experience. As Baudrillard has pointed out, "the generalized consumption of images, of facts, of information aims also to conjure away the real with signs of the real, to conjure away history with the signs of change, etc."[84] The "experience" of the *bagnard* was a point of literary commodification, eliciting reactions of horror, indignation, and mystification in the reader. His life existed—at least for the general public—within a narrative structure whose sole purpose was titillation. That escapes from the *bagne* were extremely rare was irrelevant, as was the fact that the vast majority of those imprisoned were, indeed, guilty of their crimes, for a new center of knowledge-power had emerged. The efflorescence of the mass media superseded the various discourses of criminologists, penologists, and even penal colony officials. In the words of Foucault, the *bagne* was no longer merely a "rigorous and distant form of imprisonment" but rather a site of caricatural, almost parodic, evocation that captured the imagination.[85]

This is perhaps nowhere more evident than in separate letters written by two Americans. In a missive to the Ministry of Justice, Everett Johnson of New Britain, Connecticut, noted that he had "heard and read all sorts of stories about the Island" and expressed his heartfelt desire to become a guard on Devil's Island.[86] In response to this rather peculiar request, A. Maginot, a ministerial representative, listed the basic qualifications for service and concluded with the following: "I cannot hide my surprise that such a query has been posed. . . . It seems that there has been circulating many tenacious rumors concerning the *bagne* as a result of press campaigns so fantastic that it forces us to attend to odd questions such as this."[87] Similarly, the Ministry received a letter from C. Porter Hochstadter, employed with the Pacific Mutual Life Insurance Company in Cincinnati, in which he asked if he and his wife could visit Devil's Island, "as we are planning a trip this winter that will put is in close proximity, and it has always been our desire to see this infamous place."[88] The Ministry responded with a terse note that read, in part: "This colony was not constructed for the voyages of tourists."[89] While the doors of the *bagne* may have been closed to journalists, the doors of the public imagination were now opened wide, and the fate of the institution was henceforth sealed.

Conclusion

In the last years of its life, the *bagne* came under attack not only from the press but from colonial and government officials as well. One former administrator summed it up best by remarking that "transportation is economically an absurdity, from the colonial point of view it is a scandal, and morally it is a crime."[1] As historian Gordon Wright has pointed out, the basic issue "was now out in the open. Was the *bagne* a monstrous aberration, beyond hope of reform?"[2]

To twentieth-century colonial governors who saw the *bagne* as an impediment to free colonization, the answer seemed quite clear: "The penitentiary administration manifests a retrograde spirit that is in direct opposition to our colonial efforts."[3] Indeed, the age-old battle between colonial administrators and penal colony officials persisted until its closure. In a letter to the minister of the marine, one governor noted that for a "long time" he had informed "the Ministry of the grave inconveniences that have hindered the progress of this colony and are a direct result of the autonomy which the penitentiary administration enjoys vis-à-vis the governor, particularly concerning the organization of work in the colony. This nearly complete autonomy has never produced anything useful for the colony except increased expenses for the civilian government (gendarmerie) for the surveillance of the *libérés*, who are the source of multiple inconveniences of every order."[4]

In 1908, Sen. Emile Chautemps, a former minister of the colonies, was the first parliamentarian to call for the abolition of penal transportation on the grounds that it had failed to promote colonization. "There are only a few kilometers of railroad and telegraph line as a result of years of penal labor in New Caledonia," he argued, "and in French Guiana such work has failed to produce anything of consequence."[5] Indeed, it was later estimated that convicts in New Caledonia "took two million working days to construct sixty-six kilometers of road, a method of construction that worked out at 20,000 francs a kilometer."[6] While Chautemps's bill went nowhere, on the heels of Albert Londres's newspaper series on the *bagne*, a parliamentary measure was introduced in 1925 that would have allowed judges to substitute imprisonment in France for transportation and to end the practice of *doublage*. It was not adopted. In addition, various investigatory commissions led by Gaston Monnerville, the Guianese representative in Parlement who was adamantly opposed to the practice of penal colonization, were convened during the early 1930s.[7]

As in New Caledonia nearly a half-century prior, local journalists complained that the *bagne* was an impediment to free colonization. According to Alfred Marie-Sainte, "French Guiana must rid itself of *transportés*; purify itself in order to regain its vigor so that it can replenish its land with resourceful, honest, and laborious peoples who will not hesitate to create and install trade, industry, and plantations without relying upon the manpower of criminals whose presence is a constant source of concern and worry. . . . Their pernicious occupation of French Guiana for seventy-seven years has proved more harmful than useful to a colony that could live and prosper given its fertility and abundance."[8] In a pamphlet entitled *Les parias de la Guyane*, entrepreneur Honorat Boucon, a resident of Cayenne, similarly inveighed: "For more than half a century, experience has demonstrated the failure of the *bagne* as a means of labor and colonization. . . . As to the economic situation in general, there is hardly any agriculture, industry, or commerce in Guiana. Of twelve million hectares of land, only 3,500 are currently cultivated. There was 1,571 hectares cultivated in sugarcane alone in 1836! Cotton, pepper, vanilla, cloves, nutmeg, cinnamon, all flourished but have now been abandoned. The only thing that penal colonization has ever produced is illness, epidemics, and the mortality of *transportés*."[9]

Faced with steady and seemingly unrelenting criticism, the Daladier government, by executive decree, declared on June 17, 1938, that the *bagne* be liquidated. In this decree, the prime minister remarked:

For many years, in spite of the improvements carried out in the living conditions of transported criminals, severe criticisms have been made concerning the *bagne* in French Guiana. In point of fact, the *bagne* does not appear to have any deterrent effect upon the criminals themselves and does not provide them with any means of moral reformation or rehabilitation. From another point of view, the presence in the only French colonial possession in America of a penal transport establishment is not good for the prestige of France on that continent. . . . In addition, to have any moral value, punishment should subject the prisoner to some regular work. Actually, experience shows that penal labor cannot, in the climate of French Guiana, constitute a labor force for colonization purposes. It would therefore seem vain to anticipate any alteration in the convicts themselves as a result of their work in the penitentiary . . . the *bagne* should disappear into extinction and French Guiana will then be able to adopt itself progressively to a new economy.[10]

Although the outbreak of World War II temporarily halted the closure of the *bagne*, no additional convicts were transported after 1937. The process of repatriation began in earnest in 1946, and the institution was permanently closed in 1952.[11]

What are we to make of this inauspicious denouement to a nearly century-long venture in incarceration? It is obvious that the penal colonies failed in their dual mission of reforming the man by colonizing the land. French Guiana and New Caledonia were no better off than they had been prior to the convict presence, and, as we have seen, it was not moral redemption but basic survival that was the primary concern of most *bagnards* (and, for that matter, many guards and other personnel). Yet, while this conclusion is all too clear, the history of the *bagne* itself has remained opaque and obscured, caught between myth and monolith.

A balanced consideration of the experiential and representational suggests that there were two *bagnes*: the interior, private *bagne* inhabited by the prisoners and regulated, at least ostensibly, by administrators, guards, and physicians; and the epistemic *bagne*, whose various representations were produced, maintained, manipulated, contested, and subverted by forces out-

side the institution. In other words, there was a referential and a discursive
bagne, and the two did not always coexist harmoniously.

This book has uncovered an institution fraught with administrative difficulties from the outset. Discord among penal colony, colonial, and metropolitan officials over the *bagne*'s primary objective led to a welter of ill-
conceived policy initiatives. It was at best an ineffectual instrument of
social control that reflected its human agents and subjects, all of whom
were wracked by varying degrees of hubris, self-doubt, and dread. As a result, administrators never enacted measures that were absolutely vital for
the maintenance of institutional integrity. For example, the failure to effectively professionalize the penal colony guard was critical in determining the
institution's fate, as instances of abuse and escape spoke to an ill-conceived
professional structure. The incidents that derived from this institutional
disorganization ultimately garnered the attention and scrutiny of journalists such as Londres, Niles, and many others. Perhaps more important, and
certainly most tragic, was the profound antagonism evinced between penal colony physicians and administrators, each endeavoring and failing in
their inimical efforts to control the *bagnard* by relying upon the authority
and legitimacy granted them by society at large.

It was not these various failures, however, that attracted the attention
of another group of "professionals"—criminologists, jurists, and penologists—but an institution that did not adhere to a carceral ideal that was
becoming increasingly penitential. It is important to remember that penal
colonization emerged almost simultaneously with the penitentiary as in-
novations in the early to mid-nineteenth century. As such, both addressed
what was perceived to be an ever-increasing rate of crime and recidivism in
France. Yet the element that made penal colonization initially attractive to
so many—the powerful allure of regenerative agricultural labor to counteract the perceived moral evils associated with a burgeoning urban-industrial
society—became the primary target of heated criticism from fin de siècle
theorists. As the work regimen of the shipyard *bagnes* was seen as having no
punitive or rehabilitative function in the early to mid-nineteenth century,
so penal colony labor appeared useless by the century's close.

We are therefore presented with an epistemological juxtaposition, a clash
of representations. On the one hand, colonial governors, particularly in New

Caledonia, initially portrayed penal labor, particularly agricultural work and the distribution of land concessions to released prisoners, as an effective means of rehabilitation and colonization. Penal colony administrators and metropolitan theorists, however, depicted a prison regimen of excessive softness, having no deterrent effect. Indeed, the two groups' discourses existed in a kind of symbiosis, each reinforcing the conclusions of the other.

By the early twentieth century, an additional critical perspective—that of the mass media—came on the scene, and a second epistemological conflict arose. Now we see a new *bagne* emerge within the framework of the *fait divers* and the popular autobiographical adventure tales penned by former prisoners. The penal colony of these works was a land of death inhabited by the unfortunate, the misunderstood, and the wrongly convicted. Such characterizations were seen as authoritative because they adhered to enormously popular literary and journalistic conventions that had wide currency at the time. While officials attempted to counteract this increasingly transnational image by revivifying the "tropical paradise" motif of criminologists, such characterizations acquired a totalizing position that persists to this day.[12]

Each of these perspectives had some basis in reality. Early on, prison concessionaires fared relatively well, and the basic infrastructure of both New Caledonia and French Guiana was—albeit slowly and haltingly—built by convict labor. But it was also true that some prisoners worked as domestics and enjoyed a relatively pleasant existence while the colonies themselves were floundering economically. In the twentieth century prisoners were still dying in droves, particularly in the interior jungle and timber camps in French Guiana, while others suffered the brutalities associated with prison life in main holding depots such as St. Laurent and St. Jean. Yet basic living conditions did improve as rations were increased and the punishment of the dreaded *cachot* was eliminated.

The dissonance between these facts points to a central question: Does the history of the *bagne* lie beyond our intelligibility? Its origins lie in the dim recesses of the nineteenth-century unconscious, in a culture desperately grasping for an institutional solution to a social problem (crime and recidivism) thought to be the unfortunate by-product of a new and frightening age. A palimpsest of conflicting philosophies in regard to the criminal class, the *bagne* was an institutional tabula rasa onto which a variety of fears, hopes, and dreams were inscribed. At its very essence, it was what certain people wanted it to be: a site of illusion and disillusion, prurience and abjection. Nonetheless, the answer to the question is an unequivocal "no."

When we situate these various visions of the *bagne* within their representative social and cultural settings, we see that such representations were usually motivated by narrow and often conflicting administrative interests, adhered to particular ideological or professional constructs, and were eventually mythologized in popular culture. In the long history of the overseas penal colonies we find a persistent oscillation between conceptual binaries: punishment/colonization, inhumane/humane, and perhaps most important—at least in terms of the institution's history—retribution/rehabilitation. Subsumed within this universe of conflicting images—all missing, masking, or distorting—are the vague outlines of the penal colony's raison d'être.

From the outset, its mission—to rid society of its irredeemable citizens, yet at the same time holding out that they might still be redeemed through hard work in a rural setting—was deeply conflicted. Unlike the metropolitan prison, in which confinement was justified on the basis that the institution could rehabilitate, imprisonment in the penal colony was justified on the basis that the individual could not be rehabilitated. Yet there is a persistent dialectic between a regenerative penal colony regimen and one designed to punish. In the end the delicate balance between the two swung toward the latter, in part because of larger concerns with vagabondage and petty crime and the perception that these offenses were the result of a gradual softening of all criminal penalties throughout the course of the nineteenth century.

That the *bagne* existed in tension between its design and its application is perhaps not surprising, given that most, if not all, human endeavors do so. However, by historicizing the institution, thereby wresting it from fantasy and fable, we have uncovered many of the same issues that characterize current debates over crime and punishment. Not unlike the penal colony, the modern prison is perceived as a bulwark against an encroaching tide of crime, deviance, and disorder. Indeed, the *bagne* and the prison share a simple but fundamental principle: if penal regimes are soft, then the crime rate will rise; if they are hard, then crime will be held in check or even diminish, as the threat of punishment will serve as a deterrent to the wider social collective. Of course, the practical result of this basic equation is that individuals are punished twice for their crimes, as they are not only deprived of their liberty but often endure overcrowded, debilitating, and alienating regimes that inflict deep emotional and physical distress.

In this sense this book has also raised important questions about Foucault's notion that punishment shifted from the body to the mind with the rise of modern capitalism and the birth of "helping professions" such as medicine and psychiatry in the nineteenth century. As we have seen in the penal colonies, the physical violence and punishment of the body was ever-present. What is perhaps more important, however, is that such violence persists to this day in our prisons. While public executions and displays of torture—episodes of terrorism notwithstanding—may be a thing of the past, they persist within the walls of the prison. As German historian Heinz Steinert has argued, "Alongside the discourse on punishment, the prison and their scientific 'humanization' worldwide, we still have torture; people being beaten and dying in prison. We have concentration camps: we have the death penalty in the majority of countries. There remains a lot that is not accounted for by a Foucault-type analysis of history."[13] This is nowhere more apparent than with the French overseas penal colonies, where, at the dawn of the twentieth century, the institution changed in complexion and shed any pretense of rehabilitation, serving only as a site of final atonement where the bodies, rather than the souls, of more than one hundred thousand prisoners were the ultimate loci of retribution for French society.

Notes

Introduction

1. Charrière's work is generally considered one of "historical fabrication, with very little basis in fact." Miles, *Devil's Island*, 114–15.

2. Audisio, "Recherches sur l'origine et la signification du mot bagne,'" 367.

3. For accounts within the context of crime and punishment in France, see Wright, *Between the Guillotine and Liberty*; O'Brien, *The Promise of Punishment*; Petit, *La prison, le bagne et l'histoire*; and Petit, *Histoire des galères, bagnes et prisons*. Within the colonial context, see Price, *The Convict and the Colonel*; Merle, *Expériences coloniales*; and Sénès, *La vie quotidienne en Nouvelle-Calédonie*. For popular treatments of the penal colonies, see Miles, *Devil's Island*; Pierre, *La terre de la grande punition*; Pierre, *Le Dernier Exil*; and Le Clère, *La vie quotidienne dans les bagnes*.

4. Redfield, *Space in the Tropics*.

5. Redfield was a former student of Paul Rabinow, who has written much about the concept of "modernity." See Rabinow, *French Modern*.

6. Bullard, *Exile to Paradise*.

7. Foucault, *Discipline and Punish*, 272, 279.

8. Garland, "Foucault's *Discipline and Punish*," 873.

9. Zinoman, *The Colonial Bastille*, 7.

10. The term "Other" is not used by Zinoman but is certainly applicable. The notion is drawn from Edward Said's *Orientalism*.

11. Sen, *Disciplining Punishment*, 13.

12. Hume, "Bentham's Panopticon"; Jackson, "Luxury in Punishment," 45.

13. Forster, *France and Botany Bay*.

14. Rothman, *The Discovery of the Asylum*, xx.

15. Spierenburg, *The Prison Experience*, 2.

1. France and Penal Colonization

1. O'Brien, *The Promise of Punishment*, 260.

2. Wright, *Between the Guillotine and Liberty*, 92. For information on the transportation of political prisoners to Algeria, see Rudé, *Bagnes d'Afrique*.

3. For information on the galleys, see Bamford, *Fighting Ships and Prisons*; and Bourdet-Pléville, *Justice in Chains*.

4. Zysberg, "Galley and Hard Labor Convictions in France," 115.

5. Jacques Valette, "Profil d'un bagnard de Rochefort ou la légende noire du bagne," in Petit, *La prison, le bagne et l'histoire*, 83.

6. Zysberg, "Galley and Hard Labor Convictions in France," 112.

7. Wright, *Between the Guillotine and Liberty*, 6.

8. Ministère de la Justice, *Compte générale de l'administration de la justice criminelle*, 1850, contains data on crime subsequent to 1825.

9. See Chevalier, *Laboring Classes and Dangerous Classes*.

10. Moreau-Christophe, *De la réforme des prisons en France*, 138.

11. Gillis, "Crime and State Surveillance," 314.

12. See La Berge, *Mission and Method*; Coleman, *Death Is a Social Disease*.

13. Louis Moreau-Christophe, untitled article, *Revue pénitentiaire* 1 (1843): 10.

14. Brétignières de Courteilles, *Les condamnés*, ii–iii.

15. Faucher, "La chaîne," 37.

16. Forstenzer, *French Provincial Police*, 109. See Forster, *France and Botany Bay*, 155 n. 1.

17. Appert, *Bagnes, prisons et criminels*, 3:17–18.

18. Faucher, *De la réforme des prisons*, 150.

19. Lucas, "Économie politique," 380.

20. As Ratcliffe points out in "The Chevalier Thesis Reexamined," contemporaries often did not take into account patterns of circular migration.

21. Beaumont and Tocqueville, *Du système pénitentiaire aux Etats-Unis*, 104.

22. Huerne de Pommeuse, *Des colonies agricoles*, 156.

23. The most extensive treatment of Mettray appears in Gaillac, *Les maisons de correction*.

24. Wright, *Between the Guillotine and Liberty*, 90.

25. Faucher, *De la réforme des prisons*, 150.

26. Sarraméa, *Considérations sur la maison centrale*, 113.

27. Petit, "Birth and Reform of Prisons in France," 139.

28. C. R. Ageron, *France coloniale ou parti colonial?*, cited in Petit, "Birth and Reform of Prisons in France," 139.

29. Frégier, *Des classes dangereuses*, 1:7.

30. Chevalier, *Laboring Classes and Dangerous Classes*, 433.

31. Ferrus, *Des prisonniers*, 244.

32. O'Brien, *The Promise of Punishment*, 20–21.

33. Faucher, "La chaîne," 37.

34. This brief discussion owes much to Duesterberg, "Criminology and the Social Order," 36–38.

35. For information on these organizations, see C. Duprat, "Punir et guérir."

36. Wright, *Between the Guillotine and Liberty*, 132.

37. O'Brien, *The Promise of Punishment*, 20–21.

38. Moreau-Christophe, *De la réforme des prisons*, 445.

39. On the work regime inside the nineteenth–century French penitentiary, see O'Brien, *The Promise of Punishment*, 150–90. For broader discussions of labor within the prison, see Melossi and Pavarini, *The Prison and the Factory*.

40. Jacques François Bosourdy, *Essai sur l'amélioration physique et morale des condamnés aux travaux forcés* (Paris, 1827), carton H1, Archives nationales, Centre des archives d'outre-mer, Aix-en-Provence [hereinafter AOM].

41. M. Portal, minister of the marine, quoted in Forster, *France and Botany Bay*, 166.

42. Baron Jean-Marguerite Tupinier, quoted in Russier, *Transportation et colonisation pénale*, 53–54.

43. Édouard Proust, "La transportation judiciaire et les criminels

d'habitude ou de profession," 12, *Inquest of 1872*, carton H24, AOM.

44. Appert, *Bagnes, prisons et criminels*, 3:12–13.

45. Lepelletier de la Sarthe, *Histoire générale des bagnes*, 116.

46. Fleury, "Histoire médicale," 501. See also Chassinat, *Études sur la mortalité*.

47. Alhoy, *Le bagne de Rochefort*, 41.

48. Moreau-Christophe, *De la réforme des prisons en France*, 314.

49. Lucas, *De la réforme des prisons*, 1:39.

50. Lepelletier de la Sarthe, *Histoire générale des bagnes*, 62.

51. Portal cited in Michel Pierre, "Saint-Laurent du Maroni, commune pénitentiaire," in Petit, *La prison, le bagne et l'histoire*, 91.

52. Inventory of documents communicated to the commission convened by M. Admiral Armand de Mackau, March 1, 1851, carton H1, AOM.

53. W. B. Cohen, "Malaria and French Imperialism," 23.

54. E. G., "La Guyane," *Les Antilles*, March 9, 1852, carton H1, AOM.

55. Wright, *Between the Guillotine and Liberty*, 93.

56. Pierre, *La terre de la grande punition*, 19.

57. Ministère de la Justice, *Compte générale de l'administration de la justice criminelle, 1900*.

58. Fournier, *Vision du bagne*, 13.

59. Miles, *Devil's Island*, 28–29.

60. Orgeas, *Contribution à l'étude du non-cosmopolitisme de l'homme*, 20.

61. Calmel, *La colonisation pénale*, 187.

62. Garnier, *La fièvre jaune à la Guyane*, 17.

63. *Notice sur la transportation en Guyane et en Nouvelle-Calédonie (1852–1865)*, 25, AOM.

64. *Notice sur la transportation en Guyane et en Nouvelle-Calédonie (1852–1865)*, 25, AOM.

65. Curtin, *Death by Migration*, 9–11; see also Coleman, *Yellow Fever in the North*; and François Delaporte, *The History of Yellow Fever*.

66. Report on Guiana regarding the hygiene of transportees. From the chief naval physician to the governor of French Guiana, May 9, 1866, carton H20, AOM.

67. Miles, *Devil's Island*, 28.

68. Headrick, *Tools of Empire*, 64.

69. Calmel, *La colonisation pénale*, 187.

70. Report on Guiana regarding the hygiene of transportees, May 9, 1866.

71. For an analysis of the epistemological configurations upon which such ideas were based, see Harrison, " 'The Tender Frame of Man' "; and Anderson, "Immunities of Empire."

72. Rapport sur la Guyane considerée au point de vue de l'hygiène et de la transportation.

73. Redfield, *Space in the Tropics*, 69.

74. Osborne, *Nature*, 94; see also Anderson, "Climates of Opinion."

75. Orgeas, *Contribution à l'étude du non-cosmopolitisme de l'homme*, 347; see also Redfield, *Space in the Tropics*, 203–5.

76. Cited in Franceschi, *De l'organisation locale de la transportation*, 35–36.

77. Orgeas, *Contribution à l'étude du non-cosmopolitisme de l'homme*, 347; see also Redfield, *Space in the Tropics*, 203–5.

78. *Notice sur la transportation en Guyane et en Nouvelle-Calédonie (1866–1867)*, 48, AOM. For a thorough treatment of women in the *bagnes* see Krakovitch, *Les femmes bagnards*.

79. Russier, *Transporation et colonisation pénale*, 58.

80. Cited in Kling, "L'Alcmène," 119.

81. Cormier, *La colonisation pénale*, 58.

82. Alberti, *Étude sur la colonisation à la Nouvelle-Calédonie*, 68.

83. Russier, *Transporation et colonisation pénale*, 21–22. This includes the 2,560 deported Communards arriving in the colony as of late 1873.

84. Russier, *Transporation et colonisation pénale*, 21–22.

85. Calmel, *La colonisation pénale*, 195.

86. *Notice sur la transportation en Guyane et en Nouvelle-Calédonie (1866–1867)*, 3, AOM.

87. *Notice sur la transportation en Guyane et en Nouvelle-Calédonie (1866–1867)*, 48, AOM.

2. The Recidivist of Fin de Siècle France

1. *Bulletin des lois* 931 (1885): 1120–24.

2. Wright, *Between the Guillotine and Liberty*, 39.

3. Foucault, *Discipline and Punish*, 3–7.

4. Haussonville, *Les établissements pénitentiaires*, 23.

5. Ministère de la Justice, *Compte général de l'administration de la justice criminelle, 1880*, cited in Yvernès, "La récidive," 318.

6. Lévy, "Crime, the Judicial System, and Punishment in Modern France," 89.

7. Ministère de la Justice, *Compte général de l'administration de la justice criminelle, 1880*, cited in Yvernès, "La récidive," 319–20.

8. Ministère de la Justice, *Compte général de l'administration de la justice criminelle, 1900*.

9. On the appearance of the science of statistics in the nineteenth century, see Porter, *The Rise of Statistical Thinking*.

10. Le Clère, *Histoire de la police*, 85–87.

11. Ministère de la Justice, *Compte général de l'administration de la justice criminelle, 1880*, lxxvii–lxxviii.

12. Bonneville, *De l'amelioration de la loi criminelle*, 676–87.

13. *Journal officiel*, May 21, 1875, 3574.

14. *Journal officiel*, May 21, 1875, 3574–75.

15. Aymard, *La profession du crime*, 104.

16. Reinach, *Les récidivistes*, 12.

17. Garçon, *Le code pénale*, article 271; James-Nattan, "Suite de la discussion," 999.

18. For a fascinating discussion of the vagabond in fin de siècle French culture see Matsuda, *The Memory of the Modern*, 121–41; and Wagniart, *Le vagabond à la fin du XIXe siècle*.

19. Pagnier, *Du vagabondage et des vagabonds*, 144.

20. A. Rivière, "Suite de la discussion," 988–989.

21. Macé, *Le service de la santé*, 270.

22. Robin, *Hospitalité et travail*, 4, 10.

23. M. Choppin, untitled article, *Bulletin société générale des prisons*, January 1877, 221.

24. Haussonville, *Enquête parlementaire*, 6:28.

25. Yvernès, "La récidive," 318.

26. Tarde, "La statistique criminelle du dernier demi-siècle," 63.

27. Aymard, *La profession du crime*, 102–6.

28. Cuche, "L'avenir de l'intimidation," 801–3.

29. In the British context, see Forsythe, *A System of Discipline*, 62.

30. Wright, *Between the Guillotine and Liberty*, 149.

31. Jules Leveillé, untitled article, *Bullétin société générale des prisons*, January 1889, 920.

32. Fouillée, *La France au point de vue moral*, 138.

33. Joly, *Problèmes de science criminelle*, 59–60.

34. Weber, *Peasants into Frenchmen*, 300.

35. Fourquet, "Les vagabonds criminels," 402–3.

36. Delvincourt, *La lutte contre la criminalité*, 404.

37. G. L. Duprat, *La criminalité dans l'adolescence*, 120.

38. Prins, *Criminalité et repression*, 13.

39. Bonger, *Criminality and Economic Conditions*, 120.

40. Le Bon had "a reading public no other social thinker could rival." See Nye, *The Origins of Crowd Psychology*, 3.

41. Le Bon, *The Crowd*, 149.

42. Tarde, *The Laws of Imitation*, 201.

43. Vine, "Gabriel Tarde," 231.

44. G. L. Duprat, *La criminalité dans l'adolescence*, 131.

45. Albanel, "L'enfance criminelle à Paris," 388–89.

46. In this regard, see Goldstein, "Moral Contagion"; and Barrows, *Distorting Mirrors*.

47. Tarde, *Penal Philosophy*, 386.

48. *Journal officiel*, May 21, 1875, 3574.

49. See Cole, *The Power of Large Numbers*; and Fuchs, *Poor and Pregnant in Paris*.

50. For a discussion of how degeneration theory was an ideological bridge between environmental and biological discussions of crime, see Nye, *Crime, Madness, and Politics*, 119–20; and Pick, *Faces of Degeneration*, 100.

51. Walter, "What Became of the Degenerate?" 423.

52. Le Bon, "Problèmes anthropologiques," 525, 528–29.

53. Féré, *Dégénéréscence et criminalité*, 41–42.

54. Joly, *Le crime*, 36–38.

55. Haussonville, *Enquête parlementaire*, 5:42.

56. *Journal officiel*, February 6, 1885, 36–37.

57. *Notice sur la transportation en Guyane et en Nouvelle-Calédonie, 1882–1883*, 24, AOM.

58. Pagnier, *Du vagabondage et des vagabonds*, 7.

59. Le Chartier, *Les récidivistes*, 1.

60. Delvincourt, *La lutte contre la criminalité*, 338.

61. Desportes, "Rapport sur le project de loi," 921.

62. Lacassagne, "Marche de la criminalité de 1825 à 1880," 684.

63. Le Bon, "Problèmes anthropologiques," 537–38.

64. Waldeck-Rousseau, "Rapport sur la proposition de loi," 79.

65. For a full exploration of this debate see Nye, *Crime, Madness and Politics*.

66. Ministère de la Justice, *Compte général de l'administration de la justice criminelle, 1900*, lxvi.

67. Claire, Krakovitch, and Préteux, *Établissements pénitentiaires coloniaux, 1792–1952*, 15.

68. Ministerial dispatch, July 17, 1884, carton H834, AOM.

3. The View from Above and Below

1. Regulations of the administrative service, May 10, 1855, carton H10, AOM.

2. Report of the governor of New Caledonia to the Ministry of the Marine, April 2, 1869, carton H1860, AOM.

3. Report on Randon du Landre, commandant, n.d., carton H1214, AOM.

4. Minister of the marine to the governor of French Guiana, n.d., carton H1257, AOM.

5. Report from Governor Baudin of French Guiana to the Ministry of the Marine, February 15, 1858, carton H10, AOM.

6. Regulations of the administrative service, 1870, carton H10, AOM

7. Regulations of the administrative service, 1870.

8. Regulations of the administrative service, 1870.

9. Gerth and Mills, *From Max Weber*, 196–97.

10. Belbenoit, *Dry Guillotine*, 23.

11. Miles, *Devil's Island*, 75.

12. Article 4 of Ministerial decree, November 25, 1887, carton H5346, AOM.

13. See carton H5346, AOM, for examples of such *livrets* (booklets).

14. Linon, "Les officiers du corps de santé," 44.

15. Moncelon, *Le bagne et la colonisation pénale*, 43.

16. Regulations for the disciplinary quarter on the Île St. Joseph. It was put into decree on October 5, 1889. Carton H5347, AOM.

17. Darquitain and Le Boucher, *La grande géhenne*, 28–29.

18. Ministerial dispatch, April 4, 1876, carton H11, AOM.

19. Carol, "Le bagne," 158.

20. Krarup-Nielsen, *Hell beyond the Seas*, 222.

21. Belbenoit, *Hell on Trial*, 173, 206.

22. Inspection report of M. Gayet, inspector general, February 24, 1914, carton H1856, AOM.

23. Report from the director of the penitentiary administration to the governor of New Caledonia, number 13, February 10, 1896, carton H1858, AOM.

24. Report from the director of the penitentiary administration to the governor of New Caledonia, number 13, February 10, 1896.

25. Report from the director of the penitentiary administration to the governor of New Caledonia, number 13, February 10, 1896.

26. Ministerial dispatch, August 27, 1888, report on the inspection of the establishment of Koe (New Caledonia). Observations on the employment of *garçons de famille*. Carton H1861, AOM.

27. Krarup-Nielsen, *Hell beyond the Seas*, 80.

28. Ministerial dispatch, August 27, 1888, report on the inspection of the establishment of Koe (New Caledonia).

29. Ministerial dispatch, August 27, 1888, report on the inspection of the establishment of Koe (New Caledonia).

30. Tripot, *La Guyane*, 5.

31. Albert Londres, "Premier contact avec les forçats," *Le petit parisien*, August 10, 1923, 1.

32. Confidential letter from Governor Rodier of Guyana to the minister of the colonies, December 31, 1907, carton H1862, AOM

33. Darquitain and Le Boucher, *La grande géhenne*, 40, 56.

34. Darquitain and Le Boucher, *La grande géhenne*, 56.

35. Mesclon, *Comment j'ai subi quinze ans de bagne*, 58–59.

36. Sinclair, *Loose among Devils*, 31, 34.

37. Halliburton, *New Worlds to Conquer*, 282–83.

38. Krarup-Nielsen, *Hell beyond the Seas*, 62.

39. Krarup-Nielsen, *Hell beyond the Seas*, 63.

40. Belbenoit, *Hell on Trial*, 38.

41. Belbenoit, *Dry Guillotine*, 155.

42. Seaton, *Isle of the Damned*, 58.

43. Krarup-Nielsen, *Hell beyond the Seas*, 62.

44. Rickards, *The Man from Devil's Island*, 32.

45. Seaton, *Isle of the Damned*, 58.

46. Le Clère, *La vie quotidienne dans les bagnes*, 201.

47. Price, *The Convict and the Colonel*, 98.

48. Krarup-Nielsen, *Hell beyond the Seas*, 93.

49. Seaton, *Isle of the Damned*, 58.

50. Belbenoit, *Dry Guillotine*, 152–53.

51. Seaton, *Isle of the Damned*, 56.

52. Belbenoit, *Dry Guillotine*, 45.

53. Milani and Grin, *The Convict*, 76.

54. Belbenoit, *Dry Guillotine*, 153.

55. Milani and Grin, *The Convict*, 76.

56. Seaton, *Isle of the Damned*, 56.

57. Seaton, *Isle of the Damned*, 105.

58. Liard-Courtois, *Souvenirs du bagne*, 344.

59. Albert Londres, "A Cayenne, premiers étonnements," *Le petit parisien*, August 8, 1923, 1.

60. Batzler-Heim, *Horrors of Cayenne*, 57.

61. Seaton, *Isle of the Damned*, 105.

62. Krarup-Nielsen, *Hell beyond the Seas*, 93.

63. Niles, *Condemned to Devil's Island*, 24–25; Rickards, *The Man from Devil's Island*, 32.

64. Belbenoit, *Dry Guillotine*, 51.

65. Milani and Grin, *The Convict*, 41.

66. Belbenoit, *Dry Guillotine*, 33. For information on how penal colony doctors dealt with the "plan," see Clarac, "Corps étrangers du rectum chez les condamnés à la Guyane," 456–58. I would like to thank Eric Jennings for this reference.

67. Krarup-Nielsen, *Hell beyond the Seas*, 85, 83.

68. Krarup-Nielsen, *Hell beyond the Seas*, 85.

69. Krarup-Nielsen, *Hell beyond the Seas*, 86.

70. Rickards, *The Man from Devil's Island*, 33.

71. Pierre, *La terre de la grande punition*, 311–12.

72. Governor of French Guiana to the Ministry of the Colonies, May 22, 1914, carton H1853, AOM.

73. Belbenoit, *Hell on Trial*, 270.

74. Ettighoffer, *The Island of the Doomed*, 163–64.

75. In "In the Penal Colony," Kafka writes about a metaphorical penal colony staffed by one lone officer who operates a device that engraves upon the body of the prisoner the reason for his execution. In a manner similar to *The Trial*, the story depicts a darkly oppressive and evil setting peopled by devoted and mindless automatons. Kafka implies in this story, however, that the penal colony is a thing of the past, as humankind has moved beyond such barbaric institutions.

76. Bakhtin, *Rabelais and His World*.

4. The French Penal Colony Service

1. Maroger, *Bagne*, 171.

2. Francis Carco, "La route de Devil's Island," cited in Belbenoit, *Hell on Trial*, 283.

3. Davis, *The Jungle and the Damned*, 41–42.

4. Pisier, *Les déportés de la commune*, 43 n. 1; see also Bullard, *Exile to Paradise*, 244–62. In 1880 the former Communards received an amnesty and were allowed to return to France. While the vast majority returned home, approximately 140 *déportés* remained in New Caledonia.

5. Simon Mayer, "Souvenir d'un déporté: Etape d'un forçat politique," *Le petit national*, November 4, 1879.

6. See *Reveil social*, *Le citoyen*, and *Le temps* for the full extent of the press campaign from 1879–80.

7. Testimony of Alexandre Bauche, former Communard, February 21, 1880, carton H840, AOM.

8. Testimony of Gaston Da Costa, former Communard, February 21, 1880, carton H840, AOM.

9. Testimony of Alphonse Humbert, former Communard, February 20, 1880, carton H840, AOM.

10. Testimony of Louis Le Gros, retired penal colony officer, February 14, 1880, carton H840, AOM.

11. Director of the penitentiary administration in New Caledonia to the Ministry of the Marine, November 24, 1879, carton H2078, AOM.

12. Bullard, *Exile to Paradise.*

13. Hannah Arendt, *Eichmann in Jerusalem: A Report on the Banality of Evil* (New York: Viking, 1965).

14. Primo Levi, *The Drowned and the Saved* (New York: Viking, 1989), 36.

15. Le Clère, *La vie quotidienne dans les bagnes,* 92.

16. Inspection report, November 3, 1865, p. 6, carton H24, AOM.

17. Inspector General Napoigne to the Ministry of the Marine, September 10, 1867, p. 1, carton H1257, AOM.

18. Report from Rear Admiral Gicquel de Tauche, personnel director to the Ministry of the Marine, October 24, 1867, carton H1257, AOM.

19. Governor Guillain of New Caledonia to the Ministry of the Marine, June 1, 1867, carton H1257, AOM.

20. Report from the governor of French Guiana to the Ministry of the Marine, November 29, 1861, carton H1257, AOM.

21. Governor Guillain of New Caledonia to the Ministry of the Marine, June 1, 1867.

22. Le Clère, *La vie quotidienne dans les bagnes,* 91–92.

23. Governor of French Guiana to the admiral minister of the marine, February 11, 1870, carton H1258, AOM.

24. Governor of French Guiana to the Ministry of the Marine, May 15, 1858, carton H1257, AOM.

25. Lauvergne, *Les forçats,* 269.

26. *Projet d'organisation pour un corps militaire,* 1–2.

27. Bernard Schnapper has calculated that while there were 354,000 men in the army in January 1852, there were 526,000 in January 1856. Schnapper, *Le remplacement militaire en France,* 293, 271.

28. Payne, *Police State,* 235.

29. Le Clère, *Histoire de la police,* 85.

30. Note from Captain de Vaisseau, personnel director to the Ministry of the Marine, March 28, 1867, carton H1234, AOM.

31. Report from the governor of French Guiana to the Ministry of the Marine, November 29, 1867.

32. Report from Rear Admiral Gicquel de Tauche, personnel director to the Ministry of the Marine, October 24, 1867.

33. Report from the governor of French Guiana to the Ministry of the Marine, November 29, 1861.

34. Note relating to the administrative and financial organization of transportation to Guiana, July 29, 1868, carton H10, AOM.

35. Note relating to the administrative and financial organization of transportation to Guiana, July 29, 1868.

36. Professional instruction, carton H1258, AOM.

37. Report of the commission named by the governor to examine the actual situation in regard to the corps of surveillants and to propose a project for reorganization, 1881, carton H1258, AOM.

38. Professional instruction.

39. Report from Rear Admiral Gicquel de Tauche, personnel director to the Ministry of the Marine, October 24, 1867.

40. Report from Rear Admiral Gicquel de Tauche, personnel director to the Ministry of the Marine, October 24, 1867.

41. Carlier, *Le personnel des prisons françaises*, 38.

42. Report of Rear Admiral Gicquel de Tauche, personnel director to the Ministry of the Marine, October 24, 1867.

43. Le Clère, *La vie quotidienne dans les bagnes*, 92.

44. Notes from Guard Heiss relating to the military corps of guards in the penitentiary colonies, August 27, 1875, carton H1257, AOM.

45. Report from Governor Guillain, July 25, 1869, carton H24, AOM.

46. Report from Governor de la Richerie, May 5, 1871, 2–3, carton H24, AOM.

47. Report from Governor Guillain, third trimester, 1870, carton H24, AOM.

48. Inspector general of New Caledonia to the Ministry of the Marine, July 11, 1873, carton H1861, AOM.

49. Notes from Guard Heiss relating to the military corps of guards in the penitentiary colonies, August 27, 1875.

50. Ministerial circular on the subject of penal colony wardens, April 10, 1886, carton H2028, AOM.

51. Decree concerning the disciplinary regime in the overseas establishments of hard labor, no. 9570, June 18, 1880, carton H2028, AOM.

52. Report to the governor of French Guiana from the director of the penitentiary administration, January 26, 1888, carton H1222, AOM.

53. Report to the governor of French Guiana from the director of the penitentiary administration, January 26, 1888.

54. Un Vieux Colonial, *La colonisation et le bagne*, 138.

55. Unsigned report on the functioning of guards in New Caledonia, April 19, 1881, carton H1258, AOM.

56. A. Rivière, "La colonisation pénale," 380–81.

57. Laurent, *Les châtiments corporels*, 219, 220, 222.

58. James–Nattan, "La transportation," 78–79.

59. Report of the commission named by decision of the governor to examine the actual situation of the corps of surveillants and to propose a project for reorganization, 1881.

60. Report on the reorganization of military guards, April 15, 1881, carton H1258, AOM.

61. Réne Bérenger, *Débats parlementaires*, October 24, 1884, cited in O'Brien, *The Promise of Punishment*, 269.

62. Warden Second Class Lachèze to the director of the penitentiary administration, July 13, 1880, carton H1212, AOM.

63. Warden Third Class Fouque to the director of the penitentiary administration, April 14, 1881, carton H1258, AOM.

64. Table describing the placement of guards' children, New Caledonia, 1876, carton H1234, AOM.

65. Report by inspector general of French Guiana, 1885, carton H1215, AOM.

66. Report of the commission named by decision of the governor to examine the actual situation of the corps of surveillants and to propose a project for reorganization, 1881.

67. Report on the service of transportation, 1873, carton H1861, AOM.

68. See Krakovitch, *Les femmes bagnards*.

69. Report of the commission named by decision of the governor to ex-

amine the actual situation of the corps of surveillants and to propose a project for reorganization, 1881.

70. Dispatch from the director of the penitentiary administration in French Guiana to the Ministry of the Marine: Observations relating to the guards' material settlement, July 13, 1886, carton H1861, AOM.

71. Dr. Grandmarie to the commandant of the penitentiary at St. Laurent, with regard to Gustave Octeau, guard second class, n.d., carton H1246, AOM.

72. Governor of French Guiana to the minister of the colonies with regard to Gustave Octeau, guard second class, September 28, 1905, carton H1246, AOM.

73. Report to the minister of the colonies on the demotion of Guards Reydellet and Rully, February 7, 1896, carton H1246, AOM.

74. General inspection of 1897, Register of confidential notes, carton H5187, AOM.

75. Note given to the governor of French Guiana from the penitentiary administration, May 28, 1905, carton H1234, AOM.

76. Borgnis-Desbordes, *Report on Transportation and Relegation*, 1888, carton H1214, AOM.

77. Inspector Leboul to the Ministry of the Marine, September 25, 1872, carton H1258, AOM.

78. Governor Moutet of French Guiana to the minister of the colonies, October 16, 1899, carton H1216, AOM.

79. Governor Feillet to the minister of the colonies, June 6, 1899, carton H1216, AOM.

80. Inspection general of 1878, Reorganization of corps of guards, Modifications proposed to decree of 1867, carton H1258, AOM.

81. Inspector General Bourget to the Ministry of the Marine, October 17, 1888, carton H1215, AOM.

82. Governor of French Guiana to the Ministry of the Marine, December 15, 1885, carton H1215, AOM.

83. Governor of French Guiana to the minister of the colonies, December 13, 1894, carton H1234, AOM.

84. Report of the commission named by decision of the governor to examine the actual situation of the corps of guards and to propose a project for reorganization, 1881.

85. General inspection for French Guiana, 1885, carton H1215, AOM.

86. Inspection report of the camps in New Caledonia, April 19, 1881, carton H1258, AOM.

87. Borgnis-Desbordes, *Report on Transportation and Relegation*, 1888, 20, carton H1214, AOM.

88. Griffiths, *Secrets of the Prison-House*, 230.

89. Minister of foreign affairs of the Netherlands to the Ministry of the Marine, February 8, 1899, carton H1244, AOM.

90. Dispatch from the Dutch ambassador to French Guiana, July 25, 1904, carton H1244, AOM.

91. Minister of foreign affairs for the Netherlands to the Ministry of the Marine, February 8, 1899.

92. Minister of foreign affairs for the Netherlands to the minister of French foreign affairs, December 14, 1898, carton H1244, AOM.

93. Report to the minister of the colonies from the director of the penitentiary administration, June 1, 1897, carton H1246, AOM.

94. Confidential letter from Governor Rodier of French Guiana to the minister of the colonies, December 31, 1907, carton H1862, AOM.

95. O'Brien, *The Promise of Punishment*, 222.

96. Martin, *Crime and Criminal Justice*, 264.

97. Minister of the colonies to the governor of French Guiana, November 24, 1932, professional instruction of the military guards, carton H5189, AOM.

98. Ministerial dispatch, January 28, 1899, carton H1245, AOM.

99. Report from Decoppet, director of the School of Valabre, carton H1245, AOM.

100. Notice on the functioning of the penitentiary service during the year 1926, carton H1928, AOM.

101. Craig Haney, Curtis Banks, and Philip Zimbardo, "Interpersonal Dynamics in a Simulated Prison," *International Journal of Criminology and Penology* 1 (1983): 69–97, cited in Browning, *Ordinary Men*, 167–68.

5. Tropical Medicine in the *Bagne*

1. Cousins and Hussain, *Michel Foucault*, 146.

2. Rabinow, *The Foucault Reader*, 283–84.

3. O'Brien, *The Promise of Punishment*, 48; Zinoman, *The Colonial Bastille*, 91.

4. Zinoman, *The Colonial Bastille*, 91.

5. Clarac, *Mémoirs d'un médecin*, v.

6. See Curtin, *Death by Migration*.

7. Michel, "Les Corps de santé des troupes coloniales," 190.

8. Michel, "Les Corps de santé des troupes coloniales," 185.

9. Monnais-Rousselot, *Médecine et colonization*, 258.

10. Gabriel and Metz, *History of Military Medicine*, 2:175.

11. Note from the head of the health service, December 30, 1851, carton H20, AOM.

12. Regulations on the functioning of the medical colonial service, carton H1965, AOM.

13. Note on the general inspection of health services, n.d., carton H20, AOM.

14. Report on penitentiary hospital regulations, June 1, 1909, carton H1965, AOM.

15. Report to the governor of French Guiana from the director of the penitentiary administration, July 27, 1909, carton H1965, AOM.

16. Headrick, *Tools of Empire*, 64.

17. Curtin, *Death by Migration*, 67, 137.

18. Arnold, *New Cambridge History of India*, 81.

19. Note from the head of the health service, December 30, 1861.

20. First physician of St. Laurent to the chief physician, February 19, 1900, carton H65, AOM.

21. Clarac, chief physician, to the director of the penitentiary administration, March 29, 1900, carton H65, AOM.

22. Commandant of St. Jean to the director of the penitentiary administration, February 24, 1900, carton H65, AOM.

23. Clarac, chief physician, to the director of the penitentiary administration, April 25, 1900, carton H65, AOM.

24. Chautemps, head of the penitentiary administration, to the chief physician of health service, June 6, 1895, carton H1852, AOM.

25. Note of defense, head of health service, August 6, 1895, Fonds de la direction des affaires politiques, dossier FM177/1, AOM.

26. Governor of French Guiana to the colonial undersecretary, June 9, 1892, Fonds de la direction des affaires politiques, dossier FM177/2, AOM.

27. Superior council of colonial health, meeting of August 6, 1892, Fonds de la direction des affaires politiques, dossier FM177/2, AOM.

28. Memorandum from the director of the penitentiary administration to the governor of French Guiana, January 7, 1893, Fonds de la direction des affaires politiques, dossier FM177/2, AOM.

29. Note for the health service inspection, May 27, 1895, Fonds de la direction des affaires politiques, dossier FM177/1, AOM.

30. Governor of French Guiana to the colonial undersecretary, August 1893, Fonds de la direction des affaires politiques, dossier FM177/2, AOM.

31. Miles, *Devil's Island*, 66–67.

32. Deposition, insults of medical officer Mariot against M. Jarry, officer of the penal administration, September 23, 1895, carton H1852, AOM.

33. See all reports written by Mariot from 1895 and 1896, carton H1852, AOM.

34. Moncelon, *Le bagne et la colonisation pénale*, 43.

35. Rousseau, *Un médecin au bagne*, 45. Given that it was still believed that the physical constitutions of Africans were better suited to the tropics than those of Europeans, the rations of the former were composed of manioc meal, fish, and rum, while the latter subsisted on bread, meat, and wine. Redfield, *Space in the Tropics*, 69.

36. General concerns about hygiene, December 19, 1910, carton H1965, AOM.

37. Rousseau, *Un médecin au bagne*, 49.

38. Note from the chief physician of French Guiana to the Ministry of the Marine, July 2, 1902, carton H1864, AOM.

39. Report from Physician Major Bagot to the Ministry of the Marine, carton H65, AOM.

40. French Guiana, *Annual Medical Report*, 1930, carton H1941, AOM.

41. Bérrué, Inspection report, April 21, 1918, carton H2021, AOM.

42. Nguyen, *Étude sur l'etiologie du beriberi*, 29.

43. Thereze, "Note sur le beriberi à Poulo-Condor," 16.

44. Zinoman, *The Colonial Bastille*, 95.

45. Thereze, "Note sur le beriberi à Poulo-Condor," 16.

46. Institut Colonial Français to the Ministry of the Colonies, May 2, 1920, carton H2028, AOM.

47. Arnold, *Colonizing the Body*, 99.

48. Clairin, "Les travaux forcés en 1886," 886.

49. Pain, *Colonisation pénale*, 106.

50. Henri, *Étude critique*, 25; A. Rivière, "La colonisation pénale," 381.

51. A. Duvigneau, physician first class, to the chief physician, April 29, 1892, carton H2013, AOM.

52. Curtin, *Death by Migration*, 149.

53. Duvigneau to the chief physician, April 29, 1892.

54. Duvigneau to the chief physician, April 29, 1892.

55. No records specifically demarcate the number of deaths that occurred along Colonial Route 1. As Alexander Miles has pointed out, death tolls "as high as 17,000 have been claimed but the exact number is impossible to calculate." Miles, *Devil's Island*, 84. It is safe to say, however, that morbidity among road-crew workers was quite high during its nearly half-century of construction.

56. Report from the chief physician on the sanitary state of the colonial route between Macouria and Kourou, n.d., carton H1864, AOM.

57. Rousseau, *Un médecin au bagne*, 118. See also Blin, "Sur l'ankylostomiase dans l'élément pénal de la Guyane" and "L'uncinariose chez les chercheurs d'or et les forçats du Maroni."

58. Institut Colonial Français to the Ministry of the Colonies, May 2, 1920.

59. Arnold makes this argument in regard to colonial physicians in India in *Colonizing the Body*, 100.

60. Gabriel and Metz, *A History of Military Medicine*, 2:177.

61. Michel, "Les Corps de santé des troupes coloniales," 186.

62. Michel, "Les Corps de santé des troupes coloniales," 186.

63. Henry, *French Guiana Française*, 24.

64. Ministerial report on the sanitary situation, May 19, 1924, Fonds de la direction des affaires politiques, dossier FM2737, AOM.

65. Modifications made in the rationing of prisoners' provisions, no. 121,

February 4, 1925, carton H1867, AOM. See also Espinase, chief physician, to the director of the penitentiary administration, December 19, 1923, no. 413, carton H1942, AOM.

66. Circular from the director, no. 56, On the subject of prophylactic measures against the serious afflictions ravaging Guiana, October 29, 1924, carton H2072, AOM.

67. Circular from the director, no. 56, On the subject of prophylactic measures against the serious afflictions ravaging Guiana, October 29, 1924.

68. Study on modifications in the regime of transportation, carton H2072, AOM.

69. Institut Colonial Français to the Ministry of the Colonies, May 2, 1920.

70. Conklin, *A Mission to Civilize*, 5.

71. Annual medical report, penal population, French Guiana, 1931, carton H1941, AOM.

72. Annual medical report, French Guiana, 1938, carton H1941, AOM.

73. Price, *The Convict and the Colonel*, 108.

6. The Criminological Conception of the *Bagne*

1. Teisseire, *La transportation pénale*, 372, 378–79, 402–3.

2. See also Bruyant, *Étude sur la transportation*, 8; Lajoye, *Essai sur la pénalité*, 19–21; Un Vieux Colonial, *La colonisation et le bagne*, 126; James-Nattan, "La transportation," 78–79, 81.

3. Joly, *Problèmes de science criminelle*, 151–52.

4. Tarde, *La criminalité comparée*, 86.

5. Lucas, *La transportation pénale*, 5–9.

6. Dislère, "Troisième rapport annuel," 629.

7. Teisseire, *La transportation pénale*, 374.

8. Lucas, *Du système pénale*, 330–31.

9. As the administration of the penal colonies was in the hands of the navy, governor was an appointed office. Gascher, "Regards sur l'administration coloniale."

10. Ministerial decree, January 16, 1882.

11. Ministerial decree, January 16, 1882.

12. *Notice sur la transportati en Guyane et en Nouvelle-Calédonie*, 1885, 50, AOM.

13. *Notice sur la transportation en Guyane et en Nouvelle-Calédonie*, 1882–1883, 219, AOM

14. *Notice sur la transportation en Guyane et en Nouvelle-Calédonie*, 1882–1883, 37.

15. *Notice sur la transportation en Guyane et en Nouvelle-Calédonie*, 1882–1883, 39–40.

16. Merle, *Expériences coloniales*, 142.

17. Saussol, "The Colonial Chimera," 43.

18. Delvincourt, *La lutte contre la criminalité*, 914.

19. New Caledonian delegate of the Conseil supérieur des colonies to the minister of the marine, July 23, 1884, carton H4826, AOM.

20. Lemire, *Les colonies et la question sociale*, 33.

21. *Le Néo–Calédonien*, May 1, 1883; see also May 4, May 8, 1883.

22. F. Ordinaire, "De Paris à Nouméa: Notes d'un chargé de mission," *La lanterne*, February 24, 1889.

23. "Rapport de la commission," *La libération*, May 9, 1883, 1.

24. Cited in Brou, *Peuplement et population de la Nouvelle-Calédonie*, 34.

25. Lyons, *The Totem and the Tricolour*, 49.

26. On the venal nature of the land question in New Caledonia, see Bullard, *Exile to Paradise*.

27. Leenhardt, *Notes d'ethnologie néo-calédoniennes*, 25–40; see also Leenhardt, *Gens de la Grande Terre*.

28. Dornoy, *Politics in New Caledonia*, 19.

29. Dornoy, *Politics in New Caledonia*, 36.

30. By 1889, native reserves on New Caledonia totaled less than a tenth of the island. See Lenormand, "Politique des autochtones de la Nouvelle-Calédonie," 267.

31. Connell, *From New Caledonia to Kanaky?*, 66.

32. Colombian, *La colonisation et le bagne*, 59.

33. See Guiart, *La terre est le sang des morts*; Latham, "Revolt Re-Examined."

34. Dousset-Leenhardt, *Terre natale, terre d'exil*, 151.

35. See Ministerial dispatch, July 15, 1884, January 12, May 31, 1885, carton H1241, AOM.

36. Saussol, "The Colonial Chimera," 43.

37. Vigé, *La colonisation pénale*, 10.

38. Pierre, *La terre de la grande punition*, 262.

39. Unsigned inspection report to the director of the penitentiary administration in French Guiana, April 2, 1887, carton H1864, AOM.

40. Lallier, "La gradation des peines," 9.

41. Undersecretary to the governor of French Guiana, February 9, 1887, carton H1868, AOM.

42. Saussol, "The Colonial Chimera," 43.

43. Ministerial dispatch, June 21, 1887, carton H1241, AOM.

44. Ministerial dispatch, January 6, 1888, carton H1241, AOM.

45. Ministerial dispatch, January 12, 1885, carton H1241, AOM.

46. Ministerial dispatch, June 21, 1887, carton H1241, AOM.

47. Director of penitentiary administration to the governor of French Guiana, May 27, 1883, carton H1869, AOM.

48. Brouilhet, "La transportation," 914.

49. A. Rivière, "Échelle des peines," 914.

50. Dauphiné, *Chronologie foncière et agricole*, 13–14.

51. Ministerial dispatch, August 26, 1889, carton H1864, AOM.

52. Henri, *Étude critique*, 58–59.

53. Pain, *Colonisation pénale*, 112–13.

54. Clairin, "Les travaux forcés en 1886," 888.

55. Ministerial dispatch, July 4, 1879, carton H1864, AOM.

56. Inspection report from the Île Nou, New Caledonia, April 19, 1883, carton H1861, AOM.

57. Clairin, "Les travaux forcés en 1886," 887.

58. Carol, "Le bagne," 11, 30.

59. Carol, "Le bagne," 5, 7.

60. This not-inconsiderable sum was on average two to three times the daily income of an unskilled worker in late-nineteenth-century France. See Lequin, *Les ouvriers de la région lyonnaise*, 61; and Guin, *Le mouvement ouvrier nantais*, 242.

61. Ministerial decree, August 22, 1884, carton H1861, AOM.

62. Head of the health service to the director of the penitentiary administration of French Guiana, November 7, 1884, carton H2013, AOM.

63. Director of the penitentiary administration to the governor of French Guiana, October 31, 1884, no. 435, carton H2013, AOM.

64. Report from the undersecretary of the marine to the governor of French Guiana, September 15, 1885.

65. Clairin, "Les travaux forcés en 1886," 888.

66. "Une question à Monsieur le directeur de l'administration pénitentiaire," *La France Australe*, July 20, 1889, 2.

67. These tribunals met twice a year and comprised a president (usually a naval captain), three other naval officers, and three noncommissioned officers. See Ministerial decree, June 21, 1858, carton H4879, AOM.

68. Boutinet, *De la condition des transportés aux colonies*, 220.

69. Le Clère, *La vie quotidienne dans les bagnes*, 184.

70. H. Denys, "Le bagne d'aujourd'hui," *Nouvelle revue*, April 1, 1884.

71. J. Bernier, untitled article, *L'indépendant de Nouméa*, May 28, 1887.

72. Pain, *Colonisation pénale*, 109.

73. Clairin, "Les travaux forcés en 1886," 904.

74. Ministerial dispatch, June 21, 1887, carton H1241, AOM.

75. Ministerial dispatch, June 21, 1887.

76. Cor, *Questions coloniales de la transportation*, 106–7.

77. Belbenoit, *Dry Guillotine*, 127.

78. See Leveillé, *La Guyane et la question pénitentiaire coloniale*.

79. Leveillé, *La Guyane et la question pénitentiaire coloniale*, quoted in Espeut to the undersecretary of the marine, June 7, 1889, carton H1869, AOM.

80. Unsigned inspection report, November 12, 1889, carton H1240, AOM.

81. E. Etienne, undersecretary of the marine, to the governor of French Guiana, June 21, 1887, carton H1240, AOM.

82. Ministerial dispatch, June 21, 1887.

83. Ministerial dispatch, June 21, 1887.

84. Ministerial dispatch, June 21, 1887.

85. See Dislère, *Compte-rendu des travaux*.

86. Wright, *Between the Guillotine and Liberty*, 245.

87. Ministerial decree, January 18, 1895, carton H1241, AOM.

88. Ministerial decree, September 21, 1889, carton H1241, AOM.

89. Decree of October 5, 1889, in Ministère de la Marine et des Colonies, *Lois, décrets et règlements*, 95.

90. Decree of September 4, 1891, in Ministère de la Marine et des Colonies, *Lois, décrets et règlements*, 112.

91. For an example of this Whiggish interpretation of administrative reform and penal policy in nineteenth-century England, see Leon Radzinowicz and Roger Hood, *History of English Criminal Law and Its Administration*, vol. 5, *The Emergence of Penal Policy* (London: Stevens, 1986); and Leon Radzinowicz, *Ideology and Crime* (New York: Columbia University Press, 1966).

92. Wright, *Between the Guillotine and Liberty*, 149.

93. Miles, *Devil's Island*, 29.

94. Wright, *Between the Guillotine and Liberty*, 148.

95. "Migrants were given twenty–five hectares of land, five hectares for cultivation and twenty hectares for grazing. They were also given agricultural implements and seed. They had to build their own houses." Merle, "The Foundation of Voh," 235 n. 5.

96. Saussol, "The Colonial Chimera," 43.

97. H. Rivière, *Souvenirs de la Nouvelle-Calédonie*, 205.

7. Representational Crisis

1. This term was coined by Victor Hugo; see Rickards, *The Man from Devil's Island*, 8.

2. Allen, *In the Public Eye*, 42.

3. Berenson, *The Trial of Madame Caillaux*, 209–11, 232–35.

4. Walker, *Outrage and Insight*, 1.

5. Berenson, *The Trial of Madame Caillaux*, 28; Walz, *Pulp Surrealism*, 6.

6. Nye, *Crime, Madness, and Politics*, 206.

7. Desmond, *Windows on the World*, 187.

8. Desmond, *Windows on the World*, 187.

9. Walker, *Outrage and Insight*, 6.

10. Jacques Dhur, "Les forçats propriétaires: Un défi aux honnêtes gens," *Le journal*, August 5, 1907, 1.

11. Jacques Dhur, "Le bagne: Rêve des criminals," *Le journal*, July 26, 1907, 1. See also chapter 6.

12. Note for the minister of the colonies, August 14, 1907, carton H65, AOM.

13. Note for the minister of the colonies, August 6, 1907, carton H65, AOM.

14. Paul Feillet, "Légende tenace," *La presse coloniale*, September 1, 1907, 1.

15. Wright, *Between the Guillotine and Liberty*, 184.

16. Wright, *Between the Guillotine and Liberty*, 186. For biographical treatments of Londres see Assouline, *Albert Londres*; and Mousset, *Albert Londres*.

17. Circular from the director: Ban against unauthorized visits to the camps, work areas, and disciplinary locales, March 15, 1897, carton H2072, AOM.

18. Donet-Vincent, *La fin du bagne*, 34.

19. Albert Londres, "L'arrivée d'un convoi de forçats à Saint-Laurent-du-Maroni," *Le petit parisien*, September 4, 1923, 1.

20. Albert Londres, "La route nationale numéro zero," *Le petit parisien*, August 16, 1923, 1.

21. Londres, "La route nationale numéro zero," 1.

22. Albert Londres, "Lettre ouverte . . . quelques suggestions," *Le petit parisien*, September 6, 1923, 1.

23. Londres, "Lettre ouverte . . . quelques suggestions," 1.

24. Donet-Vincent, *La fin du bagne*, 57; Wright, *Between the Guillotine and Liberty*, 186.

25. *Bulletin officiel du Ministère des colonies*, 1924, 88.

26. For information on the work of the Salvation Army in French Guiana, see Péan, *Conquêtes en terre de bagne*.

27. *Journal officiel*, September 30, 1925, 9480–88.

28. Minister of the colonies to the governor of French Guyana, n.d., carton H2021, AOM.

29. For a critical analysis of the *fait divers*, see Barthes, *Critical Essays*, 185–86.

30. Joseph Bensman and Robert Lilienfeld, "The Journalist," in *Craft*

and Consciousness: Occupational Technique and the Development of Word Images (New York: Wiley, 1973), 209–10, cited in Nye, *Crime, Madness and Politics*, 206.

31. Pierre, *La terre de la grande punition*, 79–82.

32. Londres, *L'homme qui s'évada*, 41.

33. Londres, *L'homme qui s'évada*, 295.

34. Desmond, *Windows on the World*, 59–61.

35. "Paris Apache Who Escaped from Devil's Island, French Guiana, Is Caught in Brazil," *New York Times*, July 21, 1927.

36. "200 Convicts Flee French Guiana Lumber Camp," *New York Times*, November 24, 1931.

37. "Convict Doctor Escapes from Devil's Island; Thousands Try, Few Ever Succeed in Breaks," *New York Times*, September 2, 1928; "Bougrat Reaches Safety," *New York Times*, September 8, 1928.

38. Baudrillard, *The Consumer Society*, 33.

39. See Dieudonné, *La vie des forçats*; George Batzler-Heim, *Horrors of Cayenne*; Belbenoit, *Dry Guillotine*; Belbenoit, *Hell on Trial*; Charrière, *Papillon*; Krarup-Nielsen, *Hell beyond the Seas*; Lagrange, *Flag on Devil's Island*; Roussenq, *L'enfer du bagne*; Seaton, *Isle of the Damned*; and Vaudé, *Matricule 52,306*.

40. For information on the circumstances surrounding the Dreyfus affair and biographical treatments of Dreyfus's life, see Bredin, *The Affair*; Halasz, *Captain Dreyfus*; and Burns, *Dreyfus*.

41. Albert Londres, "L'arrivée aux Iles du Salut," *Le petit parisien*, August 17, 1923, 1.

42. Dreyfus, *Letters*, 119, 137. Redfield discusses Dreyfus's internment on Devil's Island in *Space in the Tropics*, 89–90.

43. Blair Niles, "Forgotten Men of the Jungle Prisons: Portraits of Some of the Convicts Who Live in the Shadow of the 'Dry Guillotine' of French Guiana," *New York Times Magazine*, July 24, 1927, 4–5.

44. Niles, "Forgotten Men of the Jungle Prisons," 4–5.

45. Niles, *Condemned to Devil's Island*, dust jacket.

46. Allison-Booth, *Hell's Outpost*, v.

47. Allison-Booth, *Hell's Outpost*, 21.

48. Allison-Booth, *Hell's Outpost*, 243–44, 271.

49. Trevor Allen, "Isles of the Damned: Horrors of the French Penal Settlements in French Guiana," *John O'London's Weekly*, August 1, 1931, 22.

50. See dust jacket of second edition, published in 1932.

51. The offer is mentioned in a letter from the Ministry of Justice to the Ministry of the Colonies, April 17, 1931, carton H2076, AOM.

52. Paul Kingston to the president of France, forwarded to the Ministry of Justice, February 16, 1932, carton H2076, AOM.

53. Minister of the colonies to the minister of foreign affairs, May 16, 1931, carton H2076, AOM.

54. Ministry of the colonies to Paul Kingston, May 22, 1932, carton H2076, AOM.

55. M. DeJean, French ambassador to Brazil, to the Ministry of the Colonies, February 20, 1931, carton H2076, AOM.

56. Minister of justice to the minister of foreign affairs, March 4, 1931, carton H2076, AOM.

57. Minister of foreign affairs to the minister of the colonies, March 20, 1931, carton H2076, AOM.

58. Young, *Marketing Marianne*, 81, 86.

59. Miles, *Devil's Island*, 105.

60. Minister of the colonies to the governor of French Guiana, September 22, 1931, carton H2080, AOM.

61. Major M. B. Blake, "French Guiana Is a Convict's Paradise!" *Trinidad Guardian*, November 26, 1931, 1.

62. "Tales of French Guiana Penal Cruelty Are Called Twaddle by Briton," *New York Times*, November 27, 1931, 1.

63. Alexander MacGowan, "Convicts in French Guiana Build New 'Riviera,' " *New York Times*, November 28, 1931.

64. See *London Evening News*, December 3, 1931, 1; *London Times*, January 19, 1932, 1.

65. "A Guardian Woman off to Devil's Isle: Expedition Dash to Bring Back the Facts," *Trinidad Guardian*, November 26, 1931, 1.

66. Anne MacGowan, "Voyage to Devil's Island," *Trinidad Guardian*, November 27, 1931, 1.

67. Anne MacGowan, "Convicts in Straw Hats and Striped Pyjamas," *Trinidad Guardian*, November 28, 1931, 1.

68. Anne MacGowan, "How Convicts Eat and Sleep: The Truth about Colonial Penal Settlements," *Trinidad Guardian*, November 29, 1931, 1.

69. Anne MacGowan, "Doctor Dictators of the Capital of Crime," *Trinidad Guardian*, November 30, 1931, 1.

70. Maurice B. Blake, "Blake Replies to a Devil's Island Challenge," *Trinidad Guardian*, December 1, 1931, 1.

71. Telegram from Maugham to the governor of French Guiana, January 29, 1936, carton H2080, AOM.

72. For instance, see Krarup-Nielsen, *Hell beyond the Seas*, 146.

73. Interpreter Second Class Djebbari to the director of the penitentiary administration, May 10, 1934, carton H2080, AOM.

74. Report of principal guard to the commandant, May 6, 1934, carton H2080, AOM.

75. Director of the penitentiary administration to the governor of French Guiana, on the visit of Danjou and his wife, June 19, 1937, carton H2080, AOM.

76. Director of the penitentiary administration to the governor of French Guiana, June 19, 1937.

77. See Danjou, *La belle.*

78. Governor Bouge to the Ministry of the Colonies, February 5, 1932, no. 223, carton H2080, AOM.

79. Sinclair, *Loose among Devils*, 6, 15.

80. Smith, *Black Martinique*, 123.

81. Davis, *The Jungle and the Damned*, 61–62, 26.

82. Dispatch from the minister of the colonies to the governor of French Guiana, September 23, 1938, carton H2080, AOM.

83. Governor of French Guiana to the Ministry of the Colonies, September 26, 1938, carton H2080, AOM.

84. Baudrillard, *The Consumer Society*, 33.

85. Foucault, *Discipline and Punish*, 272, 279.

86. Everett Johnson to the Ministry of the Colonies, April 25, 1929, carton H2076, AOM.

87. Ministry of the Colonies to Everett Johnson, June 3, 1929, carton H2076, AOM.

88. C. Porter Hochstadter to the Ministry of Justice, July 10, 1937, carton H2080, AOM.

89. Ministry of Foreign Affairs to C. Porter Hochstadter, August 11, 1937, carton H2080, AOM.

Conclusion

1. Harmand, *Domination et colonisation*, 148.

2. Wright, *Between the Guillotine and Liberty*, 186.

3. It is noted that such complaints had been registered "for years" in a letter from the governor of French Guiana to the minister of the colonies, June 29, 1927, carton H2072, AOM.

4. Governor of French Guiana to the minister of the marine, December 8, 1920, carton H1862, AOM.

5. Emile Chautemps, "La faillite de la transportation des condamnés aux travaux forcés," *Revue bleue*, June 6, 1908, 709. See also Wright, *Between the Guillotine and Liberty*, 150–52.

6. Roberts, *History of French Colonial Policy*, 521.

7. For information on the political maneuvering surrounding the closure of the Guianese *bagne*, see Donet-Vincent, *La fin du bagne*, 111–54.

8. Alfred Marie-Sainte, "Note enquête sur la transportation coloniale," *Le courrier d'outre-mer*, November 18, 1932, 4.

9. Boucon, *Les parias de la Guyane*, 13.

10. *Journal officiel*, June 29, 1938, 7497.

11. Wright, *Between the Guillotine and Liberty*, 188.

12. Charrière's novel *Papillon*—made into a hugely successful motion picture starring Steve McQueen and Dustin Hoffman in 1973—is the foremost exemplar of this phenomenon.

13. Steinert, "The Development of 'Discipline,'" 96.

Bibliography

Primary Sources

Archives nationales, Centre des archives d'outre-mer. Aix-en-Provence, France.

Bulletin officiel de l'administration pénitentiaire en Guyane (1891–1935)

Bulletin officiel de l'administration pénitentiaire en Nouvelle-Calédonie (1889–1913)

Bulletin officiel de la transportation en Guyane (1881–90)

Bulletin officiel de la transportation en Nouvelle-Calédonie (1881–88)

Bulletin officiel du Ministère des colonies (1924)

Correspondence, rapports, décisions et dépêches. Cartons H4825–78

Fonds de la direction des affaires politiques. Dossiers 177/1, 177/2, 2191, 2737, 2975–82

Guyane, Nouvelle-Calédonie et autres pénitenciers: Gestion administratif. Cartons H1–58, H1833–58, H1955–2008, H2009–32, H5112–25

Inspection, finances, rapports. Cartons H1859–1941

Liquidation des bagnes. Cartons H2078–95

Notice sur la transportation en Guyane et en Nouvelle-Calédonie (1855–1912)

Personnel de l'administration pénitentiaires. Cartons H1212–59, H1953–54

Projet d'organisation pour un corps militaire destiné à remplacer celui des surveillants dans le service pénitentiaire de la Guyane. Cayenne: Imprimerie du gouvernement, 1855.

Suppression des bagnes. Cartons H2033–38

Published Primary Sources

Albanel, Louis. "L'enfance criminelle à Paris: Observations pratiques, cliniques et statistiques." *Revue philanthropique* 4 (1899): 385–99.

Alberti, J.-B. *Étude sur la colonisation à la Nouvelle-Calédonie: Colonisation pénale, colonisation libre.* Paris: Émile Larose, 1901.

Alhoy, Maurice. *Le bagne de Rochefort.* Paris: G. Havard, 1845.

Appert, Benjamin. *Bagnes, prisons et criminels.* 3 vols. Paris: Guilbert, 1835.

Aymard, Camille. *La profession du crime.* Paris: Librairie Hachette, 1905.

Beaumont, Gustave de, and Alexis de Tocqueville. *Du système pénitentiaire aux États-Unis, et de son application en France, suivi d'un appendice sur les colonies pénales.* Paris: Lévy, 1833.

Benoiston de Chateauneuf, Louis-François. *De la colonisation des condamnés, et de l'avantage qu'il y aurait pour la France à adopter cette mesure.* Paris, 1827.

Bentham, Jeremy. *The Works of Jeremy Bentham.* 11 vols. Ed. J. Bowring. Edinburgh: William Tart, 1843.

Berard, Alexandre. "La vagabondage en France." *Archives d'anthropologie criminelle et des sciences pénales* 13 (1898): 589–510.

Bertheau, Charles. *De la transportation des récidivistes incorrigibles.* Paris: Hachette, 1882.

Blin, G. "Sur l'ankylostomiase dans l'élément pénal de la Guyane." *Annales d'hygiène et de médecine coloniale* 17 (1914): 179–89.

———. "L'uncinariose chez les chercheurs d'or et les forçats du Maroni." *Annales d'hygiène et de médecine coloniale* 17 (1914): 149–52.

Bonger, William, ed. *Criminality and Economic Conditions.* Trans. Henry P. Horton. Boston: Little, Brown, 1915.

Bonneville, Arnould. *De l'amelioration de la loi criminelle en vue d'une justice plus prompte, plus efficace, plus glorieuse et plus moralisante.* Vol. 1. Paris: Cotillon, 1855.

Bourin-Fournet, J. *La société moderne et la question sociale.* Paris: Guillaumin, 1893.

Boutinet, Aris. *De la condition des transportés aux colonies: Étude de colonisation pénale.* Paris: Rousseau, 1889.

Brétignières de Courteilles, Louis-Hermann. *Les condamnés et les prisons ou réforme morale, criminelle, et pénitentiaire.* Paris: Perrotin, 1838.

Brouilhet, M. Francis. "La transportation." *Bullétin société générale des prisons* (November 1888): 894–914.

Bruyant, Edmond. *Étude sur la transportation.* Thèse pour Faculté de droit, Université de Paris, 1889.

Calmel, Armand. *La colonisation pénale.* Thèse pour le doctorat, Université de Bordeaux, 1899.

Carol, Jean. "Le bagne." *Revue de Paris,* November/December 1901, 10–31.

Chassinat, Raoul. *Études sur la mortalité dans les maisons centrales de force de correction, depuis 1822 jusqu'à 1837.* Paris: Librairie administrative, 1844.

Clairin, Émile. "Les travaux forcés en 1885: Ce qu'ils sont—ce qu'ils devraient être." *Bulletin société générale des prisons,* November 1885, 881–98.

Clarac, Albert. "Corps étrangers du rectum chez les condamnés à la Guyane." *Annales d'hygiène et de médecine coloniales,* July–September 1901, 455–58.

Colombian, René. *La colonisation et le bagne à la Nouvelle-Calédonie.* Paris: Challamel et Aîné, 1902.

Cor, Henri. *Questions coloniales de la transportation, considérées comme moyen de répression et comme force colonisatrice.* Thèse pour le doctorat, Université de Paris, 1895.

Corré, Armand. *Les criminels: Caractères physiques et psychologiques.* Paris: Octave Doin, 1889.

Cuche, Paul. "L'avenir de l'intimidation." *Revue pénitentiaire* 18 (1894): 800–814.

———. *Traité de science et de législation pénitentiaires.* Paris: F. Pichon et Durand Auzias, 1905.

Delvincourt, Augustin. *La lutte contre la criminalité dans les temps modernes.* Paris: E. Soye, 1897.

Desportes, F. "Rapport sur le projet de loi rélatif à la rélégation des recidivistes." *Bullétin société générale des prisons,* January 1882: 919–22.

Dislère, Paul. *Compte-rendu des travaux de la commission permanente du régime pénitentiaire pendant les années 1880 et 1890.* Melun: Imprimerie Nationale, 1891.

———. "Troisième rapport annuel de la commission de classement des récidivistes." *Bulletin société générale des prisons,* May 1889, 528–43.

Duprat, G. L. *La criminalité dans l'adolescence: Causes et remèdes d'un actual mal social actuel.* Paris: Alcan, 1909.

Duvergier, J.-B., ed. *Collection complète des lois, décrets, ordonnances, règlements, avis du Conseil d'état de 1788 à 1830.* 2nd ed. Paris: Imprimerie Nationale, 1835.

Ernouf-Bignon, Camille. *Les institutions de prévoyance dans nos populations rurales.* Paris: C. Anat, 1912.

Faucher, Léon. "La chaîne des condamnés aux travaux forcés." *Revue de Paris* 30 (1835): 32–47.

———. *De la réforme des prisons.* Paris: Angé, 1838.

Féré, Charles. *Dégéneréscence et criminalité: Essai physiologique.* 4th ed. Paris: Alcan, 1907.

Ferrus, Guillaume. *Des prisonniers, de l'emprisonnement et des prisons.* Paris: Ballière et fils, 1850.

Fleury, M. "Histoire médicale de la maladie qui a régné parmi les condamnés du bagne de Toulon." *Mémoire de l'académie royale de médecine* 3 (1833): 487–510.

Fontaine, Henri. *De la relégation des récidivistes, étude de la loi du 27 mai 1885.* Thèse pour Faculté de droit, Université de Paris, 1885.

Fouillée, Alfred. *La France au point de vue moral.* Paris: Alcan, 1900.

Fourquet, Emile. "Les vagabonds criminels." *Revue de deux mondes* 70 (December 1899): 401–5.

Franceschi, Antoine. *De l'organisation locale de la transporation.* Laval: Imprimerie E. Jamin, 1895.

Frégier, Honoré-Antoine. *Des classes dangéreuses de la population dans les grandes villes, et des moyens de les rendre meilleures.* 2 vols. Paris: J.-B. Ballière, 1840.

Garçon, Emile, ed. *Le code pénale.* Paris: Dalloz, 1955.

Garnier, M. A. *La fièvre jaune à la Guyane avant 1902 et l'epidémie de 1902.* Paris: Octave Doin, 1903.

Ginouvrier, J.-F.-T. *Tableau de l'intérieur des prisons des France, ou Études sur la situation et les souffrances morales et physiques de toutes les classes de prisonniers ou détenus.* Paris, 1824.

Griffiths, Arthur. *Secrets of the Prison-House, or Gaol Studies and Sketches.* Vol. 1. London: Chapman and Hall, 1894.

Harmand, Jules. *Domination et colonisation.* Paris: Moutet, 1910.

Haussonville, Othenin de. *Enquête parlementaire sur le régime des établissements pénitentiaire.* 5 vols. Paris: Cerf & Fils, 1873–75.

———. *Les établissements pénitentiaires en France et aux colonies.* Paris: Lévy Frères, 1875.

Henri, Edmond. *Étude critique de la transportation en guyane française: Réformes réalisables.* Thèse pour Faculté de droit, Université de Paris, 1912.

Huerne de Pommeuse, M. L.-F. *Des colonies agricoles et de leurs avantages pour assurer le secours a l'honnête indigence.* Paris: Huzard, 1832.

James-Nattan, M. "Suite de la discussion du rapport sur les mesures hospitalières destinées à empêcher les vagabonds et la mendiants de tomber dans la récidive." *Bulletin société générale des prisons,* December 1885, 985–1014.

———. "La transportation." *Bulletin société générale des prisons,* January 1885, 77–84.

Joly, Henri. *Le crime: Étude sociale.* Paris: Cerf, 1888.

———. *La France criminelle.* Paris: Cerf, 1889.

———. "Jeunes criminels parisiens." *Archives d'anthropologie criminelle et des sciences pénales* 5 (1890): 330–407.

———. *Problèmes de science criminelle.* Paris: Librairie Hachette, 1910.

Lacassagne, Alexandre. "Marche de la criminalité de 1825 à 1880: Du criminel devant la science contemporaine." *La revue scientifique* 1 (1881): 574–84.

Lajoye, Raoul. *Essai sur la penalité.* Paris: Hurtau, 1858.

Lallier, Pierre. "La gradation des peines dans le mode actuel d'exécution de la peine des travaux forcés." *Extrait du Bulletin des sciences économiques et sociales du Comité des travaux historiques et scienti-fiques,* April 1885, 1–11.

Lasègue, Charles. "Le vol aux étalages." *Archives générales de médecine* 57 (1880): 158–70.

Laurent, Emile. *Les châtiments corporels.* Lyon: Librairie Phily, 1912.

Lauvergne, Hubert. *Les forçats.* 1841. Reprint. Grenoble: Jerôme Millon, 1991.

Le Bon, Gustave. *The Crowd.* 1895. Reprint. New Brunswick nj: Transaction, 1995.

———. "Problèmes anthropologiques: La question des criminels." *Revue philosophique* 2 (1881): 519–39.

Le Chartier, J. *Les récidivistes: Choix d'une colonie pénitentiaire.* Paris, 1887.

Le Goupils, Maurice. *Un type de colonisation administrative: La crise coloniale en Nouvelle-Calédonie.* Paris: Bureaux de la Science Sociale, 1905.

Lemire, Charles. *Les colonies et la question sociale en France.* Paris: Challamel Aîné, 1885.

Lepelletier de la Sarthe, Almire. *Histoire générale des bagnes: Études à la Chiourme de Brest.* 1853. Reprint. Rennes: Découvrance, 1995.

Leveillé, Jules. *La Guyane et la question pénitentiaire coloniale.* Paris: A. Colin, 1885.

Lucas, Charles. *De la réforme des prisons, ou Théorie de l'emprisonnement.* 3 vols. Paris: Legrand and Bergounioux, 1835.

———. "Économie politique: De l'extinction de la mendicité de l'agriculture." *Le cultivateur* 15 (June 1839): 358–85.

———. *Du système pénal et du système répressif en général, de la peine du mort en particulier.* Paris: Charles Béchet, 1827.

———. *La transportation pénale, ou La politique du débarras, rapport verbal à l'occasion de la notice publiée par le ministère de la marine sur la Guyane française et la Nouvelle-Calédonie.* Orleans: Colas, 1878.

Macé, Gustave. *Le service de la santé.* Paris: Charpentier, 1890.

Michaux, Hubert-Ernest. *Étude sur la question des peines.* Paris: Challmel Aîné, 1872.

Ministère de la Justice. *Compte générale de l'administration de la justice criminelle en France.* Paris: Imprimerie Nationale, 1850, 1880, 1900.

Ministère de la Marine et des Colonies. *Lois, décrets et règlements rélatifs à la transportation, à la déportation, et à la relégation.* Melun: Imprimerie Administrative, 1904.

Molineau, Amedee. "De la suppression des bagnes." *Revue coloniale* 8 (March 1852): 243–59.

Moncelon, Léon. *Le bagne et la colonisation pénale en Nouvelle-Calédonie.* Paris: C. Bayle, 1885.

Moreau-Christophe, Louis. *De la réforme des prisons en France.* Paris: Huzard, 1835.

Nguyen, Van-Thinh. *Étude sur l'etiologie du beriberi.* Paris: Jouve, 1921.

Orgeas, J. *Contribution à l'étude du non-cosmopolitisme de l'homme: La colonisation de la Guyane par la transportation: Étude historique et démographique.* Paris: Octave Doin, 1885.

————. *La pathologie des races humaines et le problème de la colonisation: Étude anthropologique et économique faite à la Guyane française.* Paris: Octave Doin, 1885.

Pagnier, Armand. *Du vagabondage et des vagabonds: Étude psychologique, sociologique et médico-légale.* Thèse pour Faculté de médecine et de pharmacie de l'Université de Lyon, 1905.

Pain, Maurice. *Colonisation pénale: Un problème colonial.* Paris: Société des éditions scientifiques, 1898.

Parent-Duchâtelet, A. J.-B. *De la prostitution dans la ville de Paris.* 2 vols. Paris: Ballière et fils, 1835.

Perrot, Louis. *Rapport sur un projet de transportation des condamnés criminels et correctionnels et sur l'etablissement de colonies agricoles pénitentaire en Algérie et en Corse.* Paris: Imprimerie Nationale, 1852.

Poiré, Eugène. *L'émigration aux colonies.* Paris: Plon, 1897.

Prins, Adolphe. *Criminalité et répression.* Brussels: Mische et Thron, 1885.

————. *La défense sociale et les transformations du droit pénale.* Brussels: Mische et Thron, 1910.

Reinach, Joseph. *Les récidivistes.* Paris: Charpentier, 1882.

Rivière, A. "La colonisation pénale." *Bulletin société générale des prisons,* January 1885, 380–82.

———. "Échelle des peines." *Bulletin société générale des prisons,* November 1888, 914–21.

———. "Suite de la discussion du rapport sur les mésures hospitalières destinées à empêcher les vagabonds et les mendiants de tomber dans la récidive." *Bulletin société générale des prisons,* December 1885, 985–1014.

Rivière, Henri. *Souvenirs de la Nouvelle-Calédonie.* Paris: C. Lévy, 1881.

Robin, Elie. *Hospitalité et travail, ou Des moyens préventifs de combattre la mendicité et le vagabondage.* Paris: Monnerat, 1887.

Russier, Henri. *Transportation et colonisation pénale: Essai sur l'evolution des préoccupations économiques dans notre système pénitentiaire coloniale.* Paris: Vuilbert et Nony, 1904.

Sarraméa, Isidore. *Considérations sur la maison centrale d'éducation correctionnelle de Bordeaux, et sur les divers systèmes pénitentiaires appliqués en France aux jeunes détenus.* Bordeaux, 1842.

Tarde, Gabriel. *La criminalité comparée.* 5th ed. Paris: Alcan, 1905.

———. *The Laws of Imitation.* Trans. Elsie Crews Parsons. New York: Henry Holt, 1903.

———. *Penal Philosophy.* Trans. Rapelje Howell. Boston: Little, Brown, 1910.

———. "La statistique criminelle du dernier demi-siècle." *Revue philosophique* 4 (January 1883): 56–64.

Teisseire, Édouard. *La transportation pénale et la relégation, appliquées aux forçats et aux récidivistes: Étude historique, juridique et critique.* Thèse pour Faculté de droit, Université de Toulouse, 1888.

Thereze, A. "Note sur le beriberi à Poulo-Condor." *Annales de medecine et d'hygiène coloniales* 13 (1910): 15.

Tripot, J. *La Guyane: Au pays de l'or des forcats et des peaux-rouges.* Paris: Librairie Plon, 1910.

Un Vieux Colonial [pseud.]. *La colonisation et le bagne à la Nouvelle-Calédonie.* Périgueux: Imprimerie Cassard Jeune, 1902.

Vigé, André. *La colonisation pénale.* Paris: Challamel Aîné, 1910.

Waldeck-Rousseau, René. "Rapport sur la proposition de loi relative à la transportation des recidivistes." *Bulletin société générale des prisons,* December 1885, 79.

Yvernès, Emile. "La récidive." *Bulletin société générale des prisons,* March 1883, 301–18.

Secondary Sources

Allen, James Smith. *In the Public Eye: A History of Reading in Modern France, 1800–1940.* Princeton: Princeton University Press, 1991.

Allison-Booth, W. E. *Hell's Outpost: The True Story of Devil's Island.* New York: Minton, Balch, 1931.

Anderson, Warwick. "Climates of Opinion: Acclimatization in Nineteenth-Century France and England." *Victorian Studies* 35 (1992): 135–57.

———. "Immunities of Empire: Race, Disease, and the New Tropical Medicine." *Bulletin of the History of Medicine* 70 (1995): 94–118.

Arnold, David. *Colonizing the Body: State Medicine and Epidemic Disease in Nineteenth-Century India.* Berkeley: University of California Press, 1993.

———. *The New Cambridge History of India: Science, Technology, and Medicine in Colonial India.* Cambridge: Cambridge University Press, 2000.

Assouline, Pierre. *Albert Londres: Vie et mort d'un grand reporter, 1884–1932.* Paris: Balland, 1989.

Audisio, Gabriel. "Recherches sur l'origine et la signification du mot 'bagne.' " *Revue africaine* 3 (1957): 357–81.

Bakhtin, Mikhail. *Rabelais and His World.* Trans. Hélène Iswolsky. Bloomington: Indiana University Press, 1984.

Bamford, Paul. *Fighting Ships and Prisons: The Mediterranean Galleys of France in the Age of Louis XIV.* Minneapolis: University of Minnesota Press, 1973.

Bancal, Jean. "L'œuvre pénitentiaire de la restauration et de la monarchie de juillet." *Revue de science criminelle et de droit pénal comparé* 5 (1941): 219–43.

Barrows, Susanna. *Distorting Mirrors: Visions of the Crowd in Late Nine-teenth-Century France*. New Haven: Yale University Press, 1981.

Barthes, Roland. *Critical Essays*. Trans. Richard Howard. Evanston IL: Northwestern University Press, 1972.

Batzler-Heim, Georg. *Horrors of Cayenne*. Trans. Karl Bartz. New York: R. Smith, 1930.

Baudrillard, Jean. *The Consumer Society: Myths and Structures*. London: Sage, 1998.

Belbenoit, René. *Dry Guillotine: Fifteen Years among the Living Dead*. Trans. Preston Rambo. New York: Dutton, 1938.

———. *Hell on Trial*. Trans. Preston Rambo. New York: Dutton, 1940.

Berenson, Edward. *The Trial of Madame Caillaux*. Berkeley: University of California Press, 1992.

Berlière, J.-M. "The Professionalization of the Police under the Third Re-public in France, 1875–1914." In *Policing Western Europe: Politics, Professionalization, and Public Order*, ed. Clive Emsley and Barbara Weinberger, 35–54. Westport CT: Greenwood Press, 1991.

Boucon, Honorat. *Les parias de la Guyane*. Cayenne: Editions de l'aide sociale, 1933.

Bourdet-Pléville, Michael. *Justice in Chains: From the Galleys to Devil's Island*. Trans. Anthony Rippon. London: Robert Hale, 1950.

Bourdieu, Pierre. *Outline of a Theory of Practice*. Trans. Richard Nice. Cambridge: Cambridge University Press, 1977.

Bredin, Jean-Denis. *The Affair: The Case of Alfred Dreyfus*. New York: George Braziller, 1985.

Brou, Bernard. *Peuplement et population de la Nouvelle-Calédonie*. Nou-méa: Publications de la société d'études historiques, 1980.

Browning, Christopher. *Ordinary Men: Reserve Police Battalion 101 and the Final Solution in Poland*. New York: Harper, 1992.

Bullard, Alice. *Exile to Paradise: Savagery and Civilization in Paris and the South Pacific, 1790–1900*. Stanford: Stanford University Press, 2000.

Burns, Michael. *Dreyfus: A Family Affair, 1789–1945*. New York: Harper Collins, 1991.

Carlier, Christian, ed. *Le personnel des prisons françaises au XIXe siècle*. Paris: Ministère de la justice, 1987.

Charle, Christophe. *A Social History of France in the Nineteenth Century.* Trans. Miriam Kochan. Oxford: Berg, 1994.

Charrière, Henri. *Papillon.* Trans. June P. Wilson and Walter B. Michaels. New York: Pocket Books, 1971.

Chevalier, Louis. *Laboring Classes and Dangerous Classes in Paris During the First Half of the Nineteenth Century.* Trans. Frank Jellinek. Princeton: Princeton University Press, 1973.

Claire, Sylvie, Odile Krakovitch, and Jean Préteux, eds. *Établissements pénitentiaires coloniaux, 1792–1952: Série colonies H.* Paris: Archives Nationales, 1990.

———. *Terres de bagne.* Exhibition catalog. Aix-en-Provence: Centre des archives d'outre-mer, 1990.

Clapier-Vallodon, Simone. *Les médecins français d'outre-mer.* Paris: Editions anthropos, 1982.

Clarac, Albert. *Mémoires d'un médecin de la marine et des colonies, 1854–1934.* Vincennes: Service historique de la marine, 1994.

Cohen, Stanley, and Andrew Scull, eds. *Social Control and the State: Historical and Comparative Essays.* London: Basil Blackwell, 1983.

Cohen, William B. "Malaria and French Imperialism." *Journal of African History* 24 (1983): 23–35.

Cole, Joshua. *The Power of Large Numbers: Population, Politics, and Gender in Nineteenth-Century France.* Ithaca: Cornell University Press, 2000.

Coleman, William. *Death Is a Social Disease: Public Health and Political Economy in Early Industrial France.* Madison: University of Wisconsin Press, 1982.

———. *Yellow Fever in the North: The Methods of Early Epidemiology.* Madison: University of Wisconsin Press, 1987.

Conklin, Alice. *A Mission to Civilize: The Republican Idea of Empire in France and West Africa, 1895–1930.* Stanford: Stanford University Press, 1997.

Connell, John. *From New Caledonia to Kanaky?* Canberra: Australia National University Press, 1987.

Cormier, Manuel. *La colonisation pénale.* Nouméa: CTRDP, 1993.

Cousins, Mark, and Athar Hussain. *Michel Foucault.* New York: Macmillan, 1984.

Cragin, Thomas J. "Cultural Continuity in Modern France: The Representation of Crime in the Popular Press of Nineteenth-Century Paris." Ph.D. diss., Indiana University, 1995.

Curtin, Philip D. *Death by Migration: Europe's Encounter with the Tropical World in the Nineteenth Century.* Cambridge: Cambridge University Press, 1989.

————. *Disease and Empire: The Health of European Troops in the Conquest of Africa.* Cambridge: Cambridge University Press, 1998.

Danjou, Henri. *La belle.* Paris: Gallimard, 1938.

Darquitain, V., and L. Le Boucher. *La grande géhenne.* Paris: Rivière, 1928.

Dauphiné, Joel. *Chronologie foncière et agricole de la Nouvelle-Calédonie.* Paris: L'Hartmann, 1987.

Davis, Hassoldt. *The Jungle and the Damned.* New York: Little, Brown, 1952.

Delaporte, François. *The History of Yellow Fever: An Essay on the Birth of Tropical Medicine.* Trans. Arthur Goldhammer. Cambridge: MIT Press, 1991.

Desmond, Robert W. *Windows on the World: The Information Process in a Changing Society, 1900–1920.* Iowa City: University of Iowa Press, 1980.

Devèze, Michel. *Cayenne: Déportés et bagnards.* Paris: Julliard, 1955.

Dieudonné, Eugène. *La vie des forçats.* Paris: Gallimard, 1930.

Domergue, D. "French Sanitary Services in the Ivory Coast." *Revue française d'histoire d'outre-mer* 54 (1979): 103–18.

Donet-Vincent, Danielle. *La fin du bagne.* Rennes: Éditions Ouest-France, 1992.

Dornoy, Myriam. *Politics in New Caledonia.* Sydney: Sydney University Press, 1984.

Dousset-Leenhardt, Rosélene. *Terre natale, terre d'exil.* Paris: Maisonneuve & Larouse, 1975.

Dreyfus, Alfred. *The Letters of Captain Dreyfus to His Wife.* Trans. L. G. Moreau. New York: Harper and Brothers, 1899.

Duesterberg, Thomas. "Criminology and the Social Order in Nineteenth-Century France." Ph.D. diss., Indiana University, 1979.

Duprat, Catherine. "Punir et guérir: En 1819, la prison des philanthropes." In *L'impossible prison: Recherches sur le système penitentiare au XIXe siècle*, ed. Michelle Perrot, 54–123. Paris, Éditions du seuil, 1980.

Epailly, Eugène. *Saint-Martin de Ré: Bagnards pour Cayenne*. Cayenne: Imprimerie Absalon, 1987.

Ettighoffer, P. G. *The Island of the Doomed*. London: Hutchinson, 1935.

Fabian, Ann. *The Unvarnished Truth: Personal Narratives in Nineteenth-Century America*. Berkeley: University of California Press, 2000.

Forstenzer, Thomas R. *French Provincial Police and the Fall of the Second Republic: Social Fear and Counterrevolution*. Princeton: Princeton University Press, 1981.

Forster, Colin. *France and Botany Bay: The Lure of a Penal Colony*. Melbourne: Melbourne University Press, 1995.

Forsythe, William. *A System of Discipline: Exeter Borough Prison*. Exeter: University of Exeter Press, 1983.

Foucault, Michel. *Discipline and Punish: The Birth of the Prison*. Trans. Alan Sheridan. New York: Vintage Books, 1979.

———. *Madness and Civilization*. Trans. Richard Howard. New York: Pantheon Books, 1955.

Fournier, J. P. *Vision du bagne*. Camariche: Les Éditions du pélican, 1989.

Frazer, Nancy. "Michel Foucault: A Young Conservative?" *Ethics* 95 (1985): 155–84.

Fuchs, Rachel. *Poor and Pregnant: Strategies of Survival in the Nineteenth Century*. New Brunswick NJ: Rutgers University Press, 1992.

Gabriel, Richard A., and Karen S. Metz. *A History of Military Medicine*. Vol. 2, *From the Renaissance through Modern Times*. Greenwood CT: Greenwood Press, 1992.

Gaillac, Henri. *Les maisons de correction, 1830–1945*. Paris: Cujas, 1971.

Garland, David. "Foucault's *Discipline and Punish*: An Exposition and Critique." *American Bar Foundation Research Journal* 847 (1985): 870–85.

Gascher, Pierre. "Regards sur l'administration coloniale en Nouvelle-Calédonie, 1874-1894." *Le monde chrétien* 8 (January–June 1959): 79–94.

Gattrell, V. A. C., and T. B. Haddon. "Criminal Statistics and Their Interpretation." In *Nineteenth-Century Society*, ed. E. A. Wrigley, 335–95. Cambridge: Cambridge University Press, 1972.

Gerth, H. H., and C. Wright Mills, eds. *From Max Weber: Essays in Sociology*. Oxford: Oxford University Press, 1945.

Gillis, A. R. "Crime and State Surveillance in Nineteenth-Century France." *American Journal of Sociology* 95 (September 1989): 307–41.

Goldstein, Jan. "Moral Contagion: A Professional Ideology of Medicine and Psychiatry in Eighteenth and Nineteenth-Century France." In *Professions and the French State, 1700–1900*, ed. Gerald L. Geison, 181–223. Philadelphia: University of Pennsylvania Press, 1984.

Guiart, Jean. *La terre est le sang des morts: La confrontation entre blancs et noirs dans le Pacifique sud français*. Paris: Editions Anthropos, 1983.

Guin, Yannick. *Le mouvement ouvrier nantais, essai sur le syndicalisme d'action directe à Nantes et à Saint-Nazare*. Paris: Maspero, 1975.

Halasz, Nicholas. *Captain Dreyfus: The Story of Mass Hysteria*. New York: Simon and Schuster, 1955.

Halliburton, Richard. *New Worlds to Conquer*. New York: Garden City Publishing, 1929.

Harrison, Mark. " 'The Tender Frame of Man': Disease, Climate, and Racial Difference in India and the West Indies, 1750–1880." *Bulletin of the History of Medicine* 70 (1995): 58–93.

Headrick, Daniel. *The Tools of Empire: Technology and European Imperialism in the Nineteenth Century*. New York: Oxford University Press, 1981.

Henry, A. *French Guiana Française: Capital Cayenne*. Paris: Gallimard, 1935.

Holmes, Richard. *The Road to Sedan: The French Army, 1855–1870*. Atlantic Highlands NJ: Humanities Press, 1984.

Hughes, Robert. *The Fatal Shore: The Epic of Australia's Founding*. New York: Vintage Books, 1985.

Hume, L. J. "Bentham's Panopticon: An Administrative History." *Historical Studies* 15 (1973): 703–21.

Ignatieff, Michael. *A Just Measure of Pain: The Penitentiary in the Industrial Revolution, 1750–1850*. New York: Pantheon, 1978.

Jackson, R. V. "Luxury in Punishment: Jeremy Bentham and the Cost of the Convict Colony in New South Wales." *Australian Historical Studies* 23 (1988): 42–59.

Kafka, Franz. "In the Penal Colony." In *Great Short Works of Franz Kafka*, trans. Joachim Neugrochel, 189–230. New York: Simon and Schuster, 1993.

Kanya-Forstner, A. S. *The Conquest of Western Sudan: A Study in French Military Imperialism*. Cambridge: Cambridge University Press, 1959.

Kennedy, Dane. "The Perils of the Midday Sun: Climatic Anxieties in the Colonial Tropics." In *Imperialism and the Natural World*, ed. John M. MacKenzie, 118–40. Manchester: Manchester University Press, 1990.

Kling, George. "L'Alcmène: L'exploration de la Nouvelle-Calédonie, 1848–1851." *Bulletin de la société d'études historiques de la Nouvelle-Calédonie* 80 (1989): 114–29.

Krakovitch, Odile. *Les femmes bagnards*. Paris: Olivier Orban, 1990.

Krarup-Nielsen, Aage. *Hell beyond the Seas*. Garden City NJ: Garden City Publishing, 1938.

La Berge, Ann. *Mission and Method: The Early Nineteenth-Century French Public Health Movement*. Cambridge: Cambridge University Press, 1992.

Lagrange, Francis. *Flag on Devil's Island*. New York: Doubleday, 1951.

Langbein, John. "The Historical Origins of the Sanction of Imprisonment for Serious Crimes." *Journal of Legal Studies* 35 (1975): 55–58.

Latham, Linda. "Revolt Re-Examined: The 1878 Insurrection in New Caledonia." *Journal of Pacific History* 10 (1978): 48–54.

Le Boucher, L. *Ce qu'il faut connaître du bagne*. Paris: Boivin, 1930.

Le Clère, Marcel. *Histoire de la police*. Paris: Presses universitaires de France, 1954.

———. *La vie quotidienne dans les bagnes*. Paris: Librairie Hachette, 1973.

Leenhardt, Maurice. *Gens de la Grande Terre: Nouvelle-Calédonie*. Paris: Gallimard, 1937.

———. *Notes d'ethnologie néo-calédoniennes*. Paris: Institut d'ethnologie, 1930.

Lenormand, Maurice. "Politique des autochtones de la Nouvelle-Calédonie." *Journal de la société des océanistes* 17 (1953): 252–79.

Lequin, Yves. *Les ouvriers de la région lyonnaise, 1848–1914*. Lyon: Presses universitaires de Lyon, 1977.

Lévy, Réné. "Crime, the Judicial System, and Punishment in Modern France." In *Crime History and Criminal Justice in Modern History*, ed. Clive Emsley and Louis A. Knafla, 87–108. Westport CT: Greenwood Press, 1995.

Liard-Courtois, Auguste. *Souvenirs du bagne*. Paris: Charpentier, 1903.

Linon, Henri. "Les officiers du corps de santé." *Bulletin de la société d'études historiques de la Nouvelle-Calédonie* 28 (1975): 44–51.

Londres, Albert. *L'homme qui s'évada*. Paris: Editions de France, 1928.

Lyons, Martyn. *The Totem and the Tricolour*. Kensington: New South Wales Press, 1985.

Mam-Lam-Fouck, Serge. *Histoire de la société guyannaise: Les années cruciales, 1848–1945*. Paris: Éditions caribéennes, 1987.

Maroger, Mireille. *Bagne*. Paris: Denoël, 1937.

Martin, Benjamin. *Crime and Criminal Justice under the Third Republic: The Shame of Marianne*. Baton Rouge: Louisiana State University Press, 1990.

Matsuda, Matt. *The Memory of the Modern*. Oxford: Oxford University Press, 1995.

Megill, Allan. "The Reception of Foucault by Historians." *Journal of the History of Ideas* 48 (1987): 117–41.

Melossi, Dario, and Massimo Pavarini. *The Prison and the Factory: The Origins of the Penitentiary System*. Totowa NJ: Barnes and Noble, 1981.

Merle, Isabelle. *Expériences coloniales: La Nouvelle-Calédonie, 1853–1920*. Paris: Belin, 1995.

———. "The Foundation of Voh, 1892–1895: The Establishment of French Migrants on the West Coast of New Caledonia." *Journal of Pacific History* 25 (January 1991): 234–44.

Mesclon, Antoine. *Comment j'ai subi quinze ans de bagne.* Paris: A. Mesclon, 1924.

Michel, Marc. "Les Corps de santé des troupes coloniales." In *Histoire des medecins et pharmaciens de marine et des colonies,* ed. Pierre Pluchon, 180–205. Paris: Privat, 1985.

Michelet, Jean-Claude. *La guillotine sèche: Histoire du bagne de Cayenne.* Paris: Fayard, 1981.

Milani, Felix, and Micha Grin. *The Convict.* Trans. Anita Barrows. New York: St. Martin's, 1977.

Miles, Alexander. *Devil's Island: Colony of the Damned.* Berkeley: Ten Speed Press, 1988.

Miller, Michael. *The Bon Marché: Bourgeois Culture and the Department Store, 1859–1920.* Princeton: Princeton University Press, 1981.

Monnais-Rousselot, Laurence. *Médecine et colonisation: L'aventure indochinoise, 1850–1939.* Paris: CNRS Editions, 1999.

Mousset, Paul. *Albert Londres, ou L'aventure du grand reportage.* Paris: Grasset, 1972.

Niles, Blair. *Condemned to Devil's Island: The Biography of an Unknown Convict.* New York: Grosset and Dunlap, 1929.

Nye, Robert A. *Crime, Madness, and Politics in Modern France: The Medical Concept of National Decline.* Princeton: Princeton University Press, 1984.

———. *The Origins of Crowd Psychology: Gustave Le Bon and the Crisis of Mass Democracy in the Third Republic.* Beverly Hills CA: Sage, 1975.

O'Brien, Patricia. "The Kleptomania Diagnosis: Bourgeois Women and Theft in Late Nineteenth-Century France." *Journal of Social History* 17 (fall 1983): 55–77.

———. *The Promise of Punishment: Prisons in Nineteenth-Century France.* Princeton: Princeton University Press, 1982.

Payne, Howard C. *The Police State of Louis Napoleon Bonaparte, 1851–1860.* Seattle: University of Washington Press, 1954.

Péan, Charles. *Conquêtes en terre de bagne.* Strasbourg: Editions Altis, 1948.

Perrot, Michelle. "Delinquency and the Penitentiary System in Nine-teenth-Century France." In *Deviants and the Abandoned in French Society: Economies, Sociétés, Civilisations*, ed. Robert Forster and Orest Ranum, 213–45. Baltimore: Johns Hopkins University Press, 1978.

———, ed. *L'impossible prison: Recherches sur le système pénitentiaire au XIXe siècle*. Paris: Editions du seuil, 1980.

Petit, Jacques Guy. "The Birth and Reform of Prisons in France, 1791–1885." In *The Emergence of Carceral Institutions: Prisons, Galleys, and Lunatic Asylums, 1550–1900*, ed. Pieter Spierenburg, 125–47. Rotterdam, The Netherlands: Erasmus Universiteit Rotterdam, 1984.

———, ed. *Histoire des galères, bagnes et prisons: XIIIe–XXe siècles: Introduction à l'histoire pénale de la France*. Toulouse: Editions privat, 1990.

———. *La prison, le bagne et l'histoire*. Geneva: Librairie des meridiens, 1984.

Pick, Daniel. *Faces of Degeneration: A European Disorder, c. 1848–1918*. Cambridge: Cambridge University Press, 1989.

Pierre, Michel. *Le dernier exil: Histoire des bagnes et des forçats*. Paris: Gallimard, 1989.

———. *La terre de la grande punition*. Paris: Ramsay, 1982.

Pinatel, Jean. "La vie et l'œuvre de Charles Lucas." *Revue international de droit pénal* 18 (1947): 121–54.

Pirot, Robert. "L'origine et l'évolution du service de santé de la marine et des colonies: Leçons actualité." *Académie des sciences d'outre-mer* (November 1957): 441–50.

Pisier, Georges. *Les déportés de la commune et l'île des pins*. Paris: Musée de l'homme, 1971.

Porter, Theodore. *The Rise of Statistical Thinking, 1820–1900*. Princeton: Princeton University Press, 1991.

Price, Richard. *The Convict and the Colonel: A Study in Colonialism and Resistance in the Caribbean*. Boston: Beacon Press, 1998.

Rabinow, Paul. *The Foucault Reader*. New York: Pantheon, 1984.

———. *French Modern: Norms and Forms of the Social Environment*. Chicago: University of Chicago Press, 1980.

Ratcliffe, Barrie. "The Chevalier Thesis Reexamined." *French Historical Studies* 17 (fall 1991): 542–74.

Redfield, Peter. *Space in the Tropics: Convicts to Rockets in French Guiana.* Berkeley: University of California Press, 2000.

Renneville, Marc. *Crime et folie: Deux siècles d'enquêtes médicales et judiciaires.* Paris: Fayard, 2003.

Rickards, Colin. *The Man from Devil's Island.* New York: Stein and Day, 1958.

Roberts, Stephen H. *The History of French Colonial Policy, 1870–1925.* 2nd ed. London: Frank Cass, 1953.

Rothman, David. *The Discovery of the Asylum: Social Order and Disorder in the New Republic.* Boston: Little, Brown, 1971.

Rousseau, Louis. *Un médecin au bagne.* Paris: Fleury, 1930.

Roussenq, Paul. *L'enfer du bagne.* Vichy: Pucheux, 1957.

Rudé, Fernand, ed. *Bagnes d'Afrique: Trois transportés en Algérie après le coup d'état.* Paris: Maspero, 1981.

Said, Edward. *Orientalism.* London: Routledge, 1978.

Sainz, Xavier. "La Loi du bagne." *Bourbon Medical: Bulletin de la société de médecin de la Reunion* 25 (1971): 5–50.

Saussol, Alain. "The Colonial Chimera: From Annexation to the Reemergence of Kanak Identity." In *New Caledonia: Essays in Nationalism and Dependency,* ed. Michael Spencer, Alan Ward, and John Connell, 38–55. St. Lucia: Queensland University Press, 1988.

Schnapper, Bernard. *Le remplacement militaire en France: Quelques aspects politiques, économiques et sociaux du recrutement au XIXe siècle.* Paris: SEVPEN, 1958.

Seaton, George. *Isle of the Damned.* New York: Farrar, 1952.

Sen, Satardu. *Disciplining Punishment: Colonialism and Convict Society in the Andaman Islands.* Oxford: Oxford University Press, 2000.

Sénès, Jacqueline. *La vie quotidienne en Nouvelle-Calédonie, de 1850 à nos jours.* Paris: Hachette, 1985.

Shaw, A. G. L. *Convicts and the Colonies: A Study of Penal Transportation from Great Britain and Ireland to Australia and Other Parts of the British Empire.* London: Faber and Faber, 1955.

Sinclair, Gordon. *Loose among Devils.* New York: Farrar, 1935.

Smith, Nicol. *Black Martinique—Red French Guiana*. Indianapolis: Bobbs-Merrill, 1942.

Spencer, Michael, Alan Ward, and John Connell, eds. *New Caledonia: Essays in Nationalism and Dependency*. St. Lucia: Queensland University Press, 1988.

Spierenburg, Pieter. *The Prison Experience: Disciplinary Institutions and Their Inmates in Early Modern Europe*. New Brunswick NJ: Rutgers University Press, 1991.

Steinert, Heinz. "The Development of 'Discipline' according to Michel Foucault: Discourse Analysis vs. Social History." *Crime and Social Justice* 20 (1983): 83–98.

Thamar, Maurice. *Les peines coloniales et l'expérience guyanais*. Thèse pour Faculté de droit, Université de Paris, 1935.

Thompson, Virginia, and Richard Adloff. *The French Pacific Islands*. Berkeley: University of California Press, 1971.

Vaucel, M. A. "La service de santé des troupes de marine et la médecine tropicale française." *Transactions of the Royal Society of Tropical Medicine and Hygiene* 59 (1955): 225–33.

Vaudé, Raymonde. *Matricule 52,305*. Paris: Les Débats de l'histoire, 1972.

Vine, M. S. W. "Gabriel Tarde." In *Pioneers in Criminology*, ed. Hermann Mannheim, 231–44. Chicago: Quadrangle Books, 1950.

Wagniart, Jean-François. *Le vagabond à la fin du XIXe siècle*. Paris: Belin, 1999.

Walker, David H. *Outrage and Insight: Modern French Writers and the Fait Divers*. Oxford: Berg, 1995.

Walter, Richard D. "What Became of the Degenerate? A Brief History of a Concept." *Journal of the History of Medicine and Allied Sciences* 10 (1955): 422–29.

Walz, Robin. *Pulp Surrealism: Insolent Popular Culture in Early Twentieth-Century Paris*. Berkeley: University of California Press, 2000.

Ward, Alan. *Land and Politics in New Caledonia*. Canberra: Australia National University, 1982.

Weber, Eugen. *Peasants into Frenchmen: The Modernization of Rural France, 1870–1914*. Stanford: Stanford University Press, 1975.

Wiener, Martin J. *Reconstructing the Criminal: Culture, Law, and Policy in England, 1830–1914.* Cambridge: Cambridge University Press, 1990.

———. "Social Control in Nineteenth-Century Britain." *Journal of Social History* 12 (1978–79): 314–21.

Williams, Raymond. *The Long Revolution.* New York: Columbia University Press, 1973.

Williams, Rosalind. *Dream Worlds: Mass Consumption in Late Nineteenth-Century France.* Berkeley: University of California Press, 1982.

Wright, Gordon. *Between the Guillotine and Liberty: Two Centuries of the Crime Problem in France.* Oxford: Oxford University Press, 1983.

Young, Robert J. *Marketing Marianne: French Propaganda in America, 1900–1940.* New Brunswick NJ: Rutgers University Press, 2004.

Zehr, Howard. *Crime and the Development of Modern Society: Patterns of Criminality in Nineteenth-Century Germany and France.* London: Croom Helm, 1975.

Zinoman, Peter. *The Colonial Bastille: A History of Imprisonment in Vietnam, 1852–1940.* Berkeley: University of California Press, 2001.

Zysberg, André. "Galley and Hard Labor Convictions in France, 1550–1850." In *The Emergence of Carceral Institutions: Prisons, Galleys, and Lunatic Asylums, 1550–1900*, ed. Pieter Spierenburg, 78–124. Rotterdam, The Netherlands: Erasmus Universiteit Rotterdam, 1984.

———. "Galley Rowers in the Mid-Eighteenth Century." In *Deviants and the Abandoned in French Society: Economies, Sociétés, Civilisations*, ed. Robert Forster and Orest Ranum, 83–110. Baltimore: Johns Hopkins University Press, 1978.

Index

In the France Overseas series

The French Navy and the Seven Years' War
By Jonathan R. Dull

French Colonialism Unmasked
The Vichy Years in French West Africa
By Ruth Ginio

Beyond Papillon
The French Overseas Penal Colonies, 1854–1952
By Stephen A. Toth